War and the Environment: New Approaches to Protecting the Environment in Relation to Armed Conflict

The Raoul Wallenberg Institute Human Rights Library

VOLUME 45

The titles published in this series are listed at brill.com/rawa

War and the Environment:

New Approaches to Protecting the Environment in Relation to Armed Conflict

Edited by
Rosemary Rayfuse

BRILL
NIJHOFF

LEIDEN | BOSTON

ISSN 1388-3208
ISBN 978-90-04-27064-0 (hardback)
ISBN 978-90-04-27065-7 (e-book)

This book is printed on acid-free paper.

Printed by Printforce, the Netherlands

Table of Contents

Foreword

Protection of the Environment in Relation to Armed Conflicts – An Update

Marie Jacobsson*

The United Nations International Law Commission (ILC), at its sixty-third session (2011), decided to include the topic *Protection of the environment in relation to armed conflicts* in its long-term programme of work. The basis of the proposal was reproduced in an annex to the report of the Commission on the work of that session.[1] The decision was taken in the last year of the 2007–2011 ILC quinquennium.

Later that year, and in accordance with well-established practice, the United Nations General Assembly took note of the inclusion of the topic in the Commission's long-term programme of work.[2]

The election of members to the ILC for the forthcoming quinquennium (2012–2016) was held by the General Assembly in November 2011. The newly composed Commission met in May 2012. Much of the work during the first year of each ILC quinquennium focuses on planning the work of the Commission. Hence, consultations were held on the topics already placed on the long-term programme of work. The topic *Provisional application of treaties* was swiftly accepted and placed on the current programme of work, as was the *Formation and evidence of customary international law.* No decision was taken on the topic *Protection of the atmosphere.*

---

* Member of the International Law Commission; Special Rapporteur on Protection of the environment in relation armed conflicts.

1 Annex E to ILC Report 2011, UN Doc A/66/10, pp. 347 *et seq.* (Marie Jacobsson: *Protection of the Environment in relation to armed conflicts*). Rosemary Rayfuse describes the historical background in her introduction to this book. It should be recalled that the UNEP Report, *Protecting the Environment During Armed Conflict: An Inventory and Analysis of International Law* (2009), discussed how the legal framework for the protection of the environment during armed conflict might be clarified, codified and expanded. The Report recommended that the ILC "should examine the existing international law for protecting the environment during armed conflict"; see UNEP Report, Recommendation 3, p. 53.

2 UNGA Resolution 66/98 (9 December 2011), para. 7.

There was little time left to discuss the future of the topic *Protection of the environment in relation to armed conflicts.* Brief informal consultations showed that the 'new' Commission also took an interest in the topic. During the session, I was also asked by the ILC to give a presentation on the topic at the annual informal meeting with the Red Cross and Red Crescent Committee. In addition, a 'brain-storming' seminar was held at the University of Geneva and the International Law Seminar.[3]

A year later, on 28 May 2013, the Commission decided to include the topic *Protection of the environment in relation to armed conflicts* in its current programme of work and appointed me Special Rapporteur. As a consequence, consultations were held on the basis of two informal papers which I had circulated to all the members of the Commission. The purpose of the informal consultations was to initiate an informal dialogue with members of the Commission on a number of issues that could be of relevance to the consideration of this topic during the present quinquennium. The two informal papers set forth some preliminary elements which were to be read together with the syllabus containing the initial proposal for this topic, reproduced in the Commission's 2011 report.

During the informal consultations, I proposed that the topic could be addressed through a temporal perspective, rather than from the perspective of various areas of international law, such as environmental law, the law of armed conflict and human rights law, as envisaged in the United Nations Environment Programme (UNEP) Report. This approach would make the topic more manageable and easier to delineate.

The temporal phases would address legal measures taken to protect the environment before, during and after an armed conflict. Such an approach would allow the Commission to identify concrete legal issues relating to this topic that arise at the different stages of an armed conflict. Identifying such issues could then facilitate the development of concrete conclusions or guidelines.

Members of the Commission generally welcomed the approach of addressing the topic in temporal phases. Different views were expressed on the importance of each individual phase. My view, as Special Rapporteur, is that although the work will be divided into temporal phases, no strict dividing line can be drawn between the different phases. Such a dividing line would be artificial and would not correspond with how the legal rules relevant to the topic operate. The law of armed conflict, for example, consists of rules applicable before, during and after an armed conflict.

Members of the Commission supported and encouraged consultations with other United Nations organs and international organisations involved in the protection of the environment, such as UNEP, United Nations Educational, Scientific and Cultural Organization (UNESCO), United Nations High Commissioner for

---

3 Information on the annual International Law Seminar can be found at <www.unog.ch/80256EDD006AC19C/(httpPages)/519685C86E97119B80256EF30036AD9C?OpenDocument>.

Refugees (UNHCR) and the International Committee of the Red Cross (ICRC), as well as regional bodies, such as the African Union (AU), the European Union (EU), the League of Arab States and the Organisation of American States (OAS).

The 2013 Report of the International Law Commission contains a chapter reflecting on the consideration of the topic by the ILC.[4] States kindly commented on the topic on the basis of this chapter. The ideas and outline presented in the Report of the International Law Commission 2013 were generally well received by States.

The 2013 ILC Report also expresses an invitation to States to inform the Commission on "whether, in their practice, international or domestic environmental law has been interpreted as applicable in relation to international or non-international armed conflict". Examples of treaties, national legislation and case law will be particularly appreciated.[5]

The time that elapsed between the inclusion of the topic in the Commission's long-term programme of work in 2011 and the inclusion of the topic in 2013 has given me the opportunity to meet and discuss the topic with representatives of States at the UN in New York, UN bodies, international organisations, experts and academics. The interest in the topic is obvious. Representatives from organisations such as the ICRC, the International Union for Conservation of Nature (IUCN) and non-governmental organisations and associations voiced their interest informally and formally, as did representatives of UNEP and UNESCO, individual academies and institutions.

In connection with the 2013 ILC session, another 'brain-storming' seminar was held at the University of Geneva and the International Law Seminar. I also gathered a small group of academic experts in a very informal 'think-tank' meeting. When I was at the UN in New York to listen to the consideration of the 2013 ILC Report, I took the opportunity to invite States to a lunch briefing and a discussion on the topic. I also had discussions with individual representatives of States. These consultations and discussions have clearly assisted me in forming thoughts on a possible way ahead. It is my intention to continue an open dialogue. The widespread interest in the topic entails a small, but not unpleasant, risk, namely that the engaged persons and institutions will want me to include too much in my reports. I am highly aware of this, and it is incumbent on me to write the reports to be considered by the ILC in such a manner as is constructive for the purpose of the Commission's work. In the end it is the Commission that determines and decides on how to address the topic. Its considerations will be reflected in its annual reports to the United Nations General Assembly.

My first report in my capacity as Special Rapporteur will be presented to the Commission for consideration at its sixty-sixth session (2014). The focus of

---

4 Chapter IX of the Report of the International Law Commission 2013, in A/68/10, pp. 105 *et seq.*

5 For a full text of the request, see the Report of the International Law Commission 2013, in A/68/10, p. 8.

this report will be the 'first phase', namely, obligations of relevance to a potential armed conflict. Issues previously considered by the Commission that could be of relevance to the topic will be identified.

The first report will probably be the most general in nature. This is indeed the case for most first reports. As Special Rapporteur, I am indeed encouraged by the significant interest in the topic and I welcome any information, comments or analysis that are of relevance for my future work.

Introduction

Rethinking International Law and the Protection of the Environment in Relation to Armed Conflict

Rosemary Rayfuse*

1. Introduction

Truth may be the first casualty of warfare, but the environment is not far behind. Since time immemorial the environment has been a silent victim of warfare. From salting the enemy's land, to poisoning water sources, to scorched earth policies, the environment has historically been both target and weapon. It has suffered both deliberate and incidental damage and it has suffered not only during but also in preparation for, and in the aftermath of, armed conflict.

Technological developments since the 19th century have only exacerbated the potential for and reality of environment damage associated with armed conflict. Chemical defoliants such as Agent Orange, depleted uranium munitions, chemical and nuclear weapons have all caused significant environmental harms. Conventional weapons, too, have caused environmental damage through, for example, the release of toxic chemical contamination or oil spills from bombed industrial sites, and the deliberate or accidental burning of oil wells. Landmines have rendered vast areas, including agriculturally productive areas, unusable, while intentional modification of the environment through, for example, causing floods or drought, has been used as a direct weapon of war. More recently the environment has been implicated as an 'accessory' in the conduct of armed conflict with 'conflict resources' being exploited to finance armed forces and the acquisition of weapons, thereby contributing to the prolongation of a number of particularly brutal internal conflicts.

The environmental consequences of armed conflict are well documented.[1] Air, soil and water pollution, as well as habitat and species destruction, destroy

* Professor of International Law, Faculty of Law, The University of New South Wales, Australia; Conjoint Professor of International Environmental Law, Faculty of Law, Lund University, Sweden

1 *See e.g.* J. E. Austin and C. E. Bruch, *The Environmental Consequences of War: Le-*

Rosemary Rayfuse (ed.), War and the Environment: New Approaches to Protecting the Environment in Relation to Armed Conflict
Copyright 2014 Koninklijke Brill NV. Printed in The Netherlands. ISBN 978-90-04-27064-0 pp. 1-234

ecosystems and the ecosystem services upon which humans depend for their health and well-being. This destruction is expensive and sometimes irreversible. Livelihoods are undermined resulting in poverty and forced migration. Environmental protection policies are side-lined thereby weakening internal governance structures and making more difficult the achievement of a lasting and sustainable peace.[2] As Principle 24 of the Rio Declaration confirms, "[w]arfare is inherently destructive of sustainable development". States are therefore called upon to "respect international law providing protection for the environment in times of armed conflict and cooperate in its further development, as necessary."[3]

2. Traditional Approaches to Environmental Protection and Armed Conflict

Protection of the environment in times of armed conflict has traditionally been viewed through the lens of the laws of armed conflict, also referred to as international humanitarian law (IHL). Given its historic focus on protection of combatants and the obligations of occupying powers, it is hardly surprising that little is found in the early IHL treaties that could be capable of being construed as directly applicable to the environment. Perhaps the earliest rule of this sort is found in Article 23(g) of the Hague Regulations of 1907[4] which prohibits the destruction or seizure of enemy property unless required by imperative military necessity. Article 53 of the 1949 Geneva Convention (IV) relative to the Protection of Civilian Persons in Time of War,[5] similarly prohibits the destruction by an occupying power of real or personal property belonging individually or collectively to any persons, or to the State, unless absolutely necessary for military operations. Neither of these articles makes express mention of the environment although they have been taken as the origins of what is now asserted to be a customary

---

gal, Economic, and Scientific Perspectives (Cambridge University Press, 2000); A. T. Kassim and D. Barceló (eds.), *Environmental Consequences of War and Aftermath* (Springer, 2009).

2 United Nations Environment Program (UNEP), *Protecting the Environment During Armed Conflict: An Inventory and Analysis of International Law* (UNEP, 2009) (hereinafter: UNEP Report).

3 Rio Declaration on Environment and Development, Report of the United Nations Conference on the Human Environment, 3 to 14 June 1992, Rio de Janeiro, UN Doc. A/CONF.151/26 (Vol. I)

4 Convention (IV) respecting the Laws and Customs of War on Land, signed 18 October 1907

5 J.-M. Henckaerts and L. Doswald-Beck, *Customary Humanitarian International Law* (ICRC, 2005) Rule 43(B).

obligation prohibiting the destruction of any part of the natural environment unless required by military necessity.[6]

Since the 1960s protection of the environment has been addressed more specifically within the IHL framework. Jacobsson identifies three stages in this development.[7] The first stage had its origins in the confluence of public revulsion at the environmental destruction wrought during the Vietnam War with the rise of the environmental movement. This resulted in the adoption of specific articles relating to protection of the environment in IHL treaties, in particular, Articles 35(3) and 55 of the 1977 Additional Protocol I[8] to the Geneva Conventions on the laws of armed conflict and the 1976 Convention on the Prohibition of Military or Any Other Hostile Use of Environmental Modification Techniques.[9]

The second phase began with the 1990 Iraq-Kuwait war when the burning of oil wells and other environmental effects of the conflict opened the international community's eyes to the damaging effects of such warfare on the environment.[10] The UN Compensation Commission, established to deal with claims arising from the conflict, was specifically entrusted with cases relating to loss or damage to the environment and the depletion of natural resources. At the same time, the issue of protection of the environment in armed conflict was placed on the agenda of UN and the ICRC was tasked by the General Assembly to work on the issue. However, while the ICRC adopted Guidelines for Military Manuals and Instructions on the Protection of the Environment in Time of Armed Conflict,[11] no support existed for modification to or further development of existing IHL treaty provisions. Nevertheless, throughout the 1990s the issue was addressed in a number of *fora* including the 1992 Rio Conference on Environment and Development.[12]

Jacobsson places the third, and current, phase as beginning around 2010.[13] She notes that wars, such as those in Kosovo, Iraq, and Lebanon have shown the high environmental price paid by war-torn societies. At the same time, international tribunals and courts have increasingly been called upon to address issues relating to protection of the environment and fact finding missions have increasingly documented the negative effects of warfare on the environment. The

---

6 12 August 1949, 75 *UNTS* (1950) 287–417.

7 M. Jacobsson, 'Protection of the Environment in relation to armed conflicts', Annex E to Report of ILC 2011 UN Doc A/66/10 p. 351 (hereinafter: Jacobsson Report).

8 Protocol Additional to the Geneva Conventions of 12 August 1949, and relating to the protection of Victims of International Armed Conflicts, 8 June 1977, 1125 *UNTS* (1979) 3–608.

9 2 September 1976, 1108 *UNTS* (1978) 151–178.

10 Jacobsson Report, *supra* note 7, paras. 10–16.

11 Reproduced in 331 *International Review of the Red Cross* (1996).

12 Jacobsson Report, *supra* note 7, para. 12.

13 *Ibid.*, para. 17.

International Criminal Court has even been given jurisdiction over crimes which cause certain damage to the environment.[14] Nevertheless, despite growing international concern, clarification and development of IHL for the protection of the environment has continued to lag behind the more extensive development of international environmental law in general.[15]

3. Rethinking Protection of the Environment in Relation to Armed Conflict

In 2009, the United Nations Environment Program (UNEP) published its report *Protecting the Environment During Armed Conflict: An inventory and analysis of international law*,[16] in which it recommended how the legal framework for the protection of the environment during armed conflict might be clarified, codified and expanded. It is in this context that, in 2011, the International Law Commission (ILC) decided to include the topic of 'protection of the environment in relation to armed conflict' in its long-term programme of work. The objectives of the ILC are not merely to identify the extent of the legal problem but also to, *inter alia*, clarify the applicability of and relationship between IHL and other areas of international law; clarify the relationship between existing treaty law and new legal developments; provide suggestions for the development of a uniform and coherent system of legal protections; and formulate relevant rules and principles.[17]

The precise formulation of the topic by the ILC is of critical importance in that it recognises that there is more to protecting the environment, and the aspirations and needs of current and future generations, than simply treating the environment as another civilian object to be protected under existing IHL. Indeed, as recognised by the International Court of Justice (ICJ) in its Advisory Opinion on the *Legal Consequences of a Wall on the Occupied Palestinian Territory*,[18] it is no longer sufficient to look for legal answers solely within the *lex specialis* regime of the laws of armed conflict. In its recent work on the *Effects of Armed Conflicts on Treaties*[19] the ILC noted that the existence of an armed conflict does not necessarily terminate or suspend the operation of treaties. Thus, a range of treaties important to the protection of the environment may continue to operate during periods of armed conflict. Recourse must therefore also be made

---

14 Rome Statute of the International Criminal Court, 17 July 1998, UN Doc. A/CONF.183/9, Article 8.

15 Jacobsson Report, *supra* note 7, para. 19.

16 UNEP Report, *supra* note 2.

17 Jacobsson Report, *supra* note 7, para. 31.

18 *ICJ Reports* (2004) p. 178, para. 106.

19 *Draft Articles on the Effects of Armed Conflict on Treaties, with Commentaries*, adopted at the 63rd session of the ILC (2011), <untreaty.un.org/ilc/texts/instruments/English/commentaries/1_10_2011.pdf>.

to the broader corpus of international law in general, including international criminal law, international human rights law and international environmental law.

Moreover, protection of the environment in relation to armed conflict encompasses consideration of more than just the law applicable during the actual armed conflict. Environmental pressures can lead to conflict and conflict can exacerbate environmental pressures making more difficult the restoration of peace and the pursuit of sustainable development. Indeed, some rules of IHL expressly relate to measures to be taken before and after an armed conflict. Consideration must therefore be given to both the 'before' and the 'after' when examining the nature and extent of the co-existence between IHL and other areas of international law in the case of protection of the environment in relation to armed conflicts.

Some of these issues are explored in the chapters in this book. These chapters have their origins in papers presented at the Workshop on Protection of the Environment in Relation to Armed Conflict that was held on 16 and 17 February 2012 at the Faculty of Law, at Lund University in Sweden.[20] The Workshop gathered together experts from Europe, the United States and Australia, including leading academics as well as representatives from the International Committee of the Red Cross (ICRC), the Swedish, Norwegian and Danish Red Cross Societies and the Swedish and Norwegian governments, to examine the relevance and adequacy of the existing regime for environmental protection during armed conflict as well as the ability of other international legal mechanisms to contribute to the amelioration of damage to the environment arising as a result of or in relation to armed conflict. The book, like the workshop, takes as its starting point the existing IHL regime for the protection of the environment during armed conflict and then goes onto explore the application of other legal regimes that may be relevant to protection of the environment both *during* armed conflict and, as in the broader context envisaged by the ILC, *in relation to* armed conflict.

3.1. Deficiencies in the IHL Regime for the Protection of the Environment in Times of Armed Conflict

The first three chapters in this volume address the identification of lacunae in the existing IHL regime for the protection of the environment in times of armed conflict. As each of these chapters recognises, the environment may generally be protected as a civilian object. Beyond this, the environment is also subject to its own special protections in Articles 35(3) and 55 of Protocol I which forbid the use of methods or means of warfare that are intended to or may be expected to cause widespread, long-term and severe damage to the environment. However,

20 R. Rayfuse and B. Sjöstedt, *Report of the Workshop on Protection of the Environment in relation to Armed Conflict*, available at <www.jur.lu.se/Files/Environment_and_armed_conflict_Report.pdf>.

the extremely high threshold set by these articles has given rise to debates as to their efficacy as well as to the adequacy of protecting the environment as a civilian object against direct attacks but not against non-excessive collateral damage.

According to Droege and Tougas the only issue is whether the environment can ever be identified as a legitimate military objective, something they suggest is an inherently difficult task. Even if the environment, or parts thereof, might be considered a legitimate military objective and hence lawfully targeted, then other principles of IHL such as the principles of distinction, proportionality, precaution and the prohibition of destruction of property without military necessity will operate to provide protection to the environment. For example, proportionality will operate to protect the environment from excessive damage by balancing the anticipated direct military advantage with the foreseeable collateral effects while the obligation to take precaution will be particularly relevant in determining what, when, where and how to target in order to ensure the least environmental impact.

As Fleck points out, however, the inadequacy of the general principles of distinction, proportionality and precaution in ensuring effective protection of the environment is no longer disputed. Moreover, specific rules on the protection of the environment in armed conflict are almost entirely absent. Koppe seeks to overcome this deficiency by deducing the existence of a new principle – the principle of ambituity – as the legal basis for protection of the environment in times of armed conflict. According to this principle, which he identifies as a fundamental principle of the law of armed conflict, and a principle already recognised as a general principle of law and hence a general principle of international law, the environment must be protected during armed conflict and an absolute limitation exists on the necessities of war. He analogises this principle of ambituity to the principle of humanity "which provides for an absolute limitation to the necessities of war in the interest of man and civilization". He then relocates the basis of the prohibition against excessive collateral environmental damage away from the provisions of Protocol I, instead finding its emergence as a complimentary rule of customary international law in state practice since the 1990s. He concludes that "any military action which causes collateral damage to the environment would first have to be assessed under this relatively new customary prohibition; and subsequently if no breach can be established and if applicable by reference to Articles 35(3) and 55 of Protocol I".

Beyond agreeing on the inadequacy of existing IHL relating to the protection of the environment, one significant conclusion these chapters have in common is a plea for further research to clarify and improve the application of IHL norms relating to the environment. Droege and Tougas call for better application and clarification of existing IHL; for "further development of IHL in order to provide specific protection to areas of major ecological importance and to develop norms and mechanisms to address the environmental consequences of hostilities in the mid- and long term"; and for research into protections afforded by human rights and general environmental law and a clearer articulation of the relationship between these bodies of law and IHL. Koppe calls for further research into the consequences of armed conflict for the environment and its broad public dissemination. Fleck suggests the conduct of interdisciplinary case studies to "support fact-oriented evaluations of military requirements, ecological assessments and necessary legal developments" as a means of ensuring the appropriate balancing of environmental protection and military advantage in light of contemporary realities rather than outdated legal thresholds.

3.2. Options for Addressing Deficiencies in the IHL Regime for the Protection of the Environment in Times of Armed Conflict

The theme of the need for more research is carried through into the following two chapters which explore possible means of addressing at least some of the lacuna in the IHL regime identified in the first chapters. Bothe examines the ethical underpinnings and imperatives of both IHL and international environmental law, identifies commonalities between the regimes and calls for the concretisation of the principles thus identified through the further development of the law. While noting the importance of the principle of distinction and the prohibition against unnecessary suffering, he demonstrates how the interpretation of Articles 35(3) and 55 of Protocol I in accordance with the fundamental principles of environmental law, including those of intergenerational equity, precaution and prevention of transboundary harm, would result in a different outcome to interpretation according to the negotiating history of those articles. To overcome this classic demonstration of the problem of fragmentation, he argues that it is necessary to insert the core principles of international environmental law into the application of the law of armed conflict. Thus civilian environmental concerns should be considered in assessing the proportionality equation and precautionary measures should be required of persons deciding upon launching an attack. The rule prohibiting unnecessary suffering and that of military necessity should also be applied in such a way as to take account of environmental concerns and the triple qualification of environmental harm in Articles 35(3) and 55 of Protocol I must be revisited and reconsidered. In addition, hostilities must be conducted in such a way as to avoid significant damage to the environment of states not party to the conflict. Like Koppe, Bothe suggests the time may be ripe for identification and articulation of a new rule of customary international law although rather than suggesting a wholly new principled basis, he locates the rule in existing international law, requiring methods and means of warfare to be employed with 'due regard' for the environment.

Thomas focuses on the conceptual and pragmatic considerations involved in interpreting and applying the threshold of impermissible damage in Articles 35(3) and 55 of Protocol I. He notes that the threshold does not preclude the application of other IHL rules to limit environmental harm beneath the threshold and that, as a practical matter, protection of the environment during armed conflict depends on military commanders balancing military necessity against environmental and humanitarian norms. Thus, "arguments for protecting the environment should be addressed to those military decision makers who are actually in the position to make environmentally harmful decisions". He suggests a refocusing of determinations of military necessity by emphasising strategic considerations when deciding what may or may not constitute acceptable environmental damage. In other words, protection of the environment should be embedded into military operations and decision making. According to Thomas, framing military necessity in terms of strategic goals, rather than tactical operational aims, could not only help to protect the environment but could also open up discussions about the effects of environmental damage on long-term peace.

3.3. Beyond IHL: Other Legal and Institutional Mechanisms and Frameworks for Monitoring Violations and Seeking Redress

Looking beyond the IHL regime, Das explores the possibility of whether the concept of sustainable development and its substantive principles – intergenerational equity, precaution and integration – can be used to fill the gaps in IHL. Armed conflict affects both the environment and the war-torn population and can have deleterious consequences for the restoration of peace and the maintenance of the conditions necessary for sustainable development. Indeed, as Das notes, armed conflict is "the antithesis of sustainable development". Given the acceptance by the international community of the need for sustainable development, it is now arguable that damage to the environment during armed conflict must not be so extensive or severe as to unduly obstruct or interrupt that development. Thus, although the principles of IHL which protect the environment during actual armed conflict may play a crucial role in ensuring that the conditions for sustainable development continue to exist, they do not play a sufficient role. Just as Bothe argues for the integration of environmental principles into IHL, Das argues for the integration of sustainable development principles into IHL, suggesting the adoption of a new non-binding text or code or set of rules for environmental protection in armed conflict.

Lixinski examines the lessons any possible new regime on protection of the environment during armed conflict might learn from the regime for the protection of cultural property in the event of armed conflict. His framework for analysis of the relationship between the laws of armed conflict and international environmental law is provided by recourse to feminist legal theory, in particular ecofeminism which leads him to conclude that a change in attitude is needed to shift conceptions of the environment from that of a "damsel in distress" to "an important resource that needs to outlive the conflict if parties to the conflict (and humanity as a whole) are to rebound". According to Lixinski, this shift in thinking has already occurred in the case of cultural property which has received its own regime. He examines the key features of the cultural property regime, including the listing mechanism, the temporal and material application of the regime, issues of criminal responsibility and the structure of the international bureaucracy and assesses their relevance and possible application in the context of developing a future regime for safeguarding the environment in times of armed conflict.

Clearly, the applicability of multilateral environmental agreements (MEAs) during armed conflict constitutes a critical element of any discussion on protection of the environment in relation to armed conflict. Of course, many MEAs consist merely of general principles and vague obligations, the applicability of which in the context of an armed conflict may be difficult to assess. The World Heritage Convention, however, establishes an institutional framework for the protection of world heritage sites which includes a Committee to which the power to adopt binding substantive obligations is delegated. Sjöstedt provides an analysis of the role of the UNESCO World Heritage Convention in protecting the environment during armed conflict. In particular, she focuses on the cooperation between the World Heritage Committee and the United Nations peacekeeping forces deployed in the Democratic Republic of the Congo in attempting to protect the Virunga National Park from the ravages of armed conflict. She concludes that what she refers to as cooperative 'green-keeping' is a useful approach to regime interaction between IHL and international environmental law from which valuable lessons might be learned.

3.4. *Accountability for Damage to the Environment in Relation to Armed Conflicts*

The final chapter deals with issues of accountability for environmental damage with a particular focus on responsibility for predatory resource exploitation as a means of financing armed conflicts. Unsustainable patterns of resource exploitation during an armed conflict can pose particularly serious threats to the environment and to resource sustainability. As Dam-de Jong discusses, IHL provides several rules for protection of the environment as a function of its rules regarding the protection of human property. General international law also provides obligations deriving from the concept of sustainable development. However, little international law is directly applicable to resource exploitation conducted by rebel groups. The general IHL principles of distinction and proportionality as well as the prohibitions against pillage, destruction or seizure of the property of an adversary, and the taking or destruction of objects indispensable to the survival of the civilian population provide some protections, however, their wider application, particularly in the context of exploitation carried out by a government engaged in an internal armed conflict, is problematic. Governments will, of course, remain bound by their peace time obligations and therefore remain obliged to continue to respect their multilateral environmental obligations even during armed conflict. However, the applicability of these obligations to rebel groups and other individuals remains problematic. Dam de-Jong thus concludes that the current legal framework is inadequate both in its scope and in its application. Examining the sanctions regimes that have been imposed by the United

Nations Security Council for the purposes of breaking the link between resource exploitation and the continuation of armed conflicts, she concludes that, while useful, these ad hoc solutions are not necessarily sufficient. Consistent with other contributions in the volume she suggests the need for the development of clear rules on the exploitation of natural resources during armed conflict that are applicable to all parties in all armed conflicts

4. Conclusion

Protection of the environment in relation to armed conflict is not a new topic. However, with the emergence of international environmental concerns over the past five decades the topic has moved far beyond its IHL roots. As the chapters in this book demonstrate, a vast range of issues, actors and legal regimes must now be considered and some pro-active and imaginative research and thinking engaged in. This is precisely what the ILC now intends to do. These chapters are offered as a small contribution to the future consideration of this ever-important topic.

1 The Protection of the Natural Environment in Armed Conflict – Existing Rules and Need for Further Legal Protection*

Cordula Droege** and Marie-Louise Tougas***

1. Introduction: The Humanitarian Concern

Less immediately visible than the death and injury of people or the damage caused to infrastructure, the natural environment is frequently one of the casualties of war. Whether the result of deliberate acts by the belligerent parties, or incidental consequences, armed conflicts have lead to the degradation, or even destruction, of all aspects of the natural environment, including animals, vegetation, soil, water systems or even entire ecosystems. Defoliation campaigns such as the one in the Vietnam come to mind. Damage to power stations, chemical plants and other industrial installations often affect the water distribution or sewage systems, leading to serious consequences for water sources and groundwater, the soil and agricultural areas. They can lead to air pollution, ultimately affecting the health and survival of entire populations.

A particularity of environmental damage is that its impact frequently extends over large areas and continues for years or even decades after the end of the war. It has severe consequences for the civilian population, and can even lead to the displacement of entire communities, which in itself can cause stress on the environment.[1] The nature, scope and ramifications of the adverse environmental consequences of war have been well documented in the series of Post-Conflict Environmental Assessments published by the United Nations Environmental

---

* The views expressed in this article are those of the authors, and do not necessarily reflect those of the ICRC.

** Legal Adviser, International Committee of the Red Cross.

*** Legal Adviser, International Committee of the Red Cross.

1 *See e.g.* United Nations Environment Programme (hereinafter UNEP), *The Democratic Republic of Congo, Post-Conflict Environmental Assessment, Synthesis for Policy Makers*, (2011) p. 26, <postconflict.unep.ch/publications/UNEP_DRC_PCEA_EN.pdf>, visited on 26 July 2012 (which describes the consequences of the displacement of communities, such as deforestation in the new areas or wildlife poaching).

Rosemary Rayfuse (ed.), War and the Environment: New Approaches to Protecting the Environment in Relation to Armed Conflict
Copyright 2014 Koninklijke Brill NV. Printed in The Netherlands. ISBN 978-90-04-27064-0 pp. 11-234

Programme (UNEP) which, in recent years, have significantly contributed to raising awareness of the problem.[2]

The international community has been aware of the environmental degradation caused by armed conflict for many decades. In 1972, the Stockholm Declaration, adopted by the UN Conference on the Human Environment proclaimed that "[m]an and his environment must be spared the effects of nuclear weapons and all other means of mass destruction".[3] The World Charter of Nature, adopted by the UN General Assembly in 1982, stated that "[n]ature shall be secured against degradation caused by warfare or other hostile activities".[4] In 1992, the Rio Declaration reiterated that international law protecting the natural environment has to be respected in times of armed conflict.[5] The same year, the UN General Assembly adopted a resolution on the protection of the environment in times of armed conflict "stressing that destruction of the environment not justified by military necessity and carried out wantonly, is clearly contrary to existing international law".[6] In 2011, the Parliamentary Assembly of the Council of Europe adopted a resolution on armed conflicts and the environment.[7] At the Rio+20 summit in 2012, the international community reaffirmed the principles of the 1992 Rio Declaration and of Agenda 21.[8]

---

2 *See e.g.* UNEP, *The Post-Conflict Environmental Assessments on the Democratic Republic of Congo (2011), Sudan (2007, 2008), Lebanon (2007), Iraq (2007), Afghanistan (2003, 2011), Occupied Palestinian Territories (2003, 2006, 2009), Kosovo (1999)*, <www.unep.org/disastersandconflicts/Publications/tabid/54718/Default.aspx>, visited on 26 July 2012.

3 United Nations, Declaration of the United Nations Conference on the Human Environment, Stockholm, 16 June 1972 ("The Stockholm Declaration"), UN Doc. A/CONF.48/14/Rev.1, Principle 26. *See also* Principle 21.

4 United Nations General Assembly, World Charter for Nature, UN Doc. A/RES/37/7, 28 October 1982, para. 5.

5 Rio Declaration on Environment and Development, Report of the United Nations Conference on the Human Environment, 3 to 14 June 1992, Rio de Janeiro, UN Doc. A/CONF.151/26 (Vol. I), Principle 24.

6 United Nations General Assembly, *Protection of the environment in times of armed conflict*, UN Doc. A/RES/47/37, 12 November 1992.

7 Council of Europe, Parliamentary Assembly, Resolution 1851 (2011), *Armed conflicts and the environment*, adopted by Standing Committee, acting on behalf of the Assembly, 25 November 2011. *See also* Council of Europe, Doc. 12774, *Armed Conflicts and the Environment*, report of the Committee on the Environment, Agriculture and Local and Regional Affairs, Mr. R. Huseynov, rapporteur.

8 *See* United Nations Conference on Sustainable Development, *The Future We Want*, Outcome of the Conference, UN Doc. A/Conf.216/L.1, 19 June 2012, para. 16. *See also* Agenda 21, online: <www.un.org/esa/dsd/agenda21/>, visited on 1 November 2012.

Considerable research has been conducted, particularly since the Iraq-Kuwait war of 1991, on the legal protection of the environment in armed conflicts.[9] Much of this research has focused either on the specific protections provided in international humanitarian law (IHL), in particular the Convention on the prohibition of military or any hostile use of environmental modification techniques (ENMOD Convention)[10] and Protocol Additional to the Geneva Conventions of 12 August 1949, and relating to the Protection of Victims of International Armed Conflicts (AP I)[11] which contain specific provisions against harm to the natural environment, or on the applicability of international environmental law to situations of armed conflict. Rather than focus on these specific provisions, this study seeks to examine the general protections under IHL, in particular the characterisation of the natural environment as a civilian object and the legal protection flowing from this characterisation – namely the general rules on the conduct of hostilities. After addressing these general rules in section 2, section 3 briefly recalls some other relevant provisions of IHL before turning, in section 4, to possible avenues to strengthen the legal protection of the environment in armed conflict by clarifying or further developing IHL in this respect, taking into account the protection provided by international human rights law and international environmental law.

2. The Protection of the Environment as a Civilian Object under the General Rules on the Conduct of Hostilities

The natural environment is generally either explicitly or implicitly recognised as a civilian object.[12] It therefore benefits from the corresponding protections under

9 *See e.g.* N. Al-Duaij, *Environmental Law of Armed Conflict* (Transnational Publishers, New York, 2004); J. E. Austin and C. E. Bruch (eds.), *The Environmental Consequences of War* (Cambridge University Press, Cambridge, 2000); D. Guillard, *Les armes de guerre et l'environnement naturel* (L'Harmattan, Paris, 2006); K. Hulme, *War Torn Environment: Interpreting the Legal Threshold* (Martinus Nijhoff Publishers, Leiden, 2004); E. Koppe, *The Use of Nuclear Weapons and the Protection of the Environment during International Armed Conflict* (Hart Publishing, Oxford, 2008); K. Mollard-Bannelier, *La protection de l'environnement en temps de conflit armé* (Pedone, Paris, 2001); G. Plant, *Environmental Protection and the Law of War: A "Fifth Geneva" Convention on the Protection of the Environment in Time of Armed Conflict?* (Belhaven Press, London and New York, 1992); M. Tignino, *L'eau et la guerre. Éléments pour un régime juridique* (Bruylant, Bruxelles, 2011); Special Issue on Environment, 92:879 *International Review of the Red Cross* (2010).

10 G.A. Res. 72, 31st sess., Supp. No. 39, at 36, U.N.Doc. A/31/39 (1977), entered into force 5 October 1978.

11 1125 *U.N.T.S.* 3, entered into force 7 December 1978.

12 UNEP, *Protecting the Environment During Armed Conflict, An Inventory and Analysis of International Law,* (UNEP, Geneva, 2009) p. 13 (hereinafter "UNEP Report 2009"); ICRC, *Guidelines for Military Manuals and Instructions on the Protection of*

IHL, in particular the principles of distinction, proportionality and precaution. As provided in Rule 43 of the ICRC's Customary Law Study:[13]

> The general principles on the conduct of hostilities apply to the natural environment:
> A. No part of the natural environment may be attacked, unless it is a military objective.
> B. Destruction of any part of the natural environment is prohibited, unless required by imperative military necessity.
> C. Launching an attack against a military objective which may be expected to cause incidental damage to the environment which would be excessive in relation to the concrete and direct military advantage anticipated is prohibited.

The protection of the natural environment under the general principles on the conduct of hostilities has also been confirmed by the International Court of Justice which stated in its advisory opinion on the *Legality of the Use of Nuclear Weapons*:[14]

> States must take environmental considerations into account when assessing what is necessary and proportionate in the pursuit of legitimate military objectives. Respect for the environment is one of the elements that go into assessing whether an action is in conformity with the principles of proportionality.

---

the Environment in Times of Armed Conflict, reprinted in *International Review of the Red Cross* no. 818 (1996), para. 4; A. Roberts, 'The Law of War and Environmental Damage', in Austin and Bruch, *supra* note 9, p. 50; M. Bothe *et al.*, 'International law protecting the environment during armed conflict: gaps and opportunities', 92:879 *International Review of the Red Cross* (2010) p. 576; M. N. Schmitt, 'Humanitarian Law and the Environment', 28 *Denver Journal of International Law and Policy* (2000) p. 283; W. H. Boothby, *Weapons and the Law of Armed Conflict* (Oxford, 2009) p. 100.

13 J.-M. Henckaerts and L. Doswald-Beck, *Customary International Humanitarian Law* (Volumes I and II), ICRC (Cambridge University Press, Cambridge, 2005). *Note* that this rule was not put into question by the United States in its criticism of the customary law rules on the environment, which focussed on Rule 45: "[I]t is clear under the principle of discrimination that parts of the natural environment cannot be made the object of attack unless they constitute military objectives, as traditionally defined, and that parts of the natural environment may not be destroyed unless required by military necessity." J. B. Bellinger III and W. J. Haynes II, 'A US government response to the International Committee of the Red Cross study on Customary International Humanitarian Law', 89:866 *International Review of the Red Cross* (2007) p. 455.

14 The controversy over the mention of the Additional Protocol I rules in the particular context of the resort to nuclear weapons is relayed in Schmitt, *supra* note 12, p. 265, at fn 35.

As Karen Hulme writes, "the recognition of the environment as a *prima facie* civilian object has done more to protect it than any environmentally specific rule of international humanitarian law".[15] However, given that the natural environment is not a tangible object in the traditional sense of the word, and that it is transboundary in nature and seemingly limitless, the question arises as to the precise significance of considering it as a civilian object under IHL. In particular, it must be asked, how the rules governing the conduct of hostilities by the belligerent parties apply to the natural environment.

2.1. *The Natural Environment as a Civilian Object*

The term 'natural environment' should be understood in the widest sense possible. The Commentary to Article 55 of AP I explains that "[t]he concept of the natural environment should be understood in the widest sense to cover the biological environment in which a population is living … [It] includes forests and other vegetation …, as well as fauna, flora and other biological or climatic elements."[16] This, then, would include everything that is not man-made: the atmosphere, the air, the ozone layer, the oceans and other bodies of water, soil, rocks, plants and animals. While there remain some doubts as to the exact definition of the natural environment,[17] for practical purposes broad agreement on what is covered by the term is sufficient for the purposes of our discussion.

However, the very fact that the natural environment is understood in such a broad manner has created some controversy over whether it can be characterised in its totality as a civilian object. Is it really correct to say that the natural environment as a whole is a civilian object? Two arguments, in particular, have been put forward against such an understanding. First, it is it argued that the natural environment as a whole, or indeed all of its parts, cannot really be considered as an object. Traditionally, the term 'object' would be understood to refer to material things that can be seen or touched. Thus, the natural environment as the sum total of different and differing natural components and processes cannot easily be characterised as such an object.[18] Moreover, it is controversial whether all of the different parts of the natural environment can be characterised as civilian

15 K. Hulme, 'Taking care to protect the environment against damage: a meaningless obligation?', 92:879 *International Review of the Red Cross* (2010) p. 678.

16 Y. Sandoz, C. Swinarski and B. Zimmermann (eds.), *Commentary on the Additional Protocols* (ICRC, Geneva, 1987) para. 2126.

17 *See e.g.* Program on Humanitarian Policy and Conflict Research, Harvard University (HPCR), *Manual on International Law Applicable to Air and Missile Warfare* (Bern, 2010) p. 205.

18 W. Heintschel, H. von Heinegg and M. Donner, 'New Developments in the Protection of the Natural Environment in Naval Armed Conflicts', 37 *German Yearbook of International Law* (1994) p. 289. The question is left open by Schmitt, *supra* note 12, p. 283.

objects. This is put into question, for instance, in the case of the air or the ozone layer. Second, it is contended that the norms of AP I may be understood as indicating that the natural environment cannot be equated with a civilian object. The express prohibitions on environmental damage contained in Article 35(3) and Article 55 of AP I are confined to effects that are 'widespread, long-term and severe'. Thus, it would be circumventing this high threshold to hold States parties to the Protocol accountable under the general rules for all negative effects of warfare on the natural environment.[19]

These arguments are not ultimately convincing. To begin with, numerous statements and declarations by States make no distinction between *parts* of the natural environment and the natural environment *as a whole*, when referring to direct attacks, destruction or incidental damage. For instance, the Final Declaration adopted by the International Conference for the Protection of War Victims of 1993 reaffirms "the rules of international humanitarian law applicable during armed conflicts protecting … the natural environment, either against *attacks on the environment as such* or against wanton destruction causing serious environmental damage".[20] In Resolution 687 of 1991, the Security Council held Iraq liable for "any direct loss, damage, including *environmental damage*, and the depletion of natural resources" as a consequence of its invasion of Kuwait.[21] In 1992, the UN General Assembly stressed that "the destruction of the environment, not justified by military necessity and carried out wantonly, is clearly contrary to existing international law".[22] With respect to the North Atlantic Treaty Organization's (NATO) bombing campaign in the war in Kosovo in 1999, NATO stated that, when making targeting decisions, it took into account "all possible collateral damage, be it environmental, human or to the civilian infrastructure".[23] There is therefore nothing in the practice or statements of States that would indicate that they do not consider all of the natural environment to be protected as a civilian object.

Moreover, the system of international humanitarian law requires that everything that can be the subject of an attack or destruction be classified either as

---

19 Heintschel *et al.*, *ibid.*, p. 289.

20 International Conference for the Protection of Victims of War, Geneva, 30 August–1 September 1993, para. 10, online: <www.icrc.org/eng/resources/documents/misc/57jms8.htm>, visited 31 October 2012.

21 United Nations Security Council, Resolution 687, UN Doc. S/RES/687 (1991), 3 April 1991. For an overview of the damages caused to the Kuwait environment, *see* S. A. S. Omar *et al.*, 'The Gulf War Impact on the Terrestrial Environment of Kuwait: An Overview', in Austin and Bruch, *supra* note 9, p. 316.

22 GA Resolution 47/37, *supra* note 6, para. 55.

23 Statement quoted in C. Hedges, 'Serbian Town Bombed by NATO Fears Effects of Toxic Chemicals', *New York Times*, 14 July 1999. For further statements by States, *see ICRC Customary Law Study*, *supra* note 13, pp. 848 *et seq.*

a civilian object or as a military objective. IHL clearly states that civilian objects are all objects which are not military objectives.[24]

Lastly, the relationship between the general proportionality principle and the specific protection of Article 55 of AP I must be understood in light of their different scopes of application. Under the general rules on the conduct of hostilities, the natural environment is protected against direct attack and against excessive damage, but only as long as it remains a civilian object and only relatively to the concrete and direct military advantage. Article 55 of AP I has a different purpose and scope of application: it sets an absolute limit to the damage that is tolerated for the natural environment.

Proceeding, therefore, from the recognition that the natural environment – whether in its entirety or as the sum total of its parts – is a civilian object, how do the rules on the conduct of hostilities apply to it?

2.2. *The Principle of Distinction*

As a consequence of the natural environment qualifying as civilian object, no part of it may be attacked, unless it is a military objective.[25] The weakness of the general protection afforded to civilian objects to protect the natural environment is often highlighted, with the argument that civilian objects are all too likely to become military objectives.[26] However, the transformation of a civilian object into a military objective is not as simple and frequent as might at first sight seem to be the case. Indeed, only those objects which fulfil the criteria laid out in Article 52(2) of AP I, a provision that reflects customary IHL, can be qualified as military objectives. According to these criteria, military objectives are limited to those objects which by their nature, location, purpose or use make an effective contribution to military action; *and* whose total or partial destruction, capture or neutralisation, in the circumstances ruling at the *time*, offers a definite military advantage. Thus, there must be a close nexus between the potential target and 'military action'.

The term 'military action' denotes the enemy's war fighting capabilities. This nexus is established through the four criteria of nature, location, purpose or use. 'Nature' refers to the intrinsic character of an object. No part of the natural environment is a military objective by nature. However, according to these criteria, in a given situation of hostilities, parts of the natural environment may make an effective contribution to military action by virtue of their particular location,

---

24 Article 52(1) AP I, *supra* note 11; Rule 9 of the *ICRC Customary Law Study, supra* note 13.

25 *See* Article 52(1) AP I, *supra* note 11; Rules 7, 10, 43(A) of the *ICRC Customary Law Study, supra* note 13.

26 S. Vöneky, *Die Fortgeltung des Umweltvölkerrechts in internationalen bewaffneten Konflikten* (Berlin, 2001) p. 46; Bothe *et al., supra* note 12, p. 577, who call this a 'gap'; UNEP Report 2009, *supra* note 12, p. 13.

their purpose or their present use.[27] For example, a hill can become a military objective by location if it is militarily necessary to seize it or to prevent the enemy from seizing it. A forest can become a military objective by use, if troops are hiding in or under its cover. On the other hand, while not excluded *per se*, it is difficult to see how the air, the ozone layer, the soil or underground water resources could make an effective contribution to military action by their use, purpose or location. As long as this is not the case, all these parts of the natural environment remain civilian objects, and must be protected against direct attack (and against excessive incidental damage). In addition, critical thought must be given to the assertion that an area becomes a military objective once armed forces are located in it.[28] In each case it is necessary to make clear which particular 'area' is meant. Thus, in certain instances, such as where the very characteristics of the natural environment of the area are directly used to contribute to military action (such as the foliage of a forest), the area might be liable to become a military objective. However, the concept of an 'area' is a rather broad one, encompassing, for example, a city or a large forest; areas which do not become military objectives simply because combatants are located therein.

It is also important to remember that the contribution to military action must be both effective and, following from the reference to 'military action', must be directed towards the actual war-fighting capabilities of a party to the conflict. If an object merely contributes towards the war-sustaining capability of a party to the conflict (the general war effort), it does not qualify as a military objective. In addition, an attack on the object in question must bring about 'a *definite* military advantage', meaning that the advantage must be concrete and perceptible as opposed to merely hypothetical or speculative. From the word 'military', it can be inferred that the anticipated advantage must not be of a merely political nature. Even when the military advantage is derived from an 'attack as a whole' it constitutes a finite, limited event that must not be confused with the entire war. Finally, the definite military advantage must be offered 'in the circumstances ruling at the time'. If the destruction of a given object does not yet offer, or no longer offers, a definite military advantage, the object does not constitute a military objective and must not be attacked.

In the UNEP report *Protecting the Environment during Armed Conflict*, two questions are put forward. First, "does undermining a country's morale and political resilience constitute a sufficiently definite military advantage?"; and second, "would a protected area [affected by the illegal exploitation of high-value

27 *See* the Declaration of the United Kingdom upon ratification of AP I: "In relation to Article 52, that a specific area of land may be a military objective if, because of its location or other reasons specified in the Article, its total or partial destruction, capture or neutralisation in the circumstances ruling at the time offers definite military advantage." *See e.g.* the similar declarations of France, Italy, The Netherlands, and Germany upon ratification of AP I.

28 Bothe *et al.*, *supra* note 12, p. 576.

natural resources] be considered an acceptable target, considering that revenue from this illegal trade was contributing to the war effort?"[29] The answer to both of these questions is *no*. Undermining a country's morale and political resilience is a political and not a military advantage, and the exploitation of natural resources might constitute a war sustaining activity, but it does not, as such, make a direct effective contribution to military action.

Finally, it is important to bear in mind that once an object has been identified as a military objective on the basis of the criteria laid out above, the attacker does not have unlimited licence to attack this object. Indeed, even if a military objective has been properly identified, an attack may still be prohibited under other IHL rules, for example, if it would lead to excessive incidental civilian casualties and/or damage to civilian objects and thus be contrary to the principle of proportionality. In addition, if the attack is intended, or may be expected, to cause widespread, long-term and severe damage to the natural environment, it would still be prohibited by Article 35(3) of AP I[30] even if it constitutes a military objective.

2.3. *The Principle of Proportionality*

As a civilian object, the natural environment must not only be protected against direct attack, but also against so-called 'collateral damage'[31] that is excessive. Thus, launching an attack against a military objective which may be expected to cause incidental damage to the natural environment which would be excessive in relation to the concrete and direct military advantage anticipated is prohibited.[32]

For the protection of the natural environment, which is often affected indirectly rather than directly by the hostilities,[33] it is of particular importance that

---

29 UNEP Report 2009, *supra* note 12, p. 13.

30 Recognised as a rule of customary international humanitarian law (Rule 45 of the *ICRC Customary Law Study, supra* note 13).

31 For instance, Article 13(c) of the *San Remo Manual on International Law Applicable to Armed Conflicts at Sea and Explanation*, L. Doswald-Beck (ed.) (International Institute of Humanitarian Law, Grotius Publications, Cambridge University Press, Cambridge, 1995) (hereinafter "*San Remo Manual*") defines collateral damage as "the loss of life of, or injury to, civilians or other protected persons, and damage to or the destruction of the natural environment or objects that are not in themselves military objectives".

32 Article 51(5)(b) AP I, *supra* note 11; Rules 14, 43 of the *ICRC Customary Law Study, supra* note 13.

33 For instance, massive movement of refugees and internally displaced persons often has important environmental consequences such as deforestation and uncontrolled exploitation of natural resources. Large refugee camps can pose a challenge in terms of waste management, water and sanitation. *See, for instance*, UNEP, *Desk Study on the Environment in Liberia* (2004) and UNEP, *Environmental Considerations of Human Displacement in Liberia: A Guide for Decision-maker and Practitioners* (2006).

when balancing the anticipated concrete and direct military advantage against the expected incidental loss of civilian life, injury to civilians, damage to civilian objects, or a combination thereof, the *foreseeable reverberating effects* of the attack on the civilian population and civilian objects must also be taken into consideration.

The principle of proportionality is thus particularly relevant when the destruction of or damage to military objectives is likely to have indirect adverse effects on the natural environment. This is particularly clear for facilities that are military objectives and contain chemical substances whose release could damage the natural environment. However, frequently even more remote damage will be foreseeable and will have to be taken into account in the proportionality assessment. For example, if an electricity network is targeted because it is being used by the adversary as a military objective, past experience has shown that the destruction of electricity networks can lead to serious disruption of sewage or waste water treatment systems, and, in turn, very seriously harm the quality of the water and soil. This should certainly be taken into account in the proportionality assessment. In this respect, it would be advisable to conduct a prior assessment of the environmental consequences before launching attacks, including the expected consequences of weapons and ammunitions used. This is proposed for instance in the Joint NATO Doctrine for Environmental Protection during NATO Led Military Activities, which states that:

> 1. While meeting their military mission, NATO Forces should be committed to taking all reasonably achievable measures to protect the environment. To achieve this, commanders must know how NATO led military activities affect and are affected by the environment. Environmental planning is an essential process to ensure appropriate environmental protection. An Environmental Management System is a useful tool to support the commander in this task.
>
> …
>
> 3. Environmental damage may be an inevitable consequence of operations. However, environmental planning should minimise these effects without compromising either operational or training requirements. While operational requirements are paramount, it is only by including environmental considerations early in the planning process that an informed decision can be taken about the full consequences of proposed actions.[34]

34 Joint NATO Doctrine for Environmental Protection During NATO Led Military Activities (STANAG-7141) (Edition 5), available online: <nsa.nato.int/nsa/nsdd/listpromulg.html>, visited 27 July 2012; *see also Environmental Guidebook for Military Operations,* developed by a multinational working group consisting of representatives from defence organizations from the United States and Sweden, 2008, available online: <www.defmin.fi/files/1256/Guidebook _final_printing_version.pdf> visited 27 July 2012.

It is clear, however, that the principle of proportionality suffers from a number of limitations. First, as in all applications of the principle of proportionality, there remains a measure of uncertainty about what can be considered as excessive incidental damage to civilian objects as compared to the concrete and direct military advantage. This problem might be exacerbated when trying to measure an immediate military advantage to an adverse effect on the natural environment which, though foreseeable, might be remote in time or space. For instance, the bombardment of the Pancevo industrial complex and of a petroleum refinery in Novi Sad by NATO forces during the war in Kosovo in 1999 lead to the release of some 80,000 tons of crude oil into the soil and of many tonnes of other toxic substances.[35] This led the Committee established to review the NATO campaign to state that "[i]t is difficult to assess the relative values to be assigned to the military advantage gained and harm to the natural environment, and the application of the principle of proportionality is more easily stated than applied in practice".[36] During the Lebanon war in 2006, the bombardment of the El Jyieh power plant south of Beirut led to the release of an estimated 12,000 to 15,000 tons of fuel into the Mediterranean Sea. The General Assembly expressed its deep concern about the environmental consequences but did not express a view about a violation of IHL.[37]

Second, while it is by now undisputed that reverberating effects must be taken into account, there remains some discussion as to how far this obligation goes.[38] How far down the environmental chain must the attacker assess the harm? For example, while destruction or damage to a small element of the natural environment (a small part of a naturally protected area) might not be considered excessive (and indeed negligible) as compared to a given military advantage, the secondary effects of this damage or destruction (the disappearance of an animal species whose livelihood depends on these trees and the effects of the disappearance of this species on the wider ecosystem) might be considered excessive. In such instances, of course, the question of the foreseeability of these second and third-order effects arises. The Special Committee established to study the bombing campaign by NATO in 1999 mentions some of the difficulties in this respect and notes that

35 Hulme, *supra* note 9, p. 188.

36 The International Criminal Tribunal for Former Yugoslavia (ICTY), *Final Report to the Prosecutor by the Committee Established to Review the NATO Bombing Campaign Against the Federal Republic of Yugoslavia*, 13 June 2000, para. 19.

37 UNEP Report 2009, *supra* note 12, p. 23; *see also* UN General Assembly Resolution 61/194 of 20 December 2006, UN Doc. A/RES/61/194, paras. 1–3; *and* Resolution 62/188 of 19 December 2007, UN Doc. A/RES/62/188, paras. 1–4.

38 *See e.g. Commentary to the Air and Missile Warfare Manual*, *supra* note 17, Rule 14, Comment 4.

> [i]t would be necessary to know the extent of the knowledge possessed by NATO as to the nature of the Serbian military-industrial targets (and thus the likelihood of environmental damage flowing from their destruction), the extent to which NATO could reasonably have anticipated such environmental damage (for instance, could NATO have reasonably expected that toxic chemicals of the sort allegedly released into the environment by the bombing campaign would be stored alongside that military target?), and whether NATO could reasonably have resorted to other (and less environmentally damaging) methods for achieving its military objective of disabling the Serbian military-industrial infrastructure.[39]

Again, "knowledge of the environment is constantly increasing, and there is a growing understanding of long-term risks attendant to disruption of ecosystems";[40] as such knowledge increases, so does the foreseeability of reverberating effects. Thus, it is necessary to more carefully consider the interpretation to be given to 'excessive incidental damage' to the natural environment. M. Bothe and others suggest that expert groups should analyse typical scenarios and develop a set of criteria for determining proportionality.[41] Having said this, there is also a measure of subjectivity in valuing competing considerations during the proportionality assessment. The value attributed to the natural environment will undoubtedly vary considerably among different belligerent parties to an armed conflict, and will probably evolve over time as the consciousness of the importance of healthy ecosystems for our survival increases.[42]

Third, there is an absolute limit to the incidental damage that can be caused to the natural environment. The use of methods or means of warfare which are intended, or may be expected, to cause widespread, long-term and severe dam-

---

39 *Final Report by the Committee Established to Review the NATO Bombing Campaign*, *supra* note 36, para 24. Serbia and Montenegro, in its claim against the legality of the NATO bombing campaign before the International Court of Justice, on the other hand, alleged that Belgium "has violated … the obligation to protect the environment" and requested the Court to adjudge and declare that "by taking part in the bombing of oil refineries and chemical plants, the Kingdom of Belgium has acted against the Federal Republic of Yugoslavia in breach of its obligation not to cause considerable environmental damage" and "by taking part in the use of weapons containing depleted uranium, the Kingdom of Belgium has acted against the Federal Republic of Yugoslavia in breach of its obligation not to use prohibited weapons and not to cause far-reaching health and environmental damage". *Case concerning the Legality of the use of Force (Serbia and Montenegro* v. *Belgium)* (Preliminary objections), Judgment of 15 December 2004, *ICJ Reports* 2004, at paras. 1 and 22.

40 Y. Dinstein, *The Conduct of Hostilities under the Law of International Armed Conflict* (Cambridge University Press Cambridge, 2004) p. 177.

41 Bothe *et al.*, *supra* note 12, p. 578.

42 M. Bothe, 'The Protection of the Environment in Times of Armed Conflict. Legal rules, uncertainty and possible developments', 34 *German Yearbook of International Law* (1991) pp. 54–62.

age to the natural environment is prohibited.[43] The high threshold of this rule is frequently criticised, as indeed it appears to be so high that it has been almost meaningless in protecting the natural environment in practice.[44] Traditionally, 'long-term' is understood to refer to decades, 'widespread' is understood to refer to several hundred square kilometres and 'severe' means a serious disruption of the ecosystem or, in relation to Article 55, refers to the prejudice to the health or survival of the population.[45] A number of commentators even questioned whether the environmental destruction resulting from the burning of oil wells in Kuwait by Iraq during the 1991 Gulf War reached the threshold of widespread, long-term and severe damage to the natural environment.[46] In other words, these cumulative criteria imply that the norm in question only protects the natural environment against exceptionally catastrophic events, sometimes referred to as 'ecocide'.

Given our contemporary understanding of the natural environment, several of these aspects do not necessarily make sense. For instance, it is now known that the extinction of a particular species can have dramatic consequences for a particular ecosystem, and ultimately the population living in the area even if its eradication is not widespread (for instance if the species does not live in an area which covers several hundred square kilometres). It is also argued that certain core aspects of the natural environment should be protected absolutely (not merely by the principle of proportionality), and not only against widespread, long-term and severe damage.[47] Some commentators therefore suggest that the Article 55 AP I standard should be interpreted so as to lower its threshold thereby making it more practically meaningful.[48] The International Committee of the Red Cross (ICRC) has also suggested that consideration be given to the need to strengthen this provision. In short, it is recognised that each of the three criteria ('widespread, longterm and severe') establishes a high, yet imprecise, threshold. The meaning of these terms should therefore be more clearly defined in order to improve the effectiveness of the norm. In addition, given the often more limited geographical scope of non-international armed conflicts, the appropriateness of this threshold for such conflicts calls for examination.[49]

---

43 Articles 35(3) and 55(1) AP I, *supra* note 11; Rule 45 of the *ICRC Customary Law Study, supra* note 13.

44 Bothe *et al.*, *supra* note 12, p. 576.

45 Sandoz *et al.*, *supra* note 16, para. 1452 and fn 117.

46 *See* the references of the positions in Vöneky, *supra* note 26, p. 42, at fn 50.

47 *Ibid.*, p. 74.

48 Hulme, *supra* note 15, p. 690.

49 Report prepared by the ICRC for the 31st International Conference of the Red Cross and Red Crescent, "Strengthening legal protection for victims of armed conflicts", Geneva, October 2011, p. 15.

2.4. The Principle of Precaution

The principle of precaution relates both to the principle of distinction and the principle of proportionality. It requires that those who plan or decide upon an attack must do everything feasible to verify that the targets are military objectives.[50] It also imposes a duty on parties to the conflict to take constant care to spare civilian objects, including the natural environment.[51] Thus, means and methods of warfare must be employed with due regard to the protection and preservation of the natural environment.[52] This seems to be widely accepted[53] and reflects the international community's increasing recognition of the natural environment as an 'essential interest'.[54] As the Commentary to the ICRC Customary Law Study explains, the principle of precaution was included in Rule 44 to show that the protection of the natural environment stems not only from the application of the rules on civilian objects but also from a recognition of the need to provide particular protection to the natural environment as such.[55] However, the extent to which these norms really impose different obligations in practice is not entirely settled.[56]

The following discussion focuses on the general IHL rules that flow from the principle of precaution. In this respect, two aspects of the principle of precaution are of particular relevance. First, each party to the conflict must take all feasible precautions in the choice of means and methods of warfare with a view to avoiding, and in any event to minimising, incidental loss to the natural environment as a civilian object.[57] Second, when a choice is possible between several military objectives for obtaining a similar military advantage, the objective to be selected

---

50 Article 57(2)(a)(i) AP I, *supra* note 11; Rule 16 of the *ICRC Customary Law Study, supra* note 13.

51 Article 57(1) AP I, *supra* note 11; Rule 15 of the *ICRC Customary Law Study, supra* note 13.

52 Rule 44 of the *ICRC Customary Law Study, supra* note 13.

53 *See* practice related to Rule 44 of the *ICRC Customary Law Study*, online: <www.icrc.org/customary-ihl/eng/docs/v2_rul_rule44>, visited 27 July 2012.

54 *See* International Court of Justice, *Case Concerning the Gabčikovo-Nagymaros Protect (Hungary* v. *Slovakia)*, Judgment of 15 September 1997, [1997] *ICJ Reports* 7, para. 53.

55 *ICRC Customary Law Study*, Volume I, p. 147, *supra* note 13. The term due regard seems to be taken from the *San Remo Manual*, para. 44, which in turn was inspired by the Law of the Sea Convention (*see San Remo Manual, supra* note 31, at 44.7, 44.9).

56 *See also* a discussion of the different standards in Hulme, *supra* note 15, pp. 685 *et seq.*, who, however, does not analyse the difference between the due regard obligation and the constant care obligation.

57 Article 57(2)(a)(ii) AP I, *supra* note 11; Rules 17, 44 of the *ICRC Customary Law Study, supra* note 13.

must be the one on which the attack may be expected to cause the least danger to the natural environment.[58]

The principle of precaution therefore imposes certain duties of precaution on belligerent parties to take measures to protect the natural environment. In this respect advance information gathering is crucial.[59] Appropriate information gathering may, for example, require belligerents, whenever feasible:

- to seek the relevant information about quantity, toxicity, possibility of avoiding leaks, and so on if attacking a target that may contain, for example, toxic substances;
- to gather the necessary information about the environmental conditions surrounding specific military operations, for instance the proximity of rivers, underground aquifers, sensitive natural habitats, vulnerable species;
- to choose, as between several military targets, those targets the attack on which will cause the least danger to the natural environment;
- to assess the environmental impact of the weaponry to be used in the context of the particular natural environment concerned and to possibly use available alternative weaponry that reduces the risk of environmental damage;
- to change the timing of the attack if this can contribute to reducing harm to the natural environment;
- to give warnings before the attack, if time permits, to allow for measures to safeguard the natural environment.

Having said this, the fact that effects on the natural environment are often more complex to assess than, for example, the destruction of civilian infrastructure surrounding a military target, raises the question as to how onerous the burden of feasible precautions can be in practice. Thus, whether certain means or methods of warfare will have reverberating effects on the natural environment might not be easily foreseeable for the military commander deciding upon the attack. The principle of precaution would presumably not require a commander, especially in the heat of battle, to conduct an environmental impact assessment at the moment of deciding upon the attack. At the tactical level, a reasonable commander is merely required to take into account all the information reasonably available to him.[60] This limitation notwithstanding, the inclusion of relevant

58 Article 57(3) AP I, *supra* note 11; Rule 21 of the *ICRC Customary Law Study*, *supra* note 13.

59 *See also* Hulme, *supra* note 9, p. 82, with a number of similar suggestions on relevant factors to be taken into account under the obligation of care in Article 55(1) AP I.

60 *See* the Declaration of the United Kingdom upon ratification of AP I: "In relation to Articles 51 to 58 inclusive, that military commanders and others responsible for planning, deciding upon or executing attacks necessarily have to reach decisions on the basis of their assessment of the information from all sources which is available to them at the relevant time."

factors into military manuals and directives could conceivably contribute to raising the awareness of commanders to the need to assess the impact on the natural environment if relevant information is available and can be considered in the time available. This would be more readily the case, for instance, in situations where attacks, such as planned airstrikes, are planned in advance. However, as discussed in the next section, the relatively onerous burden of a more thorough environmental impact assessment would appear only to be required at the time of the development or acquisition of certain weapons with the result from any such impact assessments being included in the rules and directions governing the use of those weapons.

2.5. *Review of New Weapons, Means and Methods of Warfare*

Article 36 of Additional Protocol I provides that "[i]n the study, development, acquisition or adoption of a new weapon, means or method of warfare, a High Contracting Party is under an obligation to determine whether its employment would, in some or all circumstances, be prohibited by this Protocol or by any other rule of international law applicable to the High Contracting Party". Beyond the specific obligation it imposes on States parties to the Protocol, all States have an interest in assessing the legality of new weapons, whether or not they are party to AP I. Such assessments will contribute to ensuring that the State's armed forces can conduct hostilities in accordance with that State's international obligations.

Considering the obligation to avoid excessive incidental damage to the natural environment, States should arguably take measures when studying, developing, acquiring or adopting new weapons to assess the *potential* impact of a weapon on the natural environment, including its secondary effects on the air, water, soil, fauna or flora, in light of the characteristics of the weapons, such as its components, impact area, and so on. Such an assessment would, of course, by its nature remain at a relatively abstract level, as environmental effects will depend on the concrete characteristics of the natural environment in a particular area of hostilities. Nonetheless, assessment of the potential impact of a certain weapon if deployed in certain types of natural environment would arguably go a long way towards complying with the obligations of proportionality and precaution. This knowledge could then be translated into specific rules and directions on the use of the weapon, which would govern or even restrict its use in certain environments.

As suggested in the ICRC *Guide to the Legal Review of New Weapons, Means and Methods of Warfare*,[61] in determining the effects on the natural environment of the weapon under review, and in particular whether the weapon is expected to cause excessive incidental damage to the natural environment or widespread,

61 ICRC, *A Guide to the Legal Review of New Weapons, Means and Methods of Warfare: Measures to Implement Article 36 of Additional Protocol I of 1977* (Geneva, 2006) p. 17.

long-term and severe damage to the natural environment, the relevant questions to be considered include:

- Have adequate scientific studies on the effects on the natural environment been conducted and examined?
- What type and extent of damage are expected to be directly or indirectly caused to the natural environment?
- How long is the damage expected to last; is it practically/economically possible to reverse the damage, *i.e.* to restore the natural environment to its original state; and what would be the time needed to do so?
- What is the direct or indirect impact of the environmental damage on the civilian population?
- Is the weapon specifically designed to destroy or damage the natural environment, or to cause environmental modification?

This determination is, of course, without prejudice to the *absolute* prohibition imposed by Article 35(3) of AP I to employ means and methods of warfare which are intended or may be expected to cause widespread, long-term and severe damage to the natural environment regardless of the military advantage obtained.[62] Furthermore, it should be kept in mind that some rules and principles of international environmental law may also apply to weapons testing, military training and weapons destruction or disposal outside the context of armed conflicts.[63]

2.6. Prohibition of Destruction of Property without Military Necessity

It is a customary rule of IHL, based on Article 23(g) of the Hague Regulations of 1907, that it is prohibited to destroy or seize enemy property, including its natural resources, unless required by imperative military necessity.[64] A similar rule exists in the law of occupation,[65] and the "extensive destruction and appropriation of property, not justified by military necessity and carried out unlawfully and wantonly" constitutes a grave breach of the Convention (IV) relative to the Protection

---

62 *See also* Article 55 AP I, *supra* note 11; Rule 45 of the *ICRC Customary Law Study, supra* note 13. The customary nature of this rule and its applicability in non-international armed conflict is subject to debate (*see e.g.* Bellinger III and Haynes II, *supra* note 13, p. 443 and J.-M. Henckaerts, 'Customary International Humanitarian Law: a response to US comments', in the same volume, p. 473).

63 On this issue, *see* Guillard, *supra* note 9, pp. 187–205. *See also* section 4.4 *infra*.

64 Rule 50 *ICRC Customary Law Study, supra* note 13, applicable in international and non-international armed conflict.

65 Article 53, Convention (IV) relative to the Protection of Civilian Persons in Time of War, Geneva, 12 August 1949, 75 *U.N.T.S.* 287, entered into force 21 October 1950 (GC IV).

of Civilian Persons in Time of War (GC IV).[66] Accordingly, it is now recognised as a rule of customary international law that the destruction of any part of the natural environment is prohibited, unless required by imperative military necessity.[67] It has been argued that the rules protecting 'enemy' property in Article 23(g) of the Hague Regulation[68] and occupied territory as provided for in Article 53 of GC IV are inadequate to provide protection to the natural environment because neither the natural environment as a sum total nor some parts of the natural environment, such as migratory bird species or straddling fish stocks,[69] or the high seas, outer space and the ozone layer, fall entirely within the territory or jurisdiction of a State.[70] However, as demonstrated in the ICRC's *Study on Customary International Humanitarian Law* as well as the *San Remo Manual on Naval Warfare* and the *HPCR Manual on Air and Missile Warfare*, it would appear that today the natural environment in all its parts is considered to be protected by customary law against destruction if those parts do not constitute military objectives.[71] This rule has an additional value when compared with Articles 35(3) and 55 of AP I because it prohibits the destruction of parts of the natural environment regardless of the level of damage, subject, of course, to imperative military necessity. By way of example, although there was some controversy as to whether the destruction of oil wells during the Gulf War of 1991 reached the level of widespread, long-term and severe damage,[72] there seems to have been wide agreement that it amounted to a violation of the prohibition against the destruction of enemy property without imperative military necessity.[73]

---

66 *Ibid.*, Article 147; it also constitutes a war crime in international and non-international armed conflict under the Rome Statute of the International Criminal Court, 2187 *U.N.T.S.* 90, entered into force 1 July 2002, Article 8(2)(a)(iv) and 8(2)(e)(xii) (Rome Statute).

67 Rule 43(B) of the *ICRC Customary Law Study*, *supra* note 13. *See also* para. 44 of the *San Remo Manual*, *supra* note 31: "Damage to or destruction of the natural environment not justified by military necessity and carried out wantonly is prohibited."; Rule 88 of the HPCR *Manual on International Law Applicable to Air and Missile Warfare*, *supra* note 17: "The destruction of the natural environment carried out wantonly is prohibited." However, *see* objection to the term 'imperative' by Boothby, *supra* note 12, p. 100 but without explanation for the objection or reference to the wording of Article 23(g) of the Hague Regulations.

68 And Rule 50 of the *ICRC Customary Law Study*, *supra* note 13.

69 These are the questions asked by Schmitt, *supra* note 12, p. 296.

70 Vöneky, *supra* note 26, p. 30; Roberts, *supra* note 12, p. 57.

71 *See* the commentary to the *Manual on International Law Applicable to Air and Missile Warfare*, which gives an example the destruction of the Baltic Sea (Commentary to Rule 88, para. 3), *supra* note 17.

72 Boothby, *supra* note 12, p. 97.

73 *See e.g.* US Department of Defence, *Final Report to Congress on the Conduct of the Persian Gulf War, Appendix O, The Role of the Law of War*, 10 April 1992, 31 *International Legal Materials* (1992) pp. 636–637; Dinstein, *supra* note 40, p. 218. Arguably

3. Other Existing IHL Norms Contributing to the Protection of the Natural Environment

Before discussing how the legal IHL framework for the protection of the natural environment could be further strengthened, it should be recalled that IHL also contains a number of specific norms that contribute either directly or indirectly to the protection of the natural environment.

By way of example, the ENMOD prohibits the use of military or any other hostile use of environmental modification techniques having widespread, long-lasting or severe effects as the means of destruction, damage or injury to any other State party. These are techniques which manipulate natural process and thereby change the dynamics, composition or structure of the Earth, including its biota, lithosphere, hydrosphere and atmosphere, or of outer space. In addition, Articles 35(3) and 55 of AP I prohibit resort to methods or means of warfare which are intended, or may be expected, to cause widespread, long-term and severe damage to the natural environment.[74]

A number of other provisions providing protection to specific objects are also relevant to the preservation of the natural environment. For example, Article 54 of AP I and Article 14 of Protocol Additional to the Geneva Conventions of 12 August 1949, and relating to the Protection of Victims of Non-International Armed Conflicts (AP II)[75] prohibits the attack, destruction, removal or rendering useless of *objects indispensable to the survival of the civilian population*, such as food-stuffs, agricultural areas for the production of food-stuffs, crops, livestock, drinking water installations and supplies and irrigation works.[76] Article 56 of AP I and Article 15 of AP II[77] prohibit the targeting of *dams, dykes and nuclear electrical generating stations (works and installations containing dangerous forces)*, even if they have become military objectives, as well as military objectives in their vicinity, if such attacks may cause the release of dangerous forces and consequent severe losses among the civilian population. For its, part, Article 60 AP I foresees the possibility of belligerent parties expressly agreeing on *demilitarised zones*, in

---

these destructions could also be considered as excessive incidental damage to the environment as compared to the concrete and direct military advantage.

74 *See also* Rule 45 of the *ICRC Customary Law Study, supra* note 13.

75 1125 *U.N.T.S.* 609, entered into force 7 December 1978. *See also* Rule 54 of the ICRC *Customary Law Study, supra* note 13.

76 *See* Eritrea-Ethiopia Claims Commission, *Partial Award, Western Front, Aerial Bombardment and Related Claims – Eritrea's Claims 1, 3, 5, 9-13, 14, 21, 25 & 26*, Decision of 19 December 2005, [2009] XXVI *Reports of International Arbitral Awards* 291, paras. 104–105: the Commission found a violation of Article 54(2) AP I, which it considered to reflect customary international law, because Ethiopia had bombarded a water reservoir which provided water to the civilian population. The decision is available at <untreaty.un.org/cod/riaa/vol_XXVI.htm>, visited 27 July 2012.

77 *See also* Rule 42 of the *ICRC Customary Law Study, supra* note 13.

which case they are precluded from extending their military operations to such zones. Such zones can be agreed upon in advance during in peacetime.[78] Other important protections include Articles 28 and 47 of the Hague Regulations,[79] Articles 33(2) of the Geneva Convention IV[80] and 4(2)(g) of AP II which prohibit pillage,[81] including of *natural resources*.[82] Finally, the so-called *Martens clause*, first formulated in the Preamble of the Hague Convention No IV,[83] stipulates that civilians and belligerents "remain under the protection and the rule of the principles of the law of nations, as they result from the usages established among civilized peoples, from the law of humanity and the dictates of public conscience". The dictates of public conscience are increasingly interpreted as including environmental concerns.[84] Indeed, as noted at the outset, during the last 40 years, as international concern for the protection of the natural environment has grown, the necessity to ensure such protection in times of armed conflict has gained more support. It is worth repeating that the 1972 Stockholm Declaration proclaims that "[m]an and his environment must be spared the effects of nuclear

78 Along these lines, the *San Remo Manual*, *supra* note 31, states in para. 11 that "[p]arties to the conflict are encouraged to agree that no hostile actions will be conducted in marine areas containing rare or fragile ecosystems or the habitat of depleted, threatened or endangered species or other forms of marine life".

79 Second Peace Conference of the Hague, 1907, Convention (IV) respecting the Laws and Customs of War on Land and its annex: Regulations concerning the Laws and Customs of War on Land, 36 Stat. 2277, 1 Bevans 631, 205 Consol. T.S. 277, 3 Martens Nouveau Reccueil (ser. 3) 461, entered into force 26 January 1910 (Hague Regulations and Hague Convention IV).

80 *Supra* note 65.

81 *See also* Rule 52 of the *ICRC Customary Law Study*, *supra* note 13, and Article 8(2)(b)(xvi) of the Rome Statute, *supra* note 66.

82 *See Case Concerning Armed Activities on the Territory of the Congo (Democratic Republic of the Congo* v. *Uganda)*, Judgment of 19 December 2005, *ICJ Reports* 2005, para. 245, in which the Court found that the looting, plundering and exploitation of natural resources was a violation of *jus in bello* and noted the prohibition of pillage in Article 47 of the Hague Regulations of 1907, *supra* note 79, and Article 33 of GC IV, *supra* note 65. *See also* the accusation on the ground of pillage by the United Nations War Crimes Commission of ten German administrators of Polish forest during German occupation (1939–1944) for their involvement in the "wholesale cutting of Polish timber to an extent far in excess of what was necessary to preserve the timber resources of the country" in *History of the United Nations War Crimes Commission and the Development of the Laws of War* (compiled by the United Nations War Crimes Commission, London, 1948) at p. 496.

83 *Supra* note 79. *See also* Article 1(2) AP I, *supra* note 11, and preamble, AP II, *supra* note 75.

84 ICRC *Guidelines for Military Manuals and Instructions on the Protection of the Environment in Times of Armed Conflict*, *supra* note 12, para. 7; Roberts, *supra* note 12, p. 52.

weapons and all other means of mass destruction".[85] The 1982 World Charter of Nature states, *inter alia*, that "[n]ature shall be secured against degradation caused by warfare or other hostile activities".[86] The 1992 Rio Declaration reiterates that international law protecting the natural environment must be respected in times of armed conflict.[87] This is again reiterated by the UN General Assembly in its resolution on the protection of the environment in times of armed conflict, also adopted in 1992, in which it "stress[ed] that destruction of the environment not justified by military necessity and carried out wantonly, is clearly contrary to existing international law".[88] A resolution in similar terms was adopted by the Parliamentary Assembly of the Council of Europe in 2011,[89] and in 2012 the principles of the Rio Declaration and of Agenda 21 were reaffirmed.[90]

IHL norms concerning weapons are also highly relevant for the protection of the natural environment in that they restrict the use of certain substances which can have harmful effects on the environment or require the clearing of dangerous or potentially hazardous remnants.[91] Relevant examples here include:

- The Protocol for the Prohibition of the Use of Asphyxiating, Poisonous or Other Gases, and of Bacteriological Methods of Warfare of 1925;[92]
- The prohibition of the use of poison or poisoned weapons;[93]
- The Convention on the Prohibition of the Development, Production and Stockpiling of Bacteriological (Biological) and Toxin Weapons and on their Destruction of 1972;[94]
- The Protocol on Prohibitions or Restrictions on the Use of Incendiary Weapons (Protocol III to the Convention on Prohibitions or Restrictions on the Use of Certain Conventional Weapons Which May be Deemed to be

---

85 Stockholm Declaration, *supra* note 3, Principle 26. *See also* Principle 21.

86 World Charter for Nature, *supra* note 3, para. 5.

87 Rio Declaration, *supra* note 5, Principle 24.

88 GA Resolution 47/37, *supra* note 6.

89 Council of Europe, Resolution 1851 (2011), *supra* note 7.

90 *See* "The Future We Want", United Nations Conference on Sustainable Development, *supra* note 8, at para. 16 and Agenda 21, *supra* note 8.

91 On this issue, *see* Guillard, *supra* note 9.

92 Geneva, 94 *L.N.T.S.* 65, entered into force 8 February 1928.

93 Article 23(a) of the Hague Regulations of 1907, *supra* note 79; Rule 72 of the *ICRC Customary Law Study*, *supra* note 13; the UNEP Report 2009, *supra* note 12, argues that the poisoning of water wells might be considered an 'inhumane' means of warfare. This is, in a way, a superfluous consideration, considering the very clear prohibition of the use of poison under all circumstances. It also constitutes a war crime under Article 8(2)(b)(xvii) of the Rome Statute of the International Criminal Court, *supra* note 66.

94 Apr. 10, 1972, 26 *U.S.T.* 583, 1015 *U.N.T.S.* 163, entered into force 25 March 1975. *See* also Rule 73 of the *ICRC Customary Law Study*, *supra* note 13.

Excessively Injurious or to Have Indiscriminate Effects);[95] Article 2(4) of the Protocol states: "It is prohibited to make forests or other kinds of plant cover the object of attack by incendiary weapons except when such natural elements are used to cover, conceal or camouflage combatants or other military objectives, or are themselves military objectives.";

- The Protocol on Explosive Remnants of War (Protocol V to the Convention on Prohibitions or Restrictions on the Use of Certain Conventional Weapons Which May be Deemed to be Excessively Injurious or to Have Indiscriminate Effects) of 2003;[96] and
- The Convention on the Prohibition of the Development, Production, Stockpiling and Use of Chemical Weapons and on their Destruction of 1993.[97]

These norms, which are only briefly recalled here, are all relevant in practice and may help to prevent some of the worst humanitarian consequences on the environment. Nevertheless, it is argued that more may be required.

4. Further Strengthening the Protection of the Natural Environment through Clarifying or Developing the Law

The preceding sections have sought to outline the protections afforded to the environment by the general rules on the conduct of hostilities which flow from the recognition that the environment is a civilian object and from the more specific rules that contribute to environmental protection as an aspect of the protection of the civilian population and civilian objects. Nevertheless, as highlighted above, a number of deficiencies or uncertainties remain which hinder the more effective protection of the environment in times of armed conflict. As argued here, some of these deficiencies can be rectified by clarifying some areas of the law. This is consistent with the calls made by other commentators and institutions to clarify and extend the law, including that of the Secretary-General of the United Nations, who, on the occasion of the International Day for Preventing the Exploitation of the Environment in War and Armed Conflict, called on Member States

> to clarify and expand international law on environmental protection in times of war. Existing legal instruments should be adapted to reflect the predominantly internal nature of today's armed conflicts. We need also to consider mechanisms for monitoring violations and recommending sanctions and actions for enforcement, recovery and compensation. Furthermore, national legislation must fully reflect

95 1342 *U.N.T.S.* 171, 19 *I.L.M.* 1534, entered into force 2 December 1983.

96 U.N. Doc. CCW/MSP/2003/2 (27 November 2003), entered into force 16 May 2006.

97 1974 *U.N.T.S.* 3, entered into force 29 April 1997; *see also* Rule 74 of the *ICRC Customary Law Study*, *supra* note 13.

provisions of international criminal law that allow for the prosecution of environmental violations during armed conflict.[98]

Building on this, in November 2011, the ICRC suggested two particular areas for improvement: the need to better protect certain areas of environmental importance, and the need to find mechanisms and procedures to address the environmental consequences of hostilities.

4.1. Clarifying the Rules on the Conduct of Hostilities Protecting Civilian Objects and Their Application to the Natural Environment

In terms of clarifying the law, considerable work remains to be done to address the deficiencies and uncertainties in the law of armed conflict in relation to protection of the environment. As is clear from the foregoing, more reflection is required to determine when a part of the natural environment can become a military objective, especially by distinguishing its use for military action and for war-sustaining activity. In addition, lessons learned regarding incidental damage to the natural environment during past conflicts should be gathered in order to see which incidental effects, especially indirect second and third-order effects, can follow from certain types of attacks. This can serve to make these reverberating effects more readily foreseeable for those who plan an attack in the future. More research could also be undertaken to assess how the precautionary principle, taken from environmental law, can provide guidance for the legal understanding and practical implementation of the meaning of *incidental damage* and *feasible precautions* with respect to the natural environment, particularly in the absence of scientific certainty. Importantly, further clarification of the extent and limits of the three terms '*widespread*, *long-term* and *severe*', taking into account contemporary knowledge about the effects of harm on the natural environment, might contribute to making this absolute threshold more meaningful in practice. Moreover, the question should also be asked whether the threshold is necessarily appropriate for all non-international armed conflicts. Finally, it is clear that additional specific rules should be contemplated with respect to certain installations containing dangerous substances, such as oil wells or power plants, or factories containing dangerous chemicals or pollutants, in order to make such installations the object of heightened protection, along the lines of the existing rule on works and installations containing dangerous forces.

---

98 *See e.g.* Message of the UN Secretary-General, Ban Ki-moon, on the occasion of the International Day for Preventing the Exploitation of the Environment in War and Armed Conflict, 6 November 2009, available online at <www.un.org/en/events/environmentconflictday/ sg_message_2009.shtml>, visited 27 July 2012.

4.2. *Protection of Certain Areas of Major Ecological Importance*

Beyond clarification of the rules relating to protection of the environment as a civilian object, however, special consideration should be given to the protection of areas of major ecological importance which are vulnerable to the adverse consequences of hostilities. By way of example, the oil spill caused by the bombardment of the El Jyieh power plant in Lebanon in 2006 affected the Palm Islands nature reserve and a number of archeologically significant areas in Byblos.[99] Similarly, the consequences of the conflict in the Democratic Republic of the Congo on areas of unique ecosystems and habitat for fauna and flora are well-documented.[100] One way of protecting such areas could be to place them off-limits for all military activity. By doing so these areas could not be attacked directly, although they might suffer incidental damage as a result of fighting and the presence of military activity.

Such a proposal was already made at the time of drafting of the Additional Protocols. A Working Group of Committee III submitted a draft Article 48 ter providing that "[p]ublicly recognized nature reserves with adequate markings and boundaries declared as such to the adversary shall be protected and respected except when such reserves are used specifically for military purposes".[101] The proposal was not, however, adopted. In 1995, the International Union for the Conservation of Nature (IUCN) produced a Draft Convention on the Prohibition of Hostile Military Activities in Protected Areas, which provided among other things that "[e]ach resolution adopted by the Security Council under Chapter VII of the UN Charter, in response to a situation of armed conflict shall include a list of the relevant internally protected areas, thereby designated as no-target areas in which all hostile military activities shall not be permitted during the armed conflict in question". Similar proposals have also been made by UNEP.[102] The ICRC, too, has recently reiterated the suggestion that to avoid the consequences of hostilities certain fragile environments or areas of major ecological importance, such as groundwater aquifers, national parks and habitats of endangered species, should be off-limits to any form of military activity. According to the ICRC such areas should be delineated and designated as demilitarised zones before an armed conflict occurs, or at the latest when the fighting breaks out, thereby barring all military action and the presence of combatants and military materiel.

A similar system of specially protected areas already exists for cultural property. The Second Protocol to the Hague Convention of 1954 for the Protection of

---

99 UNEP, *Lebanon Post Conflict Environmental Assessment* (2007), p. 134.

100 UNEP, *The Democratic Republic of Congo, Post-Conflict Environmental Assessment, Synthesis for Policy Makers*, *supra* note 1.

101 Sandoz *et al.*, *supra* note 16, Article 5, paras. 2138 *et seq.*

102 UNEP Report 2009, *supra* note 12, p. 54.

Cultural Property in the Event of Armed Conflict[103] establishes a system of so-called 'enhanced protection', under which cultural property of special significance for humanity is entered on a list and the parties to the Protocol undertake never to use it to back up military operations.[104] A similar system of listed sites also exists in the Convention Concerning the Protection of the World Cultural and Natural Heritage of 1972,[105] which requires States "[n]ot to take any deliberate measures which might damage directly or indirectly the cultural and natural heritage"[106] and which provides for the inscription on a 'List of World Heritage in Danger' of any world heritage endangered by "the outbreak or the threat of an armed conflict".[107] Notably, five national parks in the Democratic Republic of Congo and one in the Central African Republic are on this list.[108]

At present, however, no rule of IHL exists to confer such internationally recognised protection on specific natural areas. At best, the only option that currently exists is to establish a demilitarised zone. However, this would require agreement between the parties to the conflict. Thus, the law would need to be expanded through the adoption of new provisions aimed at providing a mechanism for territorial protection applicable to areas of major ecological importance during armed conflict.

4.3. Mechanisms to Address the Environmental Consequences of Hostilities

As previously mentioned, the environmental consequences of war may reach far beyond the hostilities in time and space. They can be felt far beyond the areas of conflict, and, as is often the case with environmental degradation, they may continue for the long term. Dealing with these consequences often requires substantial financial and technical resources which may well exceed those available to the conflict-affected countries. Thus, for example, the bombing of the power plant of El Jyieh in Lebanon in 2006 and the resulting oil pollution led the UN

103 The Hague, 26 March 1999, 2253 *U.N.T.S.* 212, entered into force 9 March 2004.

104 *Ibid.*, Article 10.

105 Paris, 16 November 1972, 1037 *U.N.T.S.* 151.

106 *Ibid.*, Article 6(3).

107 *Ibid.*, Article 11(4).

108 Hostilities in Congolese national parks are a constant matter of concern. *See for instance* 'UNESCO Director General preoccupied by fighting in World Heritage sites in eastern Congo', 29 June 2012, online: <whc.unesco.org/en/news/905/>, visited 27 July 2012. In 2000, UNESCO and the United Nations Foundation launched a pilot project of conservation of natural heritage during armed conflict, *see* online: <whc.unesco.org/en/congobiodiversity/, visited 27 July 2012. For an assessment of the impact of the conflict on the natural environment in the DRC, *see* UNEP, *The Democratic Republic of Congo. Post-Conflict Environmental Assessment. Synthesis for Policy Makers*, *supra* note 1.

General Assembly to express its deep concern over the pollution and to call upon the government of Israel "to assume responsibility for prompt and adequate compensation to the Government of Lebanon for the costs of repairing the environmental damage caused by the destruction, including the restoration of the marine environment".[109]

When harm to the natural environment occurs as a result of violations of rules of IHL in international armed conflicts, the State responsible will be liable to make reparation and to pay compensation to the harmed State.[110] However, the obligation to make reparation for harm to the natural environment cannot be found in the law of non-international armed conflicts, which today constitute the majority of conflicts.

In its report on *Strengthening Legal Protection for Victims of Armed Conflicts,* the ICRC suggests that further thought should be given to possible *mechanisms and procedures* for addressing the immediate and long-term consequences of environmental damage.[111] It is argued here that these mechanisms should be entitled to monitor the nature and extent of the damage to the natural environment caused by violations of international humanitarian law, whether in international or non-international armed conflicts. They should also be empowered to investigate alleged violations of relevant international rules and to decide on the most appropriate forms of reparation in each situation. This could imply, for example, an obligation to remove the source of harm from the affected area and to ensure decontamination.

Moreover, environmental degradation flows not only from violations, but can equally be the consequence of lawful acts of war, albeit with no less damaging impact. It is important, therefore, for the protection of both the environment and the affected population, to look beyond the legal obligation to make reparation for violations. The proposed new mechanisms should therefore also be empowered and equipped to assess the environmental damage resulting from lawful activities and to determine how such damage should be remedied. In other words, such mechanisms should provide solutions both in terms of victim assistance and in terms of restoration of the natural environment following the hostilities. In this respect the experience of the United Nations Compensation Commission (UNCC) could be relevant. The UNCC established criteria for compensation, made awards for environmental monitoring and assessment, recognised the need

---

109 UN General Assembly Resolution 61/194 of 20 December 2006, *supra* note 37, para. 3.

110 Article 3 of Hague Convention IV, *supra* note 79; Article 91 AP I, *supra* note 11; *Case Concerning the Factory at Chorzów (Merits)* PCIJ, 1928; Article 31 of the ILC's Draft Articles on Responsibility of States for Internationally Wrongful Acts, November 2001, Supplement No. 10 (A/56/10), chp.IV.E.1, available at: <www.unhcr.org/refworld/docid/3ddb8f804.html>, visited 1 November 2012.

111 Strengthening legal protection for victims of armed conflicts, ICRC Report, *supra* note 49, p. 16.

for sound scientific data to inform the review of substantive claims and acknowledged the precautionary need to identify potential risks in order to inform necessary future action, especially for the purposes of protecting human health.[112]

Finally, given the complexity of remediating environmental damage by, for example, repairing damaged plants and installations or cleaning up polluted soil and rubble, it would also be desirable to develop new norms on international assistance and cooperation. Such norms could be developed in tandem with new mechanisms or, on the contrary, independently of them. They could apply to environmental damage caused by any military operation, whether lawful or unlawful. Such new norms could be inspired by similar rules recently created for dealing with the legacy of landmines, cluster munitions and other explosive remnants of war.[113]

4.4. Complementary Protection: International Environmental Law and International Human Rights Law

This study focuses on IHL and suggestions to strengthen the protection of the environment are made within the normative framework of that body of law. While it would go beyond the realm of this analysis to address other bodies of law, it should nevertheless be briefly recalled that two other areas of law, in particular, provide complementary protection to the environment, including during armed conflict, *i.e.* international environmental law and international human rights law.

With respect to international environmental law, there are numerous treaties and customary rules of international environmental law that continue to apply during armed conflict. The obligation to take into account the rules and principles of international environment law during armed conflict was affirmed by the International Court of Justice in its advisory opinion on the *Legality of the Threat or Use of Nuclear Weapons*:

> The Court thus finds that while the existing international law relating to the protection and safeguarding of the environment does not specifically prohibit the use of nuclear weapons, it indicates important environmental factors that are properly to be taken into account in the context of the implementation of the principles and rules of the law applicable in armed conflict.[114]

---

112 UNEP Report 2009, *supra* note 12, p. 28.

113 Convention on the Prohibition of the Use, Stockpiling, Production and Transfer of Anti-Personnel Mines and on their Destruction, entered into force 1 March 1999, 2056 *UNTS* 211 / [1999] *ATS* 3 / 36 *ILM* 1507 (1997), Article 6; Convention on Cluster Munitions, 30 May 2008, 48 *ILM* 357 (2009), entered into force 1 August 2010, Article 6; Protocol on Explosive Remnants of War, *supra* note 96, Articles 7 and 8.

114 *Legality of the Threat or Use of Nuclear Weapons*, 8 July 1996, ICJ, Advisory Opinion, *ICJ Reports* 1996, para. 33.

An example of a customary international law principle pertaining to the protection of the environment which continues to apply during armed conflicts is the principle that a State shall not use or permit the use of its territory in such a manner as to cause injury in or to the territory of another.[115] Similarly, the International Law Commission (ILC) has recently noted that the existence of armed conflicts does not *ipso facto* terminate the application of treaties.[116] Only a few international environmental treaties specifically address their applicability in times of armed conflict.[117] Some do so implicitly, but the majority are silent on the issue. This has led to a discussion as to their continued applicability. The ILC has taken the position that treaties relating to the protection of the environment can be regarded as having a subject matter that leads to the assumption that they continue to apply, in whole or in part, during armed conflict.[118] However, the question has to be answered on a case-by-case basis for each treaty, as several factors have to be considered in order to ascertain whether a treaty is susceptible to termination, withdrawal or suspension in the event of an armed conflict. Among these factors are the nature of the treaty, in particular its subject matter, its object and purpose, its content, and the number of parties to the treaty, as well as the characteristics of the armed conflict, such as its territorial extent, its scale and

---

115 Also known as the *Trail Smelter principle – see Trail Smelter case (United States* v. *Canada), Reports of International Arbitral Awards*, 16 April 1938 and 11 March 1941, volume III, pp. 1905–1982; *see also Corfu Channel (United Kingdom of Great Britain and Northern Ireland* v. *Albania)* (Merits), ICJ, Judgment, *ICJ Reports* 1949, p. 22; *Legality of the Threat or Use of Nuclear Weapons*, *supra* note 114, para. 29; Stockholm Declaration, *supra* note 3, Principle 21. *See also* K. Hulme, 'Environmental protection in armed conflict', in M. Fitzmaurice, D. M. Ong and P. Merkouris (eds.), *Research Handbook on International Environmental Law* (Edward Elgar, Cheltenham, 2010) p. 595; and J. E. Vinuales, 'The Contribution of the International Court of Justice to the Development of International Environmental Law: A Contemporary Assessment', 32:1 *Fordham International Law Journal* (2008) p. 232.

116 Article 3 of the *Draft Articles on the Effects of Armed Conflicts on Treaties* adopted by the International Law Commission in 2011, ILC, "Effects of armed conflicts on treaties. Titles and texts of the draft articles on the effects of armed conflicts on treaties adopted by the Drafting Committee on second reading", UN Doc. A/CN.4/L.777, 11 May 2011; see also *Règlement concernant les effets de la guerre sur les traités*, adopted by the Institut de Droit international in 1912, Article 1.

117 See UNEP Report 2009, *supra* note 12, at 34–47. For example, Article XIX (I) of the Convention for the Prevention of Pollution of the Sea by Oil, London, 12 May 1964, provides that "[i]n case of war or other hostilities, a Contracting Government which considers that it is affected, whether as a belligerent or as a neutral, may suspend the operation of the whole or any part of the present Convention in respect of all or any of its territories. The suspending Government shall immediately give notice of any such suspension to the Bureau."

118 Article 7 and Annex thereto of the ILC Draft Articles on the Effects of Armed Conflicts on Treaties, *supra* note 116.

intensity, its duration and, in the case of non-international armed conflict, the degree of outside involvement.[119]

Many commentators have made the case for further research into the potential for international environmental treaties on the protection of the environment to apply, beyond IHL, during an armed conflict.[120] However, to date little use has been made of such an approach in practice and the potential contribution of these treaties remains to be explored. In particular, research is needed to analyse the exact legal added value of environmental treaties in comparison to the legal protections provided by IHL in armed conflict situations and to elucidate the interplay between IHL and these rules. In this respect it should be noted that in 2011 the International Law Commission included the topic of the protection of the environment in relation to armed conflict in its long-term programme.[121] The proposal foresees the clarification of the complementarity of the environmental law regime with that of humanitarian law and human rights law.[122] Clearly, further research in this area will be of real value, particularly in clarifying which treaty rules can be invoked to limit the effects of warfare on the environment.

With respect to international human rights law, it is by now fairly uncontroversial that international human rights law continues to apply during armed conflicts.[123] In terms of the protection of the environment, this is relevant because

---

119 *See for instance* Article 6 of the ILC Draft Articles on the Effects of Armed Conflicts on Treaties:

> "Factors indicating whether a treaty is susceptible to termination, withdrawal or suspension In order to ascertain whether a treaty is susceptible to termination, withdrawal or suspension in the event of an armed conflict, regard shall be had to all relevant factors, including:
>
> (a) The nature of the treaty, in particular its subject matter, its object and purpose, its content and the number of parties to the treaty; and
>
> (b) The characteristics of the armed conflict, such as its territorial extent, its scale and intensity, its duration and, in the case of non-international armed conflict, also the degree of outside involvement."

120 *See e.g.* Vöneky, *supra* note 26; Guillard, *supra* note 9; Bothe *et al.*, *supra* note 12; J. Wyatt, 'Law-making at the intersection of international environmental, humanitarian and criminal law: the issue of damage to the environment in international armed conflict', 92:879 *International Review of the Red Cross* (2010) p. 593; Tignino, *supra* note 9; Mollard-Bannelier, *supra* note 9.

121 Report of the International Law Commission, sixty-third session (23 April–3 June and 4 July–12 August 2011), UN Doc. A/66/10, at Annex E.

122 *Ibid.*, at para. 31.

123 *See, inter alia, Legality of the Threat or Use of Nuclear Weapons, supra* note 114, para. 25; *Legal Consequences of the Construction of a Wall in the Occupied Palestinian Territory*, ICJ, Advisory Opinion of 9 July 2004, *ICJ Reports* 2004; *Congo* v. *Uganda*, *supra* note 82, para. 216. On the interplay between IHL and international human rights law *see* C. Droege, 'Elective affinities? Human rights and humanitarian law', 90:871 *International Review of the Red Cross* (2008) p. 501.

a number of human rights treaties either directly or indirectly entail a protection of the environment through different recognised rights such as the right to a clean and healthy environment, or the rights to food, water or health. For example, the African Charter on Human and Peoples' Rights provides for the right to "a general satisfactory environment favourable to their development".[124] The International Covenant on Economic, Social and Cultural Rights (ICESCR) contains a right to "the enjoyment of the highest attainable standard of physical and mental health" through, *inter alia*, the "improvement of all aspects of environmental and industrial hygiene".[125]

Human rights bodies and courts have also developed a considerable body of case law addressing environmental concerns in relation to various human rights,[126]

---

124 Article 24, African Charter on Human and Peoples' Rights, adopted 27 June 1981, OAU Doc. CAB/LEG/67/3 rev. 5, 21 I.L.M. 58 (1982), entered into force 21 October 1986.

125 Article 12, International Covenant on Economic, Social and Cultural Rights, G.A. res. 2200A (XXI), 21 U.N.GAOR Supp. (No. 16) at 49, U.N. Doc. A/6316 (1966), 993 *U.N.T.S.* 3, entered into force 3 January 1976; *see also* Article 11, European Social Charter (Revised), Council of Europe, 3 May 1996, *ETS* 163, available at: <www.unhcr.org/refworld/docid/3ae6b3678.html>, visited 1 November 2012; Article 11, Additional Protocol to the Inter-American Convention on Human Rights in the Area of Economic, Social and Cultural Rights, "Protocol of San Salvador", *O.A.S. Treaty Series* No. 69 (1988), entered into force 16 November 1999, reprinted in *Basic Documents Pertaining to Human Rights in the Inter-American System*, OEA/Ser.L.V/II.82 doc.6 rev.1 at 67 (1992); Article 24(2)(c), Convention on the Rights of the Child, G.A. res. 44/25, annex, 44 U.N. GAOR Supp. (No. 49) at 167, U.N. Doc. A/44/49 (1989), entered into force 2 September 1990; Articles 4(1), 7 and 20(3)(b), Convention Concerning Indigenous and Tribal Peoples in Independent Countries, ILO, C169, 27 June 1989, C169, available at: <www.unhcr.org/refworld/docid/3ddb6d514.html>, visited 1 November 2012.

126 For a review of the jurisprudence of international tribunals and bodies, *see* D. Shelton, 'Human Rights and the Environment: substantive rights', in Fitzmaurice, Ong and Merkouris, *supra* note 115, and D. Shelton, 'Human Rights and the Environment: Jurisprudence of Human Rights Bodies', Background Paper No. 2, Joint UNEP-OHCHR Expert Seminar on Human Rights and the Environment, 14–16 January 2002, Geneva, available online at <www2.ohchr.org/english/issues/environment/environ/bp2.htm#_ftn4>, visited 27 July 2012.

such as the right to life,[127] the right to privacy and family life,[128] or minority rights.[129] For example, the UN Human Rights Committee has recognised that damage to the environment could raise issues in respect of States' obligations to protect the right to life.[130] The UN Committee on Economic, Social and Cultural Rights has held that the right to water in Articles 11 and 12 of the International Covenant on Economic, Social and Cultural Rights (ICESCR) entails an obligation for States to refrain from "unlawfully diminishing or polluting water, for example through ... use and testing of weapons".[131] The impact of environmental damages resulting from an armed conflict on the enjoyment of the right to health was acknowledged by the Special Rapporteur of the former Commission on Human Rights on the situation of human rights in Kuwait under Iraqi Occupation:

> Warfare often affects the natural environment; such consequences do not, per se, constitute human rights violations. However, in the light of the above-mentioned positions of the General Assembly and the Committee on Economic, Social and Cultural Rights, it can be concluded that not only in peacetime but also in times of armed conflict, the deliberate causing of large-scale environmental damage which

---

127 *See e.g. Öneryildiz* v. *Turkey*, ECtHR (2004), Reports of Judgments and Decisions 2004-XII. *See also* Inter-American Commission on Human Rights, Report on the situation of human rights in Ecuador, OEA/Ser.L/V/II.96, Doc. 10 rev. 1, 24 April 1997, at chapter VIII : "The realization of the right to life, and to physical security and integrity is necessarily related to and in some ways dependent upon one's physical environment. Accordingly, where environmental contamination and degradation pose a persistent threat to human life and health, the foregoing rights are implicated."

128 *See e.g. Lopez-Ostra* v. *Spain*, ECtHR (1994), Series A, No. 303C.

129 For instance, in its Report on the situation of human rights in Brazil, OEA/Ser.L/V/II.97, Doc. 29 rev.1, 29 September 1997, Chapter VI, the Inter-American Commission on Human Rights concluded that "[t]he Yanomami people have obtained full recognition of their right to ownership of their land. Their integrity as a people and as individuals is under constant attack by both invading prospectors and the environmental pollution they create. State protection against these constant pressures and invasions is irregular and feeble, so that they are constantly in danger and their environment is suffering constant deterioration."

130 *See Communication No. 67/1980, EHP* v. *Canada*, 2 *Selected Decisions of the Human Rights Committee* (1990). In this case, Canadian citizens lodged a complaint on the ground that the storage of radioactive waste in their town threatened the right to life of present and future generations. The Committee declared the complaint inadmissible for non-exhaustion of national remedies, but "observes that the present communication raises serious issues, with regard to the obligation of States parties to protect human life (article 6 (1))", at para 8.

131 UN Committee on Economic, Social and Cultural Rights, General Comment No 15 (2002): "The right to water (arts 11 and 12, of the International Covenant on Economic, social and cultural rights", E/C.12/2002/11, 20 January 2003, para. 21. On the protection of water during armed conflict, *see* Tignino, *supra* note 9.

> severely affects the health of a considerable proportion of the population concerned, or creates risks for the health of future generations, amounts to a serious violation of the right to the enjoyment of the highest attainable standard of health as embodied in article 12 of the International Covenant on Economic, Social and Cultural Rights. However, because of the limited short-term consequences for the health of the civilian population and of the difficulties in determining the long-term impact on the health situation, it is too early to assess whether the destruction of oil-wells by the Iraqi occupying forces amounted to a violation of the right embodied in this article.[132]

Without going further into an analysis of international human rights law, these examples are mentioned to show how international human rights law can provide complementary protection to the protection afforded by IHL during armed conflict and should therefore be taken into account. Nevertheless, further research is still needed, in particular with regard to two questions: 1) in which areas would existing environmental law and human rights law have an added value in terms of the environmental consequences of armed conflicts as shown by empirical evidence; and 2) where do the norms of environmental law and /or human rights law and IHL contradict each other, so that the conflict of norms can to be resolved?[133]

5. Conclusion

As long ago as 1992, paragraph 39.6 of the Agenda 21 provided that "measures in accordance with international law should be considered to address, in times of armed conflict, large-scale destruction of the environment that cannot be justified under international law". In June 2012, the States participating in the United Nations Conference on Sustainable Development reaffirmed their commitment to fully implement Agenda 21.[134]

As discussed above, in the past decades, considerable progress has been made towards understanding the effects of hostilities on the natural environment, which progress should assist in the search for meaningful ways of strengthening protection of the environment in armed conflicts. Nevertheless, while national

---

132 *Report on the situation of human rights in Kuwait under Iraqi Occupation*, prepared by W. Kälin, Special Rapporteur to the Commission on Human Rights, in accordance with Commission resolution 1991/67, UN Doc. E/CN.4/1992/26, 16 January 1992, para. 208.

133 According to the ICRC *Guidelines for Military Manuals and Instructions on the Protection of the Environment in Times of Armed Conflict* "international environmental agreements and relevant rules of customary law may continue to apply in times of armed conflict to the extent that they are not inconsistent with the applicable law of armed conflict" (para. 5), *supra* note 12. The exact scope of application and their interplay with IHL is the subject of discussion and should be further clarified.

134 *The Future We Want*, *supra* note 8, para. 16.

legislation and military manuals incorporate the IHL obligations with regard to the environment, it seems that, compared to what might have been expected after the experience of the Gulf War in 1991, little attention has been paid to the environmental consequences of hostilities. This study notes that there is certainly scope for improvement, both by applying existing rules more conscientiously and by strengthening, clarifying and expanding the existing legal framework. Improved protection could be achieved through several avenues. As a first step what is required is the better application of existing norms of IHL with respect to the protection of the natural environment, and, where needed, their clarification. As a second step, aspects of IHL require further development, particularly in order to provide specific protection to areas of major ecological importance and to develop norms and mechanisms to address the environmental consequences of hostilities in the mid- and long term. Finally, further research on the legal protections afforded to the environment in times of armed conflict, by international environmental law and international human rights law is needed, together with a clearer articulation of the relationship between these bodies of law and IHL.

2 The Protection of the Environment in Armed Conflict: Legal Obligations in the Absence of Specific Rules

Dieter Fleck*

1. Introduction

The legal protection of the natural environment in armed conflict is characterised by a far-reaching absence of specific rules, resulting in constant challenges to the application of general norms of international humanitarian law in situations for which these principles and rules may not have been designed. The few specific provisions of international humanitarian law that currently exist for wartime protection of the environment operate only in situations that will not easily occur, even in the context of an international armed conflict.[1] Moreover, the inadequacy

---

* Former Director, International Agreements & Policy, Federal Ministry of Defence, Germany. Also, Honorary President, International Society for Military Law and the Law of War; Member of the Advisory Board of the Amsterdam Center for International Law (ACIL); Member of the Editorial Board of the *Journal of International Peacekeeping*. The author expresses his gratitude to Professor Rosemary Rayfuse for critical comments on an earlier draft of this contribution. E-mail: DieterFleck@t-online.de.

1 *See* Articles 35(3) and 55 of the 1979 Geneva Protocol I Additional to the Geneva Conventions of 12 August 1949, and Relating to the Protection of Victims of International Armed Conflicts (AP I) (prohibition of "widespread, long-term [understood by some States as 'continuing for decades'] and severe" damage to the natural environment); Articles I and II of the 1977 Convention on the Prohibition of Military or any Other Hostile Use of Environmental Modification Techniques (ENMOD) and formal Understandings thereto ("environmental modification techniques [*i.e.* 'deliberate manipulation of natural processes'] having widespread, long-lasting or severe effects" encompassing 'an area on the scale of several hundred square kilometers', 'lasting for a period of months' or a season and 'involving serious or significant disruption or harm to human life, natural and economic resources or other assets'); and Article 8(2)(b)(iv) of the Statute of the International Criminal Court (ICC Statute) ("widespread, long-term and severe damage to the natural environment which would be clearly excessive in relation to the concrete and direct overall military advantage anticipated").

Rosemary Rayfuse (ed.), War and the Environment: New Approaches to Protecting the Environment in Relation to Armed Conflict
Copyright 2014 Koninklijke Brill NV. Printed in The Netherlands. ISBN 978-90-04-27064-0 pp. 45-234

of the relevant general rules of international humanitarian law in the context of environmental protection is no longer in dispute.[2] What is nevertheless needed is a convincing translation of these general rules into military planning and implementation. In addition, the role of Multilateral Environmental Agreements (MEAs) and relevant principles should be evaluated on a case-by-case basis to ascertain the specific consequences of their applicability in both international and non-international armed conflicts.[3]

The current legal situation may be seen as disappointing in view of the progressive development of research on the complexities of environmental knowledge and ecological awareness; of policy-making with the participation of an interested civil society; and of military planning under severe constraints in terms of personnel, equipment and time. Yet an identification of existing deficiencies may provide the opportunity for realistic stock-taking. This could support practical solutions that would hardly be possible otherwise, thereby paving the way towards better implementation of existing law and enlarging consensus for the development of new rules.

This study revisits an earlier attempt to deal with the subject.[4] It will show that while only minor legal progress has been achieved in the past two decades, a number of problems and processes of international law creation in this area have become much clearer today. A defined body of customary rules applicable in international and non-international armed conflicts is now in existence,[5] although further clarifications and a careful consideration of critical approaches to existing rules and their implementation in practice are still required. To this end, this study examines the natural environment as a civilian object, the legal conditions for and consequences of its use as military objective, and the exact contents of *lex lata* (*see* below section 2), before turning to an attempt to provide realistic proposals for developments *de lege ferenda*. The reach of legal protections deriving from peacetime rules that continue to apply during armed conflict is evaluated (*see* below section 3). Finally, a more general discussion on norm-creation and related processes seems to be in order. The old argument according to which

---

2 *See* C. Droege and M.-L. Tougas, 'The Protection of the Environment in Armed Conflict – Existing Rules and Need for Further Legal Protection', in this volume.

3 *See* United Nations Environment Programme (UNEP), *Protecting the Environment during Armed Conflict. An Inventory and Analysis of International Law* (UNEP, Geneva, 2009) pp. 34–46.

4 D. Fleck, 'Legal and Policy Perspectives for the Protection of the Environment in Armed Conflict', in H. Fox and M. A. Meyer, *Effecting Compliance. Armed Conflict and the New Law, Vol. II* (The British Institute of International and Comparative Law, London, 1993) pp. 143–157.

5 J.-M. Henckaerts and L. Doswald-Beck (eds), *Customary International Humanitarian Law*(Cambridge University Press, Cambridge, 2005), with update at *Customary IHL Database*,<www.icrc.org/customary-ihl/eng/docs/home>, hereafter *CIHL*, Rules 43–45.

everything that is not expressly prohibited may be taken as permitted in international law needs to be critically re-examined (*see* below section 4). In concluding (section 5) the study addresses ways of enhancing environmental protection by both reaffirming existing rules and developing new ones.

2. The Natural Environment as a Civilian Object

In all military operations it is essential today to recognise the legal status of the natural environment as a civilian object; as a heritage of mankind that should not be damaged, misused or targeted as a military objective. In this sense environmental damage is civilian damage to which, even in armed conflict, the rule of doubt, which establishes a presumption that objects normally dedicated for civilian purposes are not used to make an effective contribution to military action, applies.[6] Both environmental damage and the concern for future generations are relevant to the proportionality equation and, since decisions are to be taken on the basis of information available at the time, a realistic probability of such damage will suffice to render an attack inadmissible. While an exhaustive definition of 'the natural environment' as such may be an ambitious task, "for practical purposes broad agreement on what is covered by the term is sufficient for the purpose of our discussion".[7] Indeed, any legal delineation of the term risks excluding aspects that are relevant for environmental protection. Limiting rules to include only excessive damage to the environment may actually have the effect of potentially jeopardising the natural environment. There is a widespread reluctance in planning and conducting military operations to take into account environmental damage other than destruction on a massive scale. Considerations pertaining to security and safety often tend to trump considerations of what might turn out to be major environmental danger in the longer term. A typical example of such deficiency is found in the recent *Harvard Manual on Air and Missile Warfare* which limits the prohibition on environmental damage to wanton destruction of the natural environment and contains only a hortative clause that "due regard ought to be given to the natural environment".[8] Given the vast expansion in knowledge of environmental processes and problems that has occurred in the past decades, together with the development of international *opino juris* relating to protection of the environment, it is submitted that the phenomenon of environmental damage should be viewed from a broader perspective today. To pretend that interna-

---

6 Article 52(3) AP I.

7 Droege and Tougas, *supra* note 2. *See also* E.V. Koppe, 'The principle of ambituity and the Prohibition of Excessive Collateral Damage to the Environment during Armed Conflict', in this volume.

8 Program on Humanitarian Policy and Conflict Research (HPCR), *Commentary on the HPCR Manual on Air and Missile Warfare* (Cambridge, Massachusetts: Harvard, 2010), Introduction to Section M, para. 8; Rules 88 and 89.

tional law has not changed in this respect since 1977 when the ENMOD Treaty and Additional Protocol I[9] were adopted would, indeed, be less than convincing.

Attacks against the natural environment, as with any attacks against civilian objects, are breaches of international humanitarian law. Difficult questions arise, however, where there is no doubt that the environment is being used to make an effective contribution to military action, for example, where mountains or dykes are used for defence, or as natural shields or for the preparation of an attack. The four constitutive criteria for military objectives – nature, location, purpose and use – remain essential for the distinction between military objectives and civilian objects. Thus, parts of the environment may well turn out to be military objectives. In such cases the principle of proportionality should condition and may even exclude a lawful attack. However, little law exists to explain how this should operate in practice, and it appears debatable whether comprehensive legal assessments have been made on the issue of environmental protection during recent armed conflicts. A lack of rational decision-making that takes into consideration ecological consequences is a frequent phenomenon during armed conflict. This underlines the need for clear and objective evaluation in retrospect, even if criminal and disciplinary investigations are, ultimately, to be based on the knowledge available to the responsible commander at the time of attack. From the destruction of oil wells in the 1991 Gulf War[10] to targeting decisions in the North Atlantic Treaty Organization's bombing campaign in former Yugoslavia 1999[11] or the bombardment of the *El Jyieh* power plant in the war in Lebanon 2006,[12] comprehensive case studies in which the nature of the attacked objectives are determined and the military advantages are weighed against civilian damages are an obvious requirement that could inform military planning in the future. In this context it is not only the issue of precautions in attack which is relevant, but also the issue of precautions taken against the effects of attacks that would have to be explored. It is important to accept that any environmental damage is to be considered in this complex equation, not only its most extreme form of 'ecocide', the catchword for wanton destruction or what has been described

---

9 For both treaties *see supra* note 1.

10 *See* United Nations Environment Programme (UNEP), *Desk Study on the Environment in Iraq*(UNEP, Geneva, 2003) <postconflict.unep.ch/publications/Iraq_DS.pdf>.

11 *See* UNEP and the United Nations Centre for Human Settlements (Habitat) (UNCHS), *Final Report: The Kosovo Conflict: Consequences for the Environment & Human Settlements* (UNEP/ UNHCS, Geneva, 1999), <postconflict.unep.ch/publications/finalreport.pdf>; ICTY, *Final Report to the Prosecutor by the Committee Established to Review the NATO Bombing Campaign Against the Federal Republic of Yugoslavia* (13 June 2000), <www.icty.org/x/file/About/OTP/otp_report _nato_bombing_en.pdf>.

12 *See* UNEP, *Lebanon Post-Conflict Environmental Assessment* (UNEP, Geneva, 2007), <postconflict.unep.ch/publications/UNEP_Lebanon.pdf>.

in Article 55(1) of AP I as 'widespread, long-term and severe'. Adopting such an approach might lead to the conclusion that the general rules of international humanitarian law are more useful in providing guidance in the planning and conduct of military operations that could affect the natural environment than any more specific principle of 'eco-protection'. Nevertheless, ascertaining the exact meaning of those general rules and their relevance for environmental protection in times of armed conflict still requires considerable interpretive effort.

As stated in Rule 43 (A) of the *ICRC Study on Customary International Humanitarian Law* (*CIHL*),[13] it is accepted today that "[n]o part of the natural environment may be attacked unless it is a military objective". Rule 43 (B) of the *CIHL* goes on to suggest that it is now a rule of customary international law that "destruction of any part of the natural environment is prohibited, unless required by imperative military necessity".[14] This text mirrors Rule 50 of the *CIHL* on the destruction or seizure of the property of an adversary, a provision that was borrowed from Article 23(g) of the 1899 and 1907 Hague Regulations respecting the Laws and Customs of War on Land.[15] A similar text has been developed with application to environmental protection in paragraph 44 of the *San Remo Manual on International Law Applicable to Armed Conflicts at Sea*.[16] However, in each of the rules referred to here the context is different and this therefore affects the meaning and reach of each provision. Hence they must be assessed separately, considering their specific purpose and implications.

The *San Remo Manual* which first introduced a prohibition on the causing of "[d]amage to or destruction of the natural environment not justified by military necessity and carried out wantonly"[17] did not do this in absolute terms or for the purpose of taking a final decision on the lawfulness of naval operations in armed conflict that might cause damage or destruction to the environment. Rather, the intention of the drafters was to explain the rule of 'due regard' which is expressed in the sentence preceding the prohibition in the following terms: "[m]ethods and means of warfare should be employed with due regard for the natural environment taking into account the relevant rules of international law".[18] As stated in the Explanations to the *San Remo Manual*, the 'due regard' formula, which was

13 *See supra* note 5.

14 Droege and Tougas, *supra* note 2.

15 Convention (II) With Respect to the Laws and Customs of War on Land, signed 29 July 1899; Convention (IV) respecting the Laws and Customs of War on Land, signed 18 October 1907.

16 International Institute of Humanitarian Law (L. Doswald-Beck, ed.), *San Remo Manual on International Law Applicable to Armed Conflicts At Sea* (Cambridge University Press, Cambridge, 1995), hereinafter "*San Remo Manual*".

17 *San Remo Manual*, para. 44, 2nd sentence.

18 *Ibid*., 1st sentence.

taken from the 1982 Law of the Sea Convention,[19] leaves "flexibility for an assessment of the conflicting interests in each particular case".[20] The authors of the Explanations referred to the general duty on States during *peacetime* not to harm the marine environment, but they also expressed their opinion that the application of this obligation in *armed conflict*, beyond the thresholds of the 'widespread, long-lasting or severe' effects called for in ENMOD and Articles 35(3) and 55 AP I,[21] was "still ambiguous and uncertain".[22] Their reference to wanton destruction not justified by military necessity was apparently intended to provide an uncontroversial rule within the context of the 'due regard' formula. It was, however, not intended as a final delineation of what was still considered, at that time, "an emerging rule forbidding the use of the marine environment as an instrument of warfare or making it an object of attack during an armed conflict at sea".[23] Thus, the purpose and meaning of that sentence in the *San Remo Manual* is descriptive rather than prescriptive. It does not provide an all-encompassing regulation. This is similar to Rule 44 of the *CIHL* where the 'due regard' formula is used again and put in the context of precautions in the conduct of military operations.

It may be noted that none of these instruments refers to the concept of 'due diligence', which is recognised as a general principle of international law.[24] Due diligence has been referred to as "the standard basis for the protection of the environment from harm".[25] However, while its application may be accepted in the general corpus of international environmental law and the law of State responsibility, its application as an obligation of conduct during armed conflict may still be considered as uncertain.

---

19 United Nations Convention on the Law of the Sea of 30 April 1982. In this Convention the 'due regard' formula is used persistently with respect to the rights and duties of other States, whereas the protection of the natural environment is normally invoked in terms of 'necessary measures', 'effective protection' and 'appropriate rules, regulations and procedures' for this end. In two instances, however, the 'due regard' formula is used in the context of environmental protection (Article 60(3) on the removal of artificial islands, installations or structures; Article 234 on laws and regulations on the prevention, reduction and control of marine pollution from vessels in ice-covered areas within exclusive economic zones). As spelled out in Article 236, the provisions of this Convention regarding the protection and preservation of the marine environment do not apply to warships and State aircraft, however States shall ensure that "such vessels or aircraft act in a manner consistent, so far as is reasonable and practicable, with this Convention".

20 *San Remo Manual, supra* note 16, Explanations, para. 44.10.

21 *See supra* note 1.

22 *San Remo Manual, supra* note 16, Explanations, para. 44.4.

23 *Ibid.*

24 *See* T. Koivurova, 'Due Diligence', *Max Planck Encyclopedia of Public International Law*, <www.mpepil.com>.

25 *See* ILC, *Articles on Prevention of Transboundary Harm from Hazardous Activities*, Commentary to Article 3, *ILC Yearbook 2001*, Vol II (2), p. 148, para. 8.

In any event Rule 43 (B) of the *CIHL* should not be understood as regulating the destruction of any part of the natural environment in independent terms, but rather as an effort to apply the general rules on the conduct of hostilities to the natural environment.[26] Rule 43 (B) is fully dependent on the rule of distinction. Hence any attacks against the natural environment as civilian objects remain prohibited, and in the event of attacks against military objectives environmental damage remains subject to the rule of proportionality. It is only in the latter context that collateral environmental damage required by imperative military necessity may be considered as justified, yet no military necessity clause is included in Articles 35(1), 54(2) or 55(1) AP I. It is true that Article 54(5) AP I allows derogation from the prohibitions of 'scorched earth' tactics by a belligerent where this is required by "imperative military necessity". But this rule is limited to the defence of territory under the own control of the defending party against foreign invasion. It does not apply to the invading party which remains fully bound by Article 54(2) and (3), unless specific objects covered by this provision are used by the defending party "in direct support of military action".[27] Thus Rule 43 (B) of the *CIHL*, which may be helpful to regulate destruction caused during military operations other than attacks, is to be applied with caution. It should not be taken as justifying attacks against civilian objects as a matter of military necessity.[28] Neither does it provide an additional ruling for attacks against military objectives, since the latter are governed by the concept of "a definite military advantage" (Article 52 AP I).[29]

In the light of these considerations the text of Rule 43 (B) of the *CIHL* leaves a number of open questions and room for interpretation. The mere fact that similar wording is used in Rule 50 of the *CIHL* in order to limit any destruction or seizure of the property of an adversary should not lead to the drawing of parallels between these two different cases. The environment is not to be equated with the adversary's property.

Interestingly, the US criticism of the *CIHL*[30] does not refer to Rules 43–44, but rather to Rule 45 which prohibits "methods or means of warfare that are intended or may be expected, to cause widespread, long-term and severe damage to the natural environment" and "[d]estruction of the natural environment … used as a weapon". This appears to support earlier assumptions that the exorbitant threshold of 'widespread, long-term and severe' damage which has been introduced into the treaty language can hardly have any relevance for normal

---

26 *CIHL*, *supra* note 5, Vol II, Part 1, Chapter 14, pp. 844–859.

27 Article 54(3) AP I.

28 *CIHL*, *supra* note 5, Vol II, Part 1, Chapter 14, pp. 844–859.

29 For supporting arguments *see* K. Hulme, 'Natural Environment', in E. Wilmshurst and S. Breau (eds.), *Perspectives on the ICRC Study on Customary International Humanitarian Law* (Cambridge University Press, Cambridge, 2007) pp. 204–237.

30 *See* E. V. Koppe, *The Use of Nuclear Weapons and the Protection of the Environment During International Armed Conflict* (Hart, Oxford, 2008) Chapter III.

military operations, except in the event of nuclear warfare where it appears to be "reasonably adequate".[31] The US position is apparently rooted in the understanding notified by the US and many of its allies according to which the "new rules introduced by Additional Protocol I" (to which Articles 35(3) and 55 AP I belong)[32] were intended to apply to conventional weapons, irrespective of other rules of international law applicable to other types of weapons. In other words, these rules do not "influence, regulate, or prohibit the use of nuclear weapons",[33] whereas in more general terms there is broad acceptance of the applicability of international humanitarian law as such to nuclear weapons.[34]

As far as conventional warfare is concerned, however, the US position is not without contradictions, as it also confirms that "parts of the natural environment cannot be made the object of attack unless they constitute military objectives, as traditionally defined, and that parts of the natural environment may not be destroyed unless required by military necessity".[35] The US also admits that Rule 45 is "desirable as a matter of policy".[36] It only denies the customary character of that rule despite the fact that the thresholds of protection contained in the rule are extremely high and hardly realistic so that the rule "may not actually have much meaning".[37] For this reason Rules 43–44 of the *CIHL* remain much more important for State practice and legal development than Rule 45.

3. Continued Application of Peacetime Obligations

Even if principles and rules of international humanitarian law fail to provide sufficient protection for the natural environment in armed conflict, peacetime international law does offer certain guidance that will be relevant not only for military planners and decision-makers, but also for combatants and civilians in

---

31 *See* E. V. Koppe, *The Use of Nuclear Weapons and the Protection of the Environment During International Armed Conflict* (Hart, Oxford, 2008) Chapter III.

32 *See* F. Kalshoven and L. Zegveld, *Constraints on the Wages of War. An Introduction to International Humanitarian Law*, 4th edition (Cambridge University Press, Cambridge, 2011) p. 118.

33 *See* statements made on ratification of or accession to AP I by Belgium, Canada, France, Germany, Italy, The Netherlands, Spain, UK, and – on signature – by the USA. *See* UK Ministry of Defence, *The Manual of the Law of Armed Conflict* (Oxford University Press, Oxford, 2004) para. 6.17.

34 *See e.g.* United States of America, *Congressional Record* 95/34, p. 85 ("The United States has long shared the view that the law of armed conflict governs the use of nuclear weapons – just as it governs the use of conventional weapons.").

35 Bellinger and Haynes, *supra* note 30, p. 455.

36 *Ibid.*

37 For this latter point *see* J.-M. Henckaerts, 'Customary International Humanitarian Law: a response to US Comments', 89:866 *International Review of the Red Cross* (2007) pp. 473–488, at p. 482.

contemporary hostilities. Rules of environmental protection have progressively developed during the recent decades. Many of these rules are important for military operations and they continue to apply in times of armed conflict. The Draft Articles on the Effects of Armed Conflicts on Treaties of the International Law Commission[38] deserve to be considered in this context. They provide in Article 7 (which is still expository in character) that an implication that treaties continue in operation, in whole or in part, during armed conflict may be seen in their subject matter. An indicative list of relevant categories of treaties is provided in the Annex of the Draft Articles. It explicitly includes treaties relating to the international protection of the environment[39] and also, using more general phraseology, multilateral law-making treaties.[40] This may lend some support for a rebuttable presumption that relevant treaty law, in particular Multilateral Environmental Agreements, continue to apply in a case of armed conflict.[41] The Commentary to the Annex specifically refers to the International Court of Justice's Advisory Opinion on *Legality of the Threat or Use of Nuclear Weapons*[42] which – irrespective of the fact that not all States have accepted Articles 35(3) and 55 AP I as being applicable to nuclear weapons – explains that "the issue is not whether treaties relating to the protection of the environment are or not applicable during an armed conflict, but rather whether the obligations stemming from these treaties were intended to be obligations of total restraint during military conflict" and that "[r] espect for the environment is one of the elements that go to assessing whether an action is in conformity with the principles of necessity and proportionality".[43]

It appears convincing to call for a case-by-case assessment of whether any intention may be inferred from a specific treaty obligation that it should continue to be effective in an armed conflict. Such intention need not be expressly stated in the treaty text; it may be implied in the parties' interests and derive from the importance of the values to be protected. Of course, treaties concluded in peacetime usually do not explicitly address that issue. Hence, an inventory of relevant treaties and international instruments should be prepared, which should include

38 ILC, Draft Articles on Effects of Armed Conflicts on Treaties, <untreaty.un.org/ilc/texts/instruments/english/commentaries/1_10_2011.pdf>; *see also* Official Records of the General Assembly, Sixty-sixth Session, Supplement No. 10 (A/66/10) chap. VI, sect. E; *Yearbook of the International Law Commission*, 2011, vol. II, Part Two; Report of the Sixth Committee (A/66/473); UNGA Res 66/98 (13 January 2012) para. 4.

39 ILC Draft Articles, *ibid.*, Annex (g).

40 *Ibid.*, Annex (c).

41 *Ibid.*, Commentary to Annex, para. 55.

42 *Legality of the Threat or Use of Nuclear Weapons*, 8 July 1996, ICJ, Advisory Opinion, paras. 29–31, *I.C.J. Reports 1996*, p. 226; 35 *International Legal Materials* (1996) p. 809.

43 *Ibid.*, para. 30.

relevant commitments under the UNESCO World Heritage Convention of1972,[44] the Stockholm Declaration of 1972,[45] the Rio Declaration of 1992,[46] and even academic proposals such as the Berlin Rules on Water Resources of 2004.[47] Where a contradiction may exist between general and specific rights and obligations, the more specific rule should be identified. For this purpose, case studies on the application of relevant rules in international and non-international armed conflicts will be most helpful.[48] These studies should include scientific evaluation by ecologists, policy considerations and operational assessments by military experts.

4. General Rules versus Specific Rules on Protection

There are not only practical considerations stemming from the fact that specific rules on environmental protection in armed conflict are almost absent. Lawyers advising military planners and commanders in the field have to rely on general norms of international humanitarian law and the rules applicable in peacetime. A constant challenge for them is the question whether and to what extent rules exist to regulate behaviour that is not expressly prohibited. The old assumption that if international law does not prohibit a particular conduct then that conduct may be considered as being permitted needs to be critically revisited in this context. Of course it is well known that international law is a field of imperfect regulation. Many existing rules lack specificity or comprehensiveness and there are opposing principles that are not fully reconciled, such as the prohibition on the use of force and self-defence; State sovereignty and human rights; international responsibility and individual rights; security and protection.

---

44 Convention Concerning the Protection of the World Cultural and Natural Heritage, adopted 16 November 1972.

45 Declaration of the United Nations Conference on the Human Environment, Stockholm, 16 June 1972.

46 Rio Declaration on Environment and Development, adopted by the United Nations Conference on Environment and Development, 14 June 1992.

47 International Law Association, Seventy-first Conference (Berlin, August 2004), *Berlin Rules on Water Resources Law*, Chapter X, <www.internationalwaterlaw.org/documents/intldocs/ILA_Berlin_Rules-2004.pdf>. For further discussion *see* O. Das, 'Environmental Protection in Armed Conflict – Filling the Gaps with Sustainable Development', in this volume.

48 *See* B. Sjöstedt, 'The Role of Multilateral Environmental Agreements in Armed Conflict: "Green-keeping" in Virunga Park – Applying the UNESCO World Heritage Convention in the Armed Conflict of the Democratic Republic of the Congo', in this volume.

Following certain lines of argument in the *Lotus* case,[49] it might be argued, and has been argued even in the law of armed conflict,[50] that due to the principle of State sovereignty there is a presumption for freedom of action in international law, unless such action is prohibited. It should be noted, however, that the *Lotus* decision, even in its historical context, does not justify such a general conclusion. The case was taken to the Permanent Court of International Justice (PCIJ) following a collision between the French steamer *Lotus* and the Turkish steamer *Boz-Kourt* which occurred on the high seas. The relevant *compromis* between the governments of the French and Turkish Republics was exclusively related to the question whether Turkey had or had not, according to the principles of international law, jurisdiction to prosecute acts committed by the captain of the *Lotus* which resulted in the death of persons on-board the *Boz-Kourt*. The French government contended that for the Turkish courts to have jurisdiction Turkey should be able to point to some title to jurisdiction recognised by international law in favour of Turkey, while the Turkish government took the view that Turkey was free to exercise jurisdiction whenever such jurisdiction did not come into conflict with a principle of international law. The Court, evenly split and only by President Huber's casting vote, decided that international law, "far from laying down a general prohibition to the effect that States may not extend the application of their laws and the jurisdiction of their courts to persons, property and acts outside their territory, ... leaves them ... a wide measure of discretion which is only limited in certain cases by prohibitive rules", rules that were, however, not applicable in the present case.[51] In his dissenting opinion Judge Loder, the former President of the PCIJ, criticised the decision stating that it was based on the "contention that under international law everything which is not prohibited is permitted",[52] a position which, however, had not been held in such general terms in the judgment itself. He argued that this contention was at variance with the spirit of international law which, because it was for the most part unwritten and lacked sanctions, rested instead on a general consensus of opinion and on the acceptance by States of rules, customs and existing conditions which they were bound to respect in their mutual relations, even though these rules were nei-

49 *The case of the S.S. "Lotus" (France* v. *Turkey)*, 7 September 1927, Permanent Court of International Justice, PCIJ Series A, No. 10 (1927).

50 *See e.g.* Y. Dinstein, *The Conduct of Hostilities under the Law of International Armed Conflict*, 2nd edition (Cambridge University Press, Cambridge, 2010) p. 85 ("It is ordinarily understood that, if international law does not prohibit a certain conduct, that conduct is lawful."). Judge Shahabuddeen, in his Dissenting Opinion to the *Legality of the Threat or Use of Nuclear Weapons* Advisory Opinion (*supra* note 42), Part II, refers to the "*Lotus* principle that a State has a right to do whatever is not prohibited under international law", but he clearly does so with interpretative constraints under the UN Charter.

51 *Lotus* case, *supra* note 49, p. 19.

52 *Ibid.*, p. 34.

ther committed to writing nor confirmed in treaties. It may be doubted whether this characterisation of international law was in any way disputed between the judges; in fact it could be used as further explanation of the judgment rather than as a counter-argument. The Court specifically examined whether there was a rule of customary international law under which Turkey was obliged to refrain from exercising jurisdiction, looking for, but not finding, evidence of situations in which States had objected to criminal proceedings in respect of collision cases before the courts of a country other than the flag State. The decision arrived at by the Court may be understood as confirming that this was a case of concurrent national jurisdiction, a matter which was not regulated at that time. However, it would go too far to conclude from this judgment that in international law everything that is not prohibited is permitted. Quite the contrary seems to be true: not everything that is not expressly prohibited may be considered as permitted. Particularly in light of Judge Shahabuddeen's comments in his dissenting opinion in the *Legality of the Threat or Use of Nuclear Weapons* Advisory Opinion, it would be useful if the International Court of Justice were to find an opportunity to clarify this important general issue.[53]

Indeed, as is evident from developments over the past 150 years, important limitations are to be observed. As stated in the 1868 St. Petersburg Declaration,[54] "the only legitimate object which States should endeavour to accomplish during war is to weaken the military forces of the enemy". Even more explicitly, Article 35 (1) AP I stipulates that "[i]n any armed conflict, the right of the Parties to the conflict to choose methods or means of warfare is not unlimited". The three main principles of international humanitarian law, *i.e.* limitation on military objectives, avoidance of unnecessary suffering and humanity, do require specific efforts to protect the natural environment in times of armed conflict in order to avoid damage and destruction that would extend beyond borders in space and time. As a matter of logic such efforts should include those circumstances where the natural environment would qualify as a military objective, and they cannot be confined only to circumstances causing 'widespread, long-term and severe' damage and destruction at a level far above existing realities.

5. Conclusions

While the present deliberations are still less than complete, it is very obvious that their impact may be more than academic. The International Committee of the Red Cross (ICRC) has initiated efforts to improve education and training on protection of the environment in armed conflicts, which fully correspond with results

53 *See supra* note 50.

54 Declaration of St. Petersburg to the Effect of Prohibiting the Use of Certain Projectiles in Wartime, signed 29 November/11 December 1868.

of scientific research.[55] The United Nations Environment Programme (UNEP) has supported inter-disciplinary cooperation to explore the environmental dimensions of armed conflicts,[56] activities that are most relevant also for post-conflict peace-building.[57] These activities should be continued. In extreme situations the Security Council might again take relevant decisions under Chapter VII of the Charter,[58] even if this would not impose more than *ad hoc* obligations on parties to the conflict and may not necessarily lead to general legal regulation.

Furthermore, it is essential for the protection of the environment in armed conflicts that efforts to enhance reaffirmation of existing principles and rules are taken as seriously as any discussion on the development of new ones. It is important to ensure that in the conduct of military operations all feasible precautions are taken to avoid, and in any event to minimise, incidental damage to the environment. Lack of scientific certainty as to the effects on the environment of certain military operations does not absolve a party to the conflict from taking such precautions. Initiatives for further legal development should be linked with scientific and ecological expertise to support effective results.

For the time being it may be stated that the general principles on the conduct of hostilities do apply to the natural environment (Rule 43 *CIHL*); methods and means of warfare must be employed with due regard to the protection and preservation of the natural environment (Rule 44 *CIHL*); the use of methods of means of warfare that are intended, or may be expected, to cause widespread, long-term and severe damage to the natural environment is prohibited; and destruction of the natural environment may not be used as a weapon (Articles 35(3) and 55(1), AP I; ENMOD; Rule 45 *CIHL*).[59]

Further interdisciplinary case studies are needed to support fact-oriented evaluations of military requirements, ecological assessments and necessary legal developments. Long-term effects of environmental damage and destruction are to be balanced against the military advantage sought rather than insisting on thresholds for legal regulation that already appeared to be escapist decades ago and which might prove counter-productive in the years to come.

---

55 *See* International Committee of the Red Cross (ICRC), *Guidelines for Military Manuals and Instructions on the Protection of the Environment in times of Armed Conflict* (ICRC, Geneva, 1994); M. Bothe *et al.*, 'International Law protecting the environment during armed conflict: gaps and opportunities', 92:879 *International Review of the Red Cross* (2010) pp. 569–592.

56 UNEP, *supra* note 3, pp. 9-11.

57 *See* United Nations Environment Programme, *From Conflict to Peacebuilding. The Role of Natural Resources and the Environment* (UNEP, Geneva, February 2009).

58 *See* Security Council Res 1857 (2008), para. 4 (g) on illicit trade of natural resources in DRC.

59 *See* the forthcoming 3rd edition of D. Fleck, *Handbook of International Humanitarian Law* (Oxford University Press, Oxford, 2013). Commentary on the relevant Sections, 467–469, will be written by S. Oeter.

3 The Principle of Ambituity and the Prohibition against Excessive Collateral Damage to the Environment during Armed Conflict

Erik V. Koppe*

1. Introduction

In recent years, relatively little attention has been paid to protection of the environment during armed conflict. Indeed, and for obvious reasons, the primary focus of attention during armed conflict has not been on the protection of flora and fauna, but rather on the protection of the victims of armed conflict. However, the consequences of warfare on the environment cannot be underestimated. The consequences of the use of anti-plant agents such as Agent Orange during the Vietnam War between 1961 and 1971,[1] the burning of oil wells and the leaking of oil into the Persian Gulf during the 1990–1991 Gulf War and the oil spill in the Mediterranean Sea following an attack on a power plant in Lebanon during the 2006 Israel-Lebanon war were devastating, not only for flora and fauna, but also for civilians. Indeed, it was these devastating consequences which triggered the debate on the need for (further) international regulation of the means and methods of warfare. The use of Agent Orange partly triggered the drafting of Articles 35(3) and 55 of Additional Protocol I (AP I) in 1977, which prohibit the use of means and methods of warfare which are intended or expected to cause widespread, long-term and severe damage to the environment.[2] More recently, this

* Assistant Professor of Public International Law, Faculty of Law and the Grotius Center for International Legal Studies, Leiden University, Leiden, The Netherlands. The author wishes to thank Dr. Heinsch, Dr. Molier and Ms. Dam, LL.M., for their comments.

1 On the legality of the United States' use of chemicals during the Vietnam War, *see* W. D. Verwey, 'Chemical Warfare in Vietnam: Legal or Illegal?', 18 *Netherlands International Law Review* (1971); W. D. Verwey, *Riot Control Agents and Herbicides in War; Their Humanitarian, Toxicological, Ecological, Military, Polemological, and Legal Aspects* (A.W. Sijthoff, Leiden, 1977).

2 *See for example* the explanatory statement of Hungary relating to its proposal to include an environmental protection provision in Additional Protocol I. CDDH/III/64, 19 March 1974 (III, 221), proposed additional paragraph, by Czechoslovakia,

Rosemary Rayfuse (ed.), War and the Environment: New Approaches to Protecting the Environment in Relation to Armed Conflict
Copyright 2014 Koninklijke Brill NV. Printed in The Netherlands. ISBN 978-90-04-27064-0 pp. 59-234

author has argued that the burning oil wells and oil spills in the Persian Gulf in 1991[3] triggered the emergence of three relatively new rules of customary international law relating to the protection of the environment during armed conflict: a prohibition of wanton destruction of the environment during armed conflict; a prohibition against excessive collateral damage to the environment during armed conflict; and the obligation to observe a general duty of care for the environment during armed conflict.[4] It is notable that the International Committee of the Red Cross (ICRC) came to a similar conclusion in its Customary International Humanitarian Law Study (CIHL Study) of 2005 (Rules 43 and 44).[5]

Although the need to protect the environment is generally recognised by States,[6] the key challenge is to observe and, if necessary, enforce these rules of *ius in bello*.[7] One way to ensure compliance with existing rules is to clarify their meaning and scope. To that end, in 2011 the International Law Commission (ILC) decided to include the "protection of the environment in relation to armed conflicts" in its long-term programme of work.[8] The ILC was of the opinion that

---

German Democratic Republic, Hungary, in: H. Levie, *Protection of War Victims: Protocol 1 to the 1949 Geneva Conventions,* Volume 3 (Oceana Publications, Dobbs Ferry, NY, 1980) p. 259.

3 These events also triggered a call for the drafting of a fifth Geneva Convention, which would be specific for the protection of the environment during armed conflict. G. Plant (ed.), *Environmental Protection and the Law of War; A 'Fifth Geneva' Convention on the Protection of the Environment in Time of Armed Conflict* (Belhaven Press, London, 1992).

4 For a discussion of emergence of such custom and the evidence on which this conclusion is based, *see* E. Koppe, *The Use of Nuclear Weapons and the Protection of the Environment during International Armed Conflict* (Hart Publishing, Oxford, 2008) pp. 246–278.

5 J.-M. Henckaerts and L. Doswald-Beck (eds.), *Customary International Humanitarian Law; Volume I and II, International Committee of the Red Cross* (Cambridge University Press, Cambridge, 2005) (also through <www.icrc.org>).

6 Please note that protection of the environment during armed conflict also follows from the *ius ad bellum* and the *ius pacis. See* Koppe, *supra* note 4, pp. 309–333 (*ius ad bellum*) and pp. 335–364 (*ius pacis*). On the relationship and overlap between *ius ad bellum* and *ius in bello, see also* E. Koppe, 'Compensation for War Damages under Jus ad Bellum', in A. de Guttry *et al.* (eds.), *The 1998–2000 War between Eritrea and Ethiopia; An International Legal Perspective* (T.M.C. Asser Press, The Hague, 2009).

7 Please note that protection of the environment during armed conflict also follows from the *ius ad bellum* and the *ius pacis. See* Koppe, *supra* note 4, pp. 309–333 (*ius ad bellum*) and pp. 335–364 (*ius pacis*). On the relationship and overlap between *ius ad bellum* and *ius in bello, see also* E. Koppe, 'Compensation for War Damages under Jus ad Bellum', in A. de Guttry *et al.* (eds.), *The 1998–2000 War between Eritrea and Ethiopia; An International Legal Perspective* (T.M.C. Asser Press, The Hague, 2009).

8 A/66/10, Report of the International Law Commission; Sixty-third session (26 April–3 June and 4 July –12 August 2011), para. 365.

discussing this topic would make a useful contribution to the codification and progressive development of international law while it would also allow the ILC to venture into fields of international law which it has hitherto not considered, such as international humanitarian law and international environmental law.

In light of the possible future work by the ILC on this topic, this study seeks to clarify the legal basis of the protection of the environment during armed conflict in general, and of the prohibition against excessive collateral damage to the environment in particular. Section 2 discusses the mutual relationship between the specific conventional and customary rules relating to the protection of the environment during armed conflict and the general or fundamental principles of the law of armed conflict. Section 3 discusses the legal basis for and scope of the prohibition against excessive collateral damage to the environment during armed conflict. The Study concludes with a brief summary, conclusion and suggestions for consideration by the ILC (section 4).

2. The Principle of Ambituity

2.1. *Introduction*

In order to understand the current legal framework in relation to the protection of the environment during armed conflict, it is pertinent to provide clarity as to its foundations. This section will first discuss the principles of the law of armed conflict in general (section 2.2) and in relation to the protection of the environment during armed conflict in particular (section 2.3). Subsequently, the relationship of the principles of the law of armed conflict to general principles of law will be discussed (section 2.4) followed by consideration of the consequences of the recognition of the principles of the law of armed conflict as general principles of law (section 2.5).

2.2. *The Principles of the Law of Armed Conflict*

It is generally agreed that the law of armed conflict is founded on four fundamental principles: the principle of military necessity; the principle of distinction; the principle of proportionality; and the principle of humanity.[9] The object and pur-

9 One may also add the general principle of chivalry (or the treachery or perfidy principle according to Greenwood) and the precautionary principle. The former prohibits the use of dishonourable means or methods of warfare, recognised in the *United States Navy Manual on the Law of Naval Warfare* of 1959. The latter is reflected in Articles 57 and 58 AP I and entails an obligation for belligerent states to take constant care to spare civilians and civilian objects during hostilities. As such the precautionary principle is a sub-principle of the principle ofnecessity and closely linked with the principles of distinction and proportionality. *See* R. Kolb and R. Hyde, *An Introduction to the International Law of Armed Conflicts* (Hart Publishing, Oxford,

pose of the law of armed conflict, and of these four principles in particular, is "alleviating as much as possible the calamities of war" as befitting civilised nations.[10]

Pursuant to the principle of military necessity States are allowed to use military force – in deviation of the law of peace[11] – in order to weaken the military forces of the enemy.[12] The inherent limitation of this objective of warfare is further reflected in the (sub-)principles of distinction and proportionality.[13] If the only legitimate object of warfare is to weaken the military forces of the enemy, it is axiomatic that States must distinguish between combatants and civilians and between military objects and civilian objects (distinction) and that they must

---

2008) p. 44. C. Greenwood, 'The law of war (international humanitarian law)', in M. Evans (ed.), *International Law*, 1st edition (Oxford University Press, 2003) p. 802.

10 St. Petersburg Declaration Renouncing the Use, in Time of War, of Explosive Projectiles Under 400 Grammes Weight, signed on 11 December 1868, entered into force on 11 December 1868, 1 *American Journal of International Law; Supplement: Official Documents* (1907) p. 95, preambular paras. 1–2.

11 A/CN.4//SER.A/1980/Add.1 (Part 2), *Yearbook of the International Law Commission*, 1980, Vol. II, Part Two, Report of the Commission to the General Assembly on the work of its thirty-second session, pp. 45–46.

12 St. Petersburg Declaration Renouncing the Use, in Time of War, of Explosive Projectiles Under 400 Grammes Weight, signed on 11 December 1868, entered into force on 11 December 1868, 1 *American Journal of International Law, Supplement: Official Documents* (1907) p. 95, preambular para. 3. This object and purpose is repeated in Article 3 of the 1880 *Oxford Manual on the Law of War on Land*, adopted by the *Institut de Droit International* (which was established in 1873), available at <www.icrc.org>. *Cf. also* the descriptions of military necessity in the 1863 Lieber Code, in which military necessity was understood as consisting of measures "which are indispensable for securing the ends of the war" (Article 14) admitting "all direct destruction of life or limb or armed enemies, and of other persons whose destruction is incidentally unavoidable in the armed contests of the war" (Article 15), available at <www.icrc.org>. The US Military Tribunal in Nuremberg ruled in the *Hostages Trial*: "Military necessity permits a belligerent … to apply any amount and kind of force to compel the complete submission of the enemy …" United States Military Tribunal (Nuremberg), *Case No. 47; The Hostages Trial; Trial of Wilhelm List and Others*; 8th July, 1947–19th February, 1948, in *The United Nations War Crimes Commission, Law Reports of Trials of War Criminals; Volume VIII* (His Majesty's Stationary Office, London, 1949) p. 66.

13 Oeter identifies two sub-principles following from the general principle of "limited warfare" (limited to what is militarily absolutely necessary in order to achieve the military objectives), one of which is the principle of distinction. S. Oeter, 'Methods and Means of Combat', in D. Fleck *et al.* (eds.), *The Handbook of International Humanitarian Law*, 2nd edition (Oxford University Press, Oxford, 2008) para. 401, nos. 2–3. According to the International Court of Justice in the *Nuclear Weapons Opinion*, however, the principle of distinction qualifies as one of the main principles of international humanitarian law. *Legality of the Threat or Use of Nuclear Weapons*, 8 July 1996, ICJ, Advisory Opinion, *I.C.J Reports 1996*, para. 78.

keep any unintentional or collateral damage to civilians and civilian objects to a minimum (proportionality). This right to use military force,[14] as reflected in the principle of military necessity, is generally limited by the principle of humanity,[15] which provides an absolute limitation on particular means and methods of warfare during armed conflict.

Together these principles form a general and systematic legal framework and a frame of reference for the law of armed conflict. Most rules of the law of armed conflict, both conventional and customary, are reflections of these principles, give expression to these principles,[16] or are the result of a compromise between these principles, in particular the principles of necessity and humanity.[17] Indeed, according to Kolb and Hyde,

> all rules of the [law of armed conflict] exist at an equilibrium point between two fundamental principles, each of which pulls in a different direction. The contents of the norms of the [law of armed conflict] are the fundamental principles made during the negotiation of treaties, or decisions made by states to adopt particular practices. The two fundamental principles are the principle of humanity on the one hand and the principle of military necessity on the other.[18]

---

14 According to Greenwood, many "supposed 'belligerent rights' are not rights in the true legal sense at all", since they often do not have correlative duties. "What the law actually confers in such a case is a liberty; the person (or state) concerned may exercise that liberty without violating the law but others are under no duty to cooperate with him or even to abstain from obstructing him. … The notion that the *ius in bello* leaves states and individuals free to act in a particular way without giving them a "right" to do so is one aspect of a fundamental principle of that law. That principle is that war (or armed conflict) is not an institution established by international law but a fact which the law has always recognized and attempted to contain. … Thus, each side in a conflict might lawfully kill the other's soldiers in open combat, not because international law gave it a right to kill but because international law left it alone to kill or not according to its ability and inclination." C. Greenwood, 'The Relationship between ius ad bellum and ius in bello', 9 *Review of International Studies* (1983) pp. 228–229.

15 St. Petersburg Declaration Renouncing the Use, in Time of War, of Explosive Projectiles under 400 Grammes Weight, preambular paras. 1, 5–6.

16 *Military and Paramilitary Activities in and against Nicaragua (Nicaragua* v. *United States of America)*, 27 June 1986, ICJ, *I.C.J. Reports 1986*, paras. 218 and 220. *See also* Oeter, *supra* note 13, para. 401, no. 1.

17 Y. Sandoz *et al.* (eds.), *Commentary on the Additional Protocols; of 8 June 1977 to the Geneva Conventions of 12 August 1949* (International Committee of the Red Cross, Martinus Nijhoff Publishers, Geneva, 1987), para. 1389. The Commentary is also available through <www.icrc.org>.

18 Kolb and Hyde, *supra* note 9, p. 43. Similarly M. Schmitt, 'Military Necessity and Humanity in International Humanitarian Law: Preserving the Delicate Balance', 50 *Virginia Journal of International Law* (2009–2010) p. 798; G. Schwarzenberger,

A general reflection of this compromise between the principle of military necessity and the principle of humanity is laid down in Article 35(1) of Additional Protocol I,[19] which provides that "the right of the Parties to the conflict to choose methods or means of warfare is not unlimited".[20] The principle of humanity is particularly reflected in Article 35(2) AP I which contains a general prohibition on "[the employment of] weapons, projectiles and materials and methods of warfare of a nature to cause superfluous injury or unnecessary suffering";[21] and it has found expression in specific prohibitions on the use of particular conventional[22] and non-conventional weapons.[23] The principles of distinction and proportionality are currently reflected in Articles 48 and 51(5)(b) AP I as well as in their

---

International Law; As Applied by International Courts and Tribunals; Volume II; The Law of Armed Conflict (Stevens & Sons, London, 1968) pp. 10–13.

19 Protocol Additional to the Geneva Conventions of 12 August 1949, and Relating to the Protection of Victims of International Armed Conflicts, opened for signature on 12 December 1977, entered into force on 7 December 1978, 1125 *UNTS*, No. 17512.

20 According to Venturini, Article 35(1) AP I mostly clearly articulates the "restraining effect" of the principle of military necessity, which "imposes a restrictive standard on the exercise of warfare: a belligerent must refrain from employing any kind or degree of violence which is not actually necessary for military purposes" and thus to achieve the goals of warfare. G. Venturini, 'Necessity in the Law of Armed Conflict and in International Criminal Law', in I. F. Dekker and E. Hey (eds.), 41 *Netherlands Yearbook of International Law* (2010) pp. 48–49.

21 According to the International Court of Justice, however, the prohibition against unnecessary suffering qualifies as a separate principle of international humanitarian law. *Nuclear Weapons Opinion*, *supra* note 13, para. 78.

22 These prohibitions include the St. Petersburg Declaration Renouncing the Use, in Time of War, of Explosive Projectiles under 400 Grammes Weight (the use of explosive projectiles under 400 grams would "uselessly aggravate the sufferings of disabled men, or render their death inevitable", and which use therefore was considered to be contrary to "the laws of humanity" (*see* preambular paras. 4 and 5)). Hague Declaration (IV, 3) on the Use of Bullets Which Expand or Flatten Easily in the Human Body, signed on 29 July 1899, entered into force 4 September 1900, D. Schindler and J. Toman (eds.), *The Laws of Armed Conflicts; A Collection of Conventions, Resolutions and Other Documents* (Martinus Nijhoff Publishers, Dordrecht, 1988) p. 109. In the Declaration's preamble, the contracting parties stated that this prohibition was "inspired by the sentiments which found expression in the Declaration of St. Petersburg". A further example is the Convention on Prohibitions or Restrictions on the Use of Certain Conventional Weapons Which May be Deemed to Be Excessively Injurious or to Have Indiscriminate Effects and Protocols, opened for signature on 10 April 1981, entered into force on 2 December 1983, 1342 *UNTS*, No. 22495.

23 Geneva Protocol for the Prohibition of the Use in War of Asphyxiating, Poisonous or Other Gases, and of Bacteriological Methods of Warfare, signed 17 June 1925, entered into force on 8 February 1928, 25 *American Journal of International Law; Supplement: Official Documents*(1931) p. 94; Convention on the Prohibition of the Development, Production, Stockpiling and Use of Chemical Weapons and on Their

customary equivalents as identified by the ICRC in its Customary International Humanitarian Law Study.[24] These rules oblige belligerents to direct their operations against military objectives only and prohibit attacks which may be expected to cause incidental loss of civilians, damage to civilian objects, or a combination thereof, which would be excessive in relation to the concrete and direct military advantage anticipated.

The relationship between these rules and the principle of necessity (which underlies the law of armed conflict) is further evidenced by the references to military necessity as a possible ground for exception from a prohibition. For example, Article 23(g) of the Hague Regulations[25] prohibits the destruction or seizure of enemy property "unless such destruction or seizure be imperatively demanded by the necessities of war". And Articles 54 and 56 AP I allow derogation on the basis of military necessity and under specific circumstances from the prohibitions on the destruction of objects which are indispensable for the survival of the civilian population and on attacking certain objects which contain dangerous forces.

2.3. *The Principles of the Law of Armed Conflict and the Protection of the Environment during Armed Conflict*

It is difficult, however, to link the above-mentioned rules relating to the protection of the environment during armed conflict to either of these fundamental principles of the law of armed conflict. In particular the general prohibition of Article 35(3) AP I cannot be deduced from the principles of necessity, distinction, proportionality or humanity, nor can it be deduced from a compromise between either of these principles. Article 35 AP I provides:

> Article 35 – Basic rules
>
> 1 In any armed conflict, the right of the Parties to the conflict to choose methods or means of warfare is not unlimited.
>
> 2 It is prohibited to employ weapons, projectiles and material and methods of warfare of a nature to cause superfluous injury or unnecessary suffering.
>
> 3 It is prohibited to employ methods or means of warfare which are intended, or may be expected, to cause widespread, long-term and severe damage to the natural environment.

Destruction, together with Annexes, opened for signature on 13 January 1993, entered into force on 29 April 1997, 1975 *UNTS*, No. 33757.

24 Henckaerts and Doswald-Beck, *supra* note 5, Rules 1–24, in particular Rules 1 and 14.

25 Hague Convention (IV) Respecting the Laws and Customs of War on Land, with annexed Regulations, signed on 18 October 1907, entered into force on 26 January 1910, 2 *American Journal of International Law; Supplement: Official Documents* (1908) p. 90.

Article 35(3) AP I qualifies as a basic rule of the law of armed conflict and provides for an absolute limitation to the necessities of war in order to protect the intrinsic value of the natural environment, irrespective of its context and relationship with man. The protection of the environment under Article 35(3) is not linked to the distinction between military and civilian objects (like its twin, Article 55 AP I), thereby excluding the principle of distinction and proportionality. The protection of the environment under Article 35(3) is not inspired by nor focused on the protection of human beings or mankind (like Article 35(2) AP I), thereby excluding the principle of humanity. Moreover – as just observed – it provides for an absolute limitation to the necessities of war (as foreseen in Article 35(1) AP I), thereby excluding the principle of military necessity as such.

Thus, in order to explain the emergence of Article 35(3) as well as the customary duty of care for the environment during armed conflict,[26] a fifth fundamental principle of the law of armed conflict must be identified.[27] This principle, already recognised by Röling,[28] reflects the common understanding of States that the environment must be protected during armed conflict,[29] and provides for an absolute limitation to the necessities of war. As such, this principle is very similar to the principle of humanity, which provides for an absolute limitation to the necessities of war in the interest of man and civilisation.

The existence of this fifth principle as a fundamental principle of the law of armed conflict not only explains the drafting of the specific rules on the protection of the environment in Additional Protocol I, in particular Article 35(3) AP I and the first sentence of Article 55(1) AP I, but it also accounts for the development of the customary rules relating to the protection of the environment during armed conflict which, as noted above, arguably emerged in the 1990s.[30]

26 Koppe, *supra* note 4, pp. 248–256. Similarly Rule 44 of the CIHL Study, which provides in part: "Methods and means of warfare must be employed with due regard to the protection and preservation of the natural environment."

27 *See* Koppe, *supra* note 4, pp. 117–118.

28 According to Verwey, Röling "submitted proposals aimed at restating traditional, but still workable, principles as well as formulating new ones ... The following new basic principles of modern *ius in bello* ought to be recognized: ... (c) *the principle of the protection of the environment* (implying a prohibition on weapons and techniques with a destructive effect on the natural balance, or which introduce destructive and irrevocable ecological processes." W. D. Verwey, 'Bert V.A. Röling (1906–1985)', in T.M.C. Asser Instituut, *The Moulding of International Law: Ten Dutch Proponents* (T.M.C. Asser Instituut, The Hague, 1995) p. 45.

29 *See supra* note 6.

30 At a recent conference organised by the Grotius Center for International Legal Studies of Leiden University launching the Grotius Center's *Jus Post Bellum* Project, Payne argued the existence of a similar norm – the norm of environmental integrity. According to Payne, worldwide efforts to restore natural resources, ecosystems and other elements of the environment in post-conflict interventions imply the existence of a norm of environmental integrity. C. R. Payne, *Just Post Bellum and the Norm of*

For consistency purposes (the principles of necessity, distinction, proportionality and humanity all have a Latin stem), it is suggested to name this principle the principle of ambituity, from the Latin word *ambitus*, which means, among other things, environment.[31]

2.4. The Principles of the Law of Armed Conflict and the General Principles of Law

The relevance of the identification of the principle of ambituity is twofold. First, it completes the general framework of the law of armed conflict and positions the conventional and customary rules in relation to the protection of the environment during armed conflict within this framework. Second, it is submitted that the principle of ambituity qualifies as a general principle of the law of armed conflict (or as one of the 'general principles of humanitarian law' as they were qualified by the International Court of Justice (ICJ) in the *Nicaragua* judgment)[32] and therefore as a general principle of law within the meaning of Article 38(1)(c) of the Statute of the ICJ (Statute). As such, it would qualify as an autonomous (and primary) source of international law.

Traditionally "the general principles of law recognized by civilized nations" were understood as referring to general principles of law *in foro domestico*, *i.e.* principles of domestic law that are common to all legal systems, such as the principle of good faith and the principle of *res iudicata*.[33] There is increasing recognition, however, that Article 38(1)(c) Statute also includes general principles of

---

Environmental Integrity, conference paper, on file with the author. *See* also <juspostbellum.com>. The role of environmental protection in *ius post bellum* situations was recently confirmed when the United States and Vietnam started cleaning up Agent Orange on part of Danang International Airport in central Vietnam, where it was stored during the Vietnam War. The US provided USD 41 million for this clean-up operation. News report through <www.reuters.com> (8 and 9 August 2012).

31 With special thanks to the present author's former teacher in classic Greek and Latin, Mr. Kluiver, and his colleague, Mr. Ossewijer.

32 *Nicaragua* v. *United States of America*, *supra* note 16, paras. 218, 220 and 255.

33 A. Pellet, 'Article 38', in A. Zimmermann *et al.*, *The Statute of the International Court of Justice; A Commentary* (Oxford University Press, Oxford, 2006) pp. 766–773.

international law.[34] This is confirmed by, among others, Mosler[35] and Gaja[36] and recently by Judge Cançado Trindade.[37] It is submitted that such recognition reflects the emancipation of public international law from a rudimentary legal order consisting mostly of bilateral contractual relationships to a developing legal order on the basis of an increasing number of multilateral (sometimes even universal) legal relationships reflecting common and even global values.[38]

---

34 As a matter of fact Tunkin argued that Article 38(1)(c) Statute ICJ only referred to general principles of international law. In 1945, the drafters of the Statute of the ICJ amended the chapeau of Article 38 of the Statute of the Permanent Court of International Justice (PCIJ) by including the phrase "whose function is to decide in accordance with international law such disputes as are submitted to it". This amendment made Tunkin come to the conclusion that the scope of Article 38(1)(c) would as from 1945 be limited to general principles of international law. G. I. Tunkin, 'General Principles of Law in International Law', in R. Marcic (eds.), *Internationale Festschrift für Alfred Verdross: zum 80. Geburtstag* (Fink, München, 1971) p. 525.

35 Mosler identified general principles of international legal relations as one category of general principles covered by Article 38(1)(c) Statute ICJ. These were "principles resulting from the sovereign equality of States (jurisdiction, immunities, self-determination), principles connected with treaties, elementary considerations of humanity, and 'generally accepted principles' related to the law of the seas, diplomatic protection and armed conflict". H. Mosler, 'General Principles of Law', in R. Bernhardt (ed.), *Encyclopaedia of Public International Law; Volume Two; East African Community to Italy-United States Air Transport Arbitration (1965)* (North-Holland Publishing Company, Amsterdam, 1995) pp. 513–514, 522–524.

36 According to Judge Gaja, the ICJ often refers to principles of international law or general principles which have no parallel in domestic law. The identification of such principles by the ICJ "whether or not it finds a parallel in municipal systems, is only rarely accompanied by an adequate demonstration of its existence in international law". G. Gaja, 'General Principles of Law', in *Max Planck Encyclopedia of Public International Law*, available at <www.mpepil.com>, paras. 17–20. Gaja refers in this context to the ICJ's recognition of the principle of *uti possidetisiuris* in the *Frontier Dispute (Burkina Faso* v. *Republic of Mali)*, Judgment of 22 December 1986, para. 24.

37 Finally, Judge Cançado Trindade concludes that "[i]n contemporary International Law, general principles of law find concrete expression not only *in foro domestico*, but also at international level. There can be no legal system without them. Always keeping their autonomy, they may find expression in other formal "sources" or manifestations of International Law (and not only treaties and custom), even though not listed in Article 38(1)(c) of the ICJ Statute, but nonetheless resorted to by the ICJ in practice." This view is not only based on an analysis of the legislative history of Article 38 Statute of the PCIJ (when the identification of principles of international law was also pursued) but also a selective review of the doctrinal developments as from the 1920s. *Case Concerning Pulp Mills on the River Uruguay (Argentina* v. *Uruguay)*, 20 April 2010, ICJ, Separate Opinion of Judge Cançado Trindade, *I.C.J. Reports 2010*, paras. 28; 26, 29–47.

38 O. Spijkers, *The United Nations, the Evolution of Global Values and International Law* (Intersentia, Cambridge, 2011). Spijkers, who defined global values as: "A global

If general principles of international law are recognised as an autonomous source of public international law under Article 38(1)(c) Statute, it is arguable that general principles of certain areas of public international law also fall under the scope of Article 38(1)(c) Statute. Indeed, according to Judge Cançado Trindade, "[t]here are, in fact, general principles of law proper to international law in general, and there are principles of Law proper to some domains of International Law, such as, *inter alia*, International Environmental Law".[39] These principles of international environmental law include the principle of prevention and precaution.[40]

It follows that the general principles underlying other specific areas of public international law also qualify as such.[41] These areas would likely include the law of treaties, the law of State responsibility, the law of international organisations or international institutional law (including the law on international administrative procedure/civil service),[42] international economic law (trade law and investment law), the law of the sea, the law of outer space, international labour law, human rights law, international criminal law[43] and the law of armed conflict.

Further clarification of the fundamental principles of the law of armed conflict as well as other areas of public international law would have several advantages. It would provide guidance to States for the further development of these

---

value is an enduring, globally shared belief that a specific state of the world, which is possible, is socially preferable, from the perspective of all human beings, to the opposite of the world" (p. 20) identified peace and security, social progress and development, human dignity, and self-determination of peoples as such. *Cf. also* the development of the European Union, which qualifies as an autonomous legal order, and which is founded on "the values of respect for human dignity, freedom, democracy, equality, the rule of law and respect for human rights, including the rights of persons belonging to minorities. These values are common to the Member States in a society in which pluralism, non-discrimination, tolerance, justice, solidarity and equality between women and men prevail." (Article 2 of the Treaty on European Union).

39 *Argentina* v. *Uruguay*, *supra* note 37, para. 48.

40 *Ibid.*, paras. 52–96.

41 In the law of the European Union, which arguably qualifies as a specific area of international law, the identification and application of general principles of (EU) law by the Court of Justice of the European Union have reached a level of sophistication similar to that of domestic legal systems. *See* T. Tridimas, *The General Principles of EU Law*, 2nd edition (Oxford University Press, Oxford, 2006).

42 *See for example*, *Bustani* v. *Organisation for the Prohibition of Chemical Weapons (OPCW)*, ILOAT Judgment 2232, 95th session, 2003, para. 16, in which the Tribunal referred to "the principles on which international organisations' activities are founded" and subsequently to "the general principles of the law of the international civil service".

43 *See for example* F. O. Raimondo, *General Principles of Law in the Decision of International Criminal Courts and Tribunals* (Martinus Nijhoff Publishers, Leiden, 2008).

areas of public international law;[44] to judges and arbitrators for the interpretation and application of public international law to a specific dispute; and to lecturers for the teaching of public international law (principles provide for a natural framework to structure a course). Further, the clarification of the fundamental principles of the various areas of public international law would reveal their mutual commonalities (unity within diversity)[45] and as such clarify the interrelationship between the various areas of public international law.[46] For example, the principle of military necessity – as one of the principles of the law of armed conflict or *ius in bello* – appears to be related to the principle of necessity which underlies the right of self-defence under *ius ad bellum*, and the principle of necessity which underlies the derogation of human rights under the various human rights treaties. And all these manifestations of necessity appear to be linked to the principle of necessity which underlies necessity as a circumstance precluding wrongfulness (reflected in Article 25 of the Articles on State Responsibility).[47]

It is suggested that the ILC should include the identification of the general principles of international law and the general principles of the various areas of public international law on its (long-term) agenda. There is no other international body with the knowledge, authority and terms of reference to accomplish such task. It appears, however, that for such task Article 1 of the Statute of the ILC[48]

---

44 Lammers calls this the formative function of the general principles of international law. J. G. Lammers, 'General Principles of Law Recognized by Civilized Nations', in F. Kalshoven *et al.* (eds.), *Essays on the Development of the International Legal Order; In Memory of Haro F. van Panhuys* (Sijthoff & Noordhoff, Alphen aan den Rijn, 1980; in cooperation with the T.M.C. Asser Institute, The Hague) p. 69.

45 Unity within diversity is the subtitle of H. G. Schermers and N. M. Blokker, *International Institutional Law*, 5th revised edition (Martinus Nijhoff Publishers, Leiden, 2011). Similarly Judge Cançado Trindade who states: "However circumscribed or specialized may one of its domains [be], its basic principles can there be found …, assuring the cohesion and unity of the Law as a whole." *Argentina* v. *Uruguay*, *supra* note 37, para. 204.

46 Indeed, as the Arbitral Tribunal in *Sempra Energy International / Argentina* observed: "International law is not a fragmented body of law as far as basic principles are concerned …" *Sempra Energy International* v. *Argentina*, 28 September 2007, ICSID ARB/02/16, Award, para. 378.

47 *See* T. Gazzini *et al.*, 'Necessity Across International Law: An Introduction', in I. F. Dekker and E. Hey (eds.), 41 *Netherlands Yearbook of International Law* (2010) pp. 8–10, in which they introduce the various contributions on the role of necessity across public international law in this special publication of the *Netherlands Yearbook*. The areas covered are the law on the use of force (Tsagourias), the law of armed conflict (Venturini), human rights law (Ryngaert), international economic law (Qureshi), international investment law (Reinisch), international environmental law (Fitzmaurice), and the law of the European Union (Koutrakos).

48 Statute of the International Law Commission 1947, adopted by the General Assembly by A/RES/174 (II) of 21 November 1947, as most recently amended by A/RES/36/39 of 18 November 1981.

would have to be amended or reinterpreted. After all, the ILC would not be engaged in the *codification* or *progressive development* of international law (which are the objects of the ILC pursuant to Article 1 and which envisage the drafting of *specific rights and obligations* in *treaty format*), but with the *identification* of *general principles* of international law.[49]

Although the general principles of (international) law and the specific rights and obligations flowing from international conventions and international custom are related, it is pertinent to keep a strict distinction between these autonomous sources of international law. After all, principles underlie rules and explain their existence.[50] Indeed, it would seem "conceptually flawed"[51] to see to what extent principles have developed into norms of customary international law and to refer to customary principles of international law.[52] General principles of law are "guiding principles of general content and, in that, they differ from the norms

---

49 It appears that, nowadays, in view of the ever extending corpus of public international law, it is possible to identify the general principles of the various areas of public international law by means of induction, similar to the induction of the principle of ambituity from the existence of Article 35(3) AP I and the customary duty of care for the environment. Induction would guarantee that the general principles of law are abstractions from positive international law and not from natural law. Schwarzenberger also suggests induction as the primary method for the identification of fundamental principles of international law, with deduction as strictly auxiliary. G. Schwarzenberger, 'The fundamental principles of international law', 87 *Recueil des Cours* (1955-I) pp. 197–198. *See also* on identification of general principles, among others, O. Elias and C. Lim, 'General principles of law, soft law and the identification of international law', 28 *Netherlands Yearbook of International Law* (1997). *Cf however* Judge Cançado Trindade, who is of the opinion that the general principles of law (including the general principles of the various domains of public international law) "emanate from human conscience, the universal juridical conscience, the ultimate material 'source' of all Law". *Argentina* v. *Uruguay, supra* note 37, paras. 191–217, in particular para. 217.

50 According to Fitzmaurice, "[a] rule answers the question 'what': a principle in effect answers the question 'why'." G. Fitzmaurice, 'The General Principles of International Law; Considered from the standpoint of the rule of law', 92 *Recueil des Cours* (1957-II) p. 7.

51 *Argentina* v. *Uruguay, supra* note 37, para. 17.

52 According to Schwarzenberger, "[i]f the principle in question is said to be based on international customary law, this terminology easily becomes misleading. It is then an abbreviation for stating more accurately that the principle is an abstraction, and nothing but an abstraction, from a number of rules which themselves bear the hallmark of this law-creating process." Schwarzenberger, *supra* note 49, p. 207. It appears that the ICJ's references to the principles of distinction and unnecessary suffering as "cardinal principles contained in the texts constituting the fabric of humanitarian law" and the "intransgressible principles of international customary law" must be interpreted as such. *Nuclear Weapons Opinion, supra* note 13, paras. 78–79. Please also note that the incorporation of fundamental principles into multilateral treaties

or rules of positive international law, and transcend them".[53] They function as "basic pillars of the international legal system" and foundations of the more specific areas of public international law. As explained above, the conventional and customary rules of the law of armed conflict are reflections or manifestations of the fundamental principles of the law of armed conflict.[54]

2.5. The Principle of Ambituity as a General Principle of Law

Recognising the fundamental principles of the law of armed conflict, including the principle of ambituity, as general principles of law has not only theoretical but also practical consequences. As a general principle of law, and therefore as an autonomous source of international law, the function of the principle of ambituity is threefold.

First, the principle of ambituity can be used to interpret existing conventional or customary rules of international law, in particular those rules which specifically protect the environment during armed conflict (perhaps by (cross) reference to related principles of international environmental law). If the meaning or scope of specific rights and obligations of belligerents during armed conflict is unclear, the principle of ambituity may be used to provide further legitimacy to a specific interpretation. For example, the principle of ambituity could support the conclusion that Article 35(3) AP I and Article 55 AP I not only protect the natural environment on land, but also the marine environment and the atmosphere.[55] Further, the principle of ambituity could be used to interpret the rules relating to non-international armed conflict in order to limit the consequences of the conduct of hostilities which are required by the necessities of war.

Second, the principle of ambituity can be used to fill any *lacunae* within the law and thereby supplement the rights and obligations of States during armed

---

may eventually influence the scope and interpretation of a fundamental principle of international law. Schwarzenberger, *supra* note 49, p. 213.

53 *Argentina* v. *Uruguay*, *supra* note 37, para. 39.

54 According to Judge Gaja a "general principle of law may be embodied in a treaty provision or become part of international customary law". It appears that conceptually, it would have been more appropriate to refer to general principles which are reflected in customary international law rather than becoming part of customary international law. Gaja, *supra* note 36, para. 24. According to Judge Cançado Trindade, rules of customary and conventional law are inspired by general principles of law. *Argentina* v. *Uruguay*, *supra* note 37, para. 17.

55 *See* Koppe, *supra* note 4, pp. 154–167. After all, Article 55 applies to certain aspects of naval and air warfare (see Article 49(3) AP I) and the basic rules on methods and means of warfare as laid down in Article 35 AP I were intended to apply to land, naval and aerial warfare. *See* International Committee of the Red Cross, *Draft Additional Protocols to the Geneva Conventions of August 12, 1949; Commentary* (ICRC, Geneva, 1973) p. 54.

conflict.[56] It is arguable that this supplementary function of the general principles of the law of armed conflict is reflected in the Martens clause, most recently articulated in Article 1(2) AP I: "In cases not covered by this Protocol or by other international agreements, civilians and combatants remain under the protection and authority of the principles of international law derived from established custom, from the principles of humanity and from dictates of public conscience." It appears that this clause, which was originally drafted in 1899 (*i.e.* before the drafting the Statute of the Permanent Court of International Justice (PCIJ)), recognises the status of the general principle of humanity as an independent source of (international) law, in addition to the relevant conventional and customary rules.[57] The principle of ambituity could play a similar role as the principle of humanity, not only with respect to international armed conflict, but also with

56 *See* Lammers, *supra* note 44, pp. 64–65, 69. Similarly, Elias and Lim, *supra* note 49, pp. 40–41. Akehurst identified similar functions of equity, namely equity *infra legem* (adapting the law to the facts in an individual case) and equity *praeter legem* (supplementary function of equity to fill gaps in the law). M. Akehurst, 'Equity and General Principles of Law', 25 *International and Comparative Law Quarterly* (1976) pp. 801–806. Similarly, under Dutch civil law the principles of reasonableness and fairness (referred to as 'good faith' before the entry into force of the new Dutch Civil Code in 1992) supplement the rights and obligations of parties under contracts or statutory law. Article 6:2(1) of the Dutch Civil Code (DCC) provides in relation to legal obligations in general (in translation): "Creditors and debtors are obliged to act towards each other pursuant to the standards of reasonableness and fairness." Article 6:248(1) DCC provides in relation to contractual obligations: "A contract does not only have the legal consequences as agreed upon by the contracting parties, but also those, which, considering the nature of the contract, follow from statutory law, custom, or the standards of reasonableness and fairness."

57 This interpretation of the Martens clause appears to be confirmed by De Preux in the Commentary to Additional Protocol I: "Military necessity means the necessity for measures which are essential to attain the goals of war, and which are lawful in accordance with the laws and customs of war. … Conversely, when the law of armed conflict does not provide for any prohibition, the Parties to the conflict are in principle free within the constraints of customary law and general principles. This is specified in [Article 1(2) AP I]. This is the Martens clause, which was already contained in essentially the same form in the Preamble of Hague Convention IV of 1907. In other words, when the Parties to the conflict do not clash with a formal prohibition of law of armed conflict, they can act freely within the bounds of the principles of international law, i.e., they have the benefit of a freedom which is not arbitrary but within the framework of law." Sandoz *et al.*, *supra* note 17, para. 1389. This interpretation appears to be rejected by Cassese by reference to the preparatory works in relation to the 1899 Hague Regulations, Martens' original intentions, and practice after 1899. A. Cassese, 'The Martens Clause: Half a Loaf or Simply Pie in the Sky?', 11 *European Journal of International Law* (2000) pp. 193–212.

respect to non-international armed conflict, which currently lacks specific obligations relating to the protection of the environment.[58]

Third, the principle of ambituity may set aside or modify existing customary and conventional rules under the law of armed conflict.[59] After all, as a general principle of law, the principle of ambituity qualifies as a primary and autonomous source of international law and the application of such principle of law may lead to a different result than the application of conventional and customary rules of international law. For purposes of legal certainty, however, it is submitted that such application of the principle of ambituity (and of other general principles of law for that matter) must be restricted to exceptional circumstances, for example if the application of conventional or customary rules leads to a result which is manifestly contrary to the object and purpose of the principle of ambituity.[60] This

---

58 Indeed it is not easy to distinguish between the interpretative function and the supplementary function of general principles of law. This grey area is also recognised in relation to the functions of the principles of reasonableness and fairness under Dutch law. A. S. Hartkamp and C. H. Sieburgh, *Mr. C. Asser's Handleiding tot de beoefening van het Nederlands Burgerlijk Recht. 6. Verbintenissenrecht. Deel I. De verbintenis in het algemeen, eerste gedeelte* (Kluwer, Deventer, 2012) no. 55–59, in particular no. 56; and *generally* A. S. Hartkamp and C. H. Sieburgh, *Mr. C. Asser's Handleiding tot de beoefening van het Nederlands Burgerlijk Recht. 6. Verbintenissenrecht. Deel III. Algemeen overeenkomstenrecht* (Kluwer, Deventer, 2010) no. 378–435.

59 Dahm, for example, writes: "Drittens aber haben die Grundsätze des Rechts eine Begrenzungs- und Gewohnheitsrecht zu zwingenden Grundsätzen des Rechts, zu elementaren Forderungen der Gerechtigkeit, zum Naturrecht in Widerspruch setzen, dort können sie nicht zur Anwendung kommen." G. Dahm, *Völkerrecht; Band I* (W. Kohlhammer Verlag, Stuttgart, 1958), p. 41. And Kolb writes: "General principles of law have an important role also when it comes to the interpretation of legal norms. ... This role of the principles can then go up to a point where the question is not any more one of interpretation, but becomes one of correction of a norm, or even of derogation. Such a derogatory function is visible mainly when it comes to general principles of *ius cogens*-character, such as the non-recourse to force." Such function was accepted by the umpire in the *Mines of Aroa* case of 1903. R. Kolb, 'Principles as Sources of International Law (with specific reference to Good Faith)', 53 *Netherlands International Law Review* (2006) p. 32. Lammers, who calls this 'the corrective function', rejects this function of general principles of law (albeit without explanation), except when principles correct other principles of law or qualifies as a peremptory norm of international law. *See* Lammers, *supra* note 44, pp. 65, 69. According to Akehurst, there is unanimous opinion that international tribunals "cannot apply equity *contra legem* in the absence of an express authorization to apply equity *contra legem* such as is found in [Article 38(2) ICJ Statute]". Akehurst, *supra* note 56, p. 807.

60 It appears that such application of the principles of the law of armed conflict was (implicitly) confirmed by the ILC when it stated that specific rules of the law of armed conflict must not apply when the necessities of war (or the principle of necessity) are absent. After all, if certain conduct is not justified by the necessities of war (which is "the underling criterion for a whole series of substantive rules of the

could mean that a belligerent may still be held responsible for acting contrary to the principle of ambituity even if his acts were for some reason not contrary to its above-mentioned conventional or customary obligations.[61]

3. The Prohibition against Excessive Collateral Damage to the Environment during Armed Conflict

3.1. *Introduction*

As noted above, the only legitimate object of warfare is to weaken the military forces of the enemy. This object and purpose is embodied in the general principle of military necessity. It follows that the civilian population and civilian objects may not be the object of attack and that any unintentional or collateral damage to the civilian population or civilian objects should be prevented. The former is embodied in the general principle of distinction; the latter is embodied in the general principle of proportionality.

Although it appears to be generally accepted that excessive collateral damage to the environment during armed conflict is prohibited, the legal basis for

law of war and neutrality") "the general rule of the law of peace prohibiting certain actions again prevails". This implies that all conduct during armed conflict must also and in last resort be assessed by the necessities of war (given by the object and purpose of warfare namely to weaken the military forces of the enemy). A/CN.4// SER.A/1980/Add.1 (Part 2), *Yearbook of the International Law Commission*, 1980, Vol. II, Part Two, *supra* note 11, pp. 45–46. Similarly N. Melzer, *Targeted Killing in International Law* (Oxford University Press, Oxford, 2008) pp. 286–289. Because of the same reason, the principle of military necessity cannot be used to justify conduct which is contrary to customary or conventional obligations under the law of armed conflict (*Kriegsraison geht vor Kriegsmanier*). *See* Sandoz *et al.*, *supra* note 17, para. 1389. Similarly Venturini, *supra* note 20, pp. 51–52. Such argument is the exact opposite of the also conceptually wrong since it implies that the principle of military necessity can also trump other fundamental principles of the law of armed conflict.

61 As such the general principle of ambituity (or any other general principle of law for that matter) would resemble the scope and functioning of the above-mentioned general principles of reasonableness and fairness in Dutch civil law. In particular, the so-called derogatory or restrictive effect of these principles may entail that contractual or even statutory rights and obligations are not applicable in a specific case, if the application of those rights and obligations would be, under the specific circumstances, unfair and unreasonable. Article 6:2 DCC provides, in relation to legal obligations (in translation): "A rule which is applicable between [creditor and debtor] pursuant to statutory law, custom or legal act, is not applicable, to the extent that this would be, under the specific circumstances, unacceptable pursuant to the standards of reasonableness and fairness." Article 6:248(2) DCC provides, in relation to contracts: "A rule which is applicable between parties pursuant to a contract, is not applicable to the extent that this would be, under the specific circumstances, unacceptable pursuant to the standards of reasonableness and fairness."

such prohibition is not self-evident. It is submitted that this prohibition does not follow from Additional Protocol I (section 3.2), but from custom (section 3.3). The scope of this prohibition is subsequently discussed in section 3.4.

3.2. *The Alleged Prohibition against Excessive Collateral Damage to the Environment under Additional Protocol I*

The general principle of proportionality is reflected in the prohibition against excessive collateral damage to the civilian population and civilian objects as recognised in treaty law and customary international law. Articles 51(4) and (5)(b) AP I, for example, provide: "Indiscriminate attacks are prohibited. ... Among others, the following types of attacks are to be considered as indiscriminate: ... (b) an attack which may be expected to cause incidental loss of civilian life, injury to civilians, damage to civilian objects, or a combination thereof, which would be excessive in relation to the concrete and direct military advantage anticipated."[62] According to the ICRC, both provisions reflect customary international law. Rule 14 of its CIHL Study provides: "Launching an attack which may be expected to cause incidental loss of civilian life, injury to civilians, damage to civilian objects, or a combination thereof, which would be excessive in relation to the concrete and direct military advantage anticipated, is prohibited."

The law of armed conflict defines civilian objects as those objects which do not qualify as military objects. Military objects are objects which "by their nature, location, purpose or use make an effective contribution to military action and whose total or partial destruction, capture or neutralisation, in the circumstances ruling at the time, offers a definite military advantage" (Article 52(2) AP I and Rule 8 CIHL Study). Therefore, if elements of the environment do not make an effective contribution to military action, these elements would qualify as a civilian object under the laws of armed conflict.[63] This conclusion is confirmed by the positioning of Article 55 AP I in Chapter III of Section I of Part IV of Additional Protocol I, which is titled 'Civilian Objects'.[64]

---

62 Further, Articles 57 and 58 AP I require parties to a conflict to take certain precautionary measures in the conduct of military operations to spare the civilian populations, civilians and civilian objects. *See also* Rules 15–24 CIHL Study.

63 Please note, however, that the formulation of Article 8(2)(b)(iv) of the Rome Statute conflicts with this view. Article 8(2)(b)(iv) qualifies, as a war crime, the international launch of an attack "in the knowledge that such attack will cause incidental loss of life or injury to civilians or damage to civilian objects or widespread, long-term and severe damage to the natural environment ...", thereby distinguishing between civilian objects and the natural environment.

64 *Similarly* Y. Dinstein, *The Conduct of Hostilities under the Law of International Armed Conflict*, 2nd edition (Cambridge University Press, Cambridge, 2010) p. 204. Please note, however, that the scope of Part IV of AP I is generally limited to civilian objects on land pursuant to Article 49(3) AP I. This limitation arguably does not apply to the protection of civilian objects under customary international law, nor does

It follows, at first sight, that because of this qualification as a civilian object, the environment is *ipso facto* protected against direct attack and against excessive collateral damage as an ordinary civilian object under Additional Protocol I.[65] This position is taken by various authors, including Bothe, Bruch, Diamond and Jensen. In a recent publication in the *International Review of the Red Cross* they state: "Elements of the environment are most often civilian objects. As such, they are protected against attacks. To that extent, the restrictive conditions of Articles 35 and 55 of Additional Protocol I do not apply. This protection is, however, shaky, as environmental elements can easily become military objectives."[66]

Substantively, the consequence of this approach is that the scope of Article 55 AP I (and Article 35(3) AP I for that matter) is limited to circumstances when the environment indeed qualifies as (or rather becomes) a military object or when any collateral damage to the environment would be justified by the military advantage to be obtained. Such damage to the environment would then generally be permitted under Additional Protocol I unless the damage is widespread, long-term and severe.

Practically, the consequence of this approach is that the legality of a(n) (planned) attack which may involve damage to the environment must first be assessed by reference to Articles 51 and 52 AP I (and their customary equivalents), and subsequently by reference to Article 55 AP I.

Schematically, an *ex post facto* assessment of the legality of an attack would look as follows:

1. Qualification of the target (the environment) as a civilian or military object (Article 52 AP I).
2. If the target (the environment) qualified as a military object, then the following would apply:

---

it apply to the protection of the natural environment under Article 35(3) AP I. *See* Koppe, *supra* note 4, pp. 154–167.

65 It is exactly for this reason that Heintschel von Heinegg and Donner conclude that the natural environment does not or rather cannot qualify as a civilian object. Furthermore, they are of the opinion that civilian objects are limited to "material things that can be seen or touched. The natural environment as the sum total of different and differing natural components and processes may not be characterizes as such an object." W. Heintschel von Heinegg and M. Donner, 'New Developments in the Protection of the Natural Environment in Naval Armed Conflicts', 37 *German Yearbook of International Law* (1994) pp. 288–289.

66 M. Bothe *et al.*, 'International law protecting the environment during armed conflict: gaps and opportunities', 92 *International Review of the Red Cross* (2010) p. 576. *See also* M. Bothe, 'The Protection of the Environment in Times of Armed Conflict; Legal Rules, Uncertainty, Deficiencies, and Possible Developments', 34 *Germany Yearbook of International Law* (1991) p. 55. Also Dinstein stipulates that "once classified as a civilian object, the natural environment must not be the object of attack". Dinstein, *supra* note 64, p. 204.

   a. The attack was lawful as a matter of principle (Article 52 AP I), unless the intended or expected damage to the target (the environment) was widespread, long-term and severe and prejudiced the health or survival of the population (Article 55 AP I).
3. If the target (the environment) qualified as a civilian object, then the following would apply:
   a. The attack was unlawful as a matter of principle (Article 52 AP I). However, if the environment was not targeted as such and the damage to the environment qualifies as acceptable (not-excessive) collateral damage, the attack would nevertheless be lawful (Article 51) unless the intended or expected damage was widespread, long-term and severe and prejudiced the health or survival of the population (Article 55 AP I).

It is submitted, however, that the better reading of the interrelationship between Articles 51/52 and 55 AP I is that Article 55 AP I specifies the protection of the environment as a civilian object and thereby supplants the general protection provided by Articles 51/52 AP I. It follows that the environment does not enjoy or can no longer enjoy such general protection as a civilian object under Additional Protocol I and that the legality of any (planned) attack involving (possible) damage to the environment must be assessed by reference to Article 55 AP I only and by reference to Article 55 AP I alone.

Schematically, an *ex post facto* assessment would then look as follows:

1. Qualification of the damaged object as (elements of) the environment.
2. If the damaged object qualifies as (elements of) the environment, then the attack was unlawful as a matter of principle provided that:
   a. the attack caused widespread, long-term and severe damage to the environment thereby prejudicing the health or survival of the population; and
   b. the attack was intended or expected to cause such damage (Article 55 AP I).

This reading is based on the fact that the drafters of Additional Protocol I chose to include a specific provision on the protection of the environment during international armed conflict in the Protocol's chapter dealing with civilian objects, which would provide for specific protection to the environment under specific and exceptional circumstances.[67] The introduction of Article 55 AP I (and Article

67 Similar provisions were included for cultural objects (Article 53 AP I), places of worship (Article 53 AP I), objects which are indispensable for the survival of the civilian population (Article 54 AP I) and installations which contain dangerous forces (Article 56 AP I), although their interaction with Article 52 AP I is not self-evident either. In particular the scope of Article 53 AP I (cultural property and places of worship) is subject of discussion. Article 53 AP I does not contain a military necessity excep-

35(3) AP I for that matter) did not follow from prior dissatisfaction with the protection of the environment during international armed conflict under the general rules on the protection of civilian objects. There was no attempt to create more legal certainty for military policy makers as to what they could and could not do during hostilities because the general rules on protection of civilian objects provided insufficient guidance.

On the contrary, the idea that the environment had to be protected during international armed conflict was new in public international law. Indeed, a general concern for the protection of the environment in general only emerged in the 1960s and was highlighted by the above-mentioned 1972 Stockholm Declaration. The inclusion of specific provisions on the protection of the environment during international armed conflict in Additional Protocol I was therefore exceptional and progressive.

The conference records of the Diplomatic Conference show that the drafters indeed intended to raise a high threshold for responsibility for damage to the environment during international armed conflict. Only the use of means or methods of warfare intended or expected to cause widespread, long-term and severe damage to the environment was considered wrongful. It appears that this cumulative standard was deliberately included to make sure that responsibility for environmental damage would be exceptional and that a tank commander whose

---

tion clause (as do Articles 54 and 56 API), which suggests, by reference to the general maxim and interpretation technique *expressio unius est exclusio alterius*, that the protection of Article 53 AP I is absolute, even if the object is used for military purposes and therefore would qualify as a military object. Such interpretation, however, is not accepted, either because of the reference to the 1954 Hague Convention and other relevant international instruments in the chapeau of Article 53, which are not prejudiced by Article 53, or because of its interaction with Article 52(2) AP I. The former argument is persuasive but only in so far states parties to these instruments are involved. *See*, for example, Kolb and Hyde, *supra* note 9, p. 146. The latter argument appears to be less persuasive, but accepted in the ICRC Commentary to Article 53, Sandoz *et al.*, *supra* note 17, paras. 2072 and 2079. *Similarly* M. Bothe *et al.*, *New Rules for Victims of Armed Conflicts; Commentary on the Two 1977 Protocols Additional to the Geneva Conventions of 1949* (Martinus Nijhoff Publishers, The Hague, 1982) pp. 333–334 (referring to the understanding of several Western delegations, and stipulating that an attack must first be assessed by reference to Article 52 AP I and only after meeting this "two-pronged test" by reference to Article 53 AP I). The latter view is also upheld by O'Keefe: "That said, if and for as long as an object covered by article 53 is used in support of the military effort contrary to paragraph (b), the legality of any attack against that object – and only that object – falls to be determined by reference to article 52(2), and will be lawful provided such use makes an effective contribution to military action and the object's total or partial destruction, capture or neutralisation, in the circumstances ruling at the time, offers a definite military advantage." R. O'Keefe, *The Protection of Cultural Property in Armed Conflict* (Cambridge University Press, Cambridge, 2006) p. 216.

tank flattened a tree would not be made a war criminal.[68] Without reference to the general protection of civilian objects under current Articles 51 and 52 AP I, "[i]t appeared to be a widely shared assumption that battlefield damage incidental to conventional warfare would not normally be proscribed by this provision".[69]

Further, it appears that the drafters intended the specific provisions relating to the protection of the environment to be the only rules which would provide such protection, irrespective of the question whether or not the environment qualified as a military or civilian object. There is no indication in the text of Additional Protocol I nor in the preparatory works that the environment is generally protected as a civilian object under Articles 51 and 52 AP I. There is no indication that Article 55 was thus intended to complement or supplement Articles 51 and 52 of Additional Protocol. And there is no indication that any assessment of damage to the environment would first have to be assessed by reference to the general rules of Articles 51 and 52 AP I or that one could fall back on either of these two general provisions when the criteria of Article 55 would not be met.

As a matter of fact, the link between the environment and civilian objects and the civilian population was not self-evident during the negotiations for Additional Protocol I. It was only decided in 1975 that Additional Protocol I would contain two separate provisions on the protection of the environment: one provision in the section on basic rules on means and methods of warfare protecting the environment *per se* and therefore characterised as eco-centric, and one provision in the section on the protection of civilian objects protecting the environment as an object which is necessary for the health and survival of the civilian population, and therefore characterised as anthropocentric.[70]

It follows that Article 55 AP I (and Article 35(3) AP I for that matter) was intended to be a stand-alone provision, providing for specific protection to the environment and that it must be interpreted as such. The legality of any (intended) attack under Additional Protocol I must therefore be assessed by reference to this provision first and by reference to this provision alone. This holds true, even though, in hindsight, Articles 51 and 52 AP I could have been a more effective basis for protecting the environment during armed conflict than Article 55 (and 35(3)) AP I.[71]

---

68 Levie, *supra* note 2, pp. 130, 272.

69 Report of Committee III, Second Session (CDDH/215/Rev 1), in H. S. Levie, *Protection of War Victims: Protocol 1 to the 1949 Geneva Conventions*, Volume 2 (Oceana Publications, Dobbs Ferry, NY, 1980) pp. 276–277.

70 Levie, *supra* note 2, pp. 269 *et seq.*; Sandoz *et al.*, *supra* note 17, para. 1449.

71 Indeed, the drafters of the 2009 UNEP report on environmental protection during armed conflict wrote: "The provisions that govern the protection of civilian objects and property could provide a more effective legal basis for protecting the environment during armed conflict than those protecting the environment *per se*, at least under existing IHL treaty law." They subsequently refer the 1907 Hague Regulations, the 1949 Geneva Convention IV and both 1977 Additional Protocols. United Nations

This interpretation of the relationship between Article 55 and Articles 51 and 52 AP I appears to be confirmed in practice. The Special Committee established by the Prosecutor of the International Criminal Tribunal for the Former Yugoslavia (ICTY) to investigate the bombings by the North Atlantic Treaty Organization (NATO) over Yugoslavia in 1999 discussed the possible damage to the environment first by reference to Articles 35(3) and 55 AP I as these were the "basic legal provisions applicable to protection of the environment in armed conflict".[72] The Committee first stated that "it would appear extremely difficult to develop a *prima facie* case upon the basis of these provisions, even assuming they were applicable" and concluded that "the environmental damage caused during the NATO bombing campaign does not reach the Additional Protocol I threshold".[73] Subsequently, the Committee assessed the alleged environmental effects of the NATO bombing campaign by reference to the general principles of necessity and proportionality, since the environmental effects "are best considered from [these] underlying principles of the law of armed conflict".[74]

The Committee did not assess the damage by reference to Articles 51 and 52 AP I as an alternative to Article 55, but instead relied on the underlying fundamental principles of necessity and proportionality (thereby confirming the autonomous status of the above-mentioned general principles of the law of armed

---

Environment Programme, *Protecting the Environment During Armed Conflict; An Inventory and Analysis of International Law*, UNEP, Nairobi, 2009, p. 16. Verwey noted that indeed, the drafting of Articles 35(3) and 55 AP I may "very well result in lowering traditional standards of protection, for, the cumulative triple standard may now render permissible what before would have been forbidden". W. D. Verwey, 'Protection of the Environment in Times of Armed Conflict: In Search of New Legal Perspective', 8 *Leiden Journal of International Law* (1995) p. 11. Bothe and Schmitt, however, stipulate that Articles 35(3) and 55 AP I were not intended to lower the general rules on the protection of civilian objects. Bothe, *supra* note 66, p. 56; M. N. Schmitt, 'Green War: An Assessment of the Environmental Law ofInternational Armed Conflict', 22 *Yale Journal of International Law* (1997) p. 73. This argument fails to convince, however, since the protection of the environment as such was of no State's concern before 1974–1977, and specific rules on the protection of the environment were only included on the basis of the given criteria.

72 International Criminal Tribunal for the Former Yugoslavia (ICTY), 'Final Report to the Prosecutor by the Committee Established to Review the NATO Bombing Campaign against the Federal Republic of Yugoslavia', 39 *International Legal Materials* (2000) para. 14.

73 *Ibid.*, para. 17.

74 *Ibid.*, paras. 18–25. Please note, however, that the committee's reference to A. P. V. Rogers, 'Zero Casualty Warfare', 82 *International Review of the Red Cross* (2000) pp. 177–178, in para. 18 is incorrect. First, the committee appears to refer to Rogers' citation of a particular section in the British Defense Doctrine, which cannot be attributed to Rogers. Second, this particular quote from the British Defense Doctrine does not refer to collateral damage to the environment (as suggested by the Committee) but generally to collateral damage to civilians and civilian objects.

conflict) and, so it appears, on the customary rules (prohibition to cause wanton destruction and excessive collateral damage) which reflect both principles. This approach is similar to the approach advocated by the present author, as will be explained further below.

Further, this interpretation of the relationship between Article 55 and Articles 51 and 52 AP I is confirmed by Heintschel von Heinegg and Donner who are of the opinion that in times of armed conflict the environment is only protected by Articles 35(3) and 55 AP I and therefore only against effects that are widespread, long-term and severe:

> Methods and means of (naval) warfare always have negative effects on the environment. The States parties to AP I can, therefore, not be said to have agreed upon a general protection of the environment against negative effects of warfare. … Finally, it would be difficult to explain why the drafters of AP I did not simply state that the term "civilian object" also comprises the environment. Instead they agreed on two independent provisions that will protect it only against damages that are 'widespread, long-term and severe'.[75]

The upside of having such a specific provision on the protection of the environment is that it provides absolute protection to the environment (including collateral damage) even when its use would have military advantages and would support military operations. The downside of having such a specific provision on the protection of the environment, however, is that it appears to be the only protection provided to the environment as a civilian object under Additional Protocol I, and that the practical application of Article 55, in view of its high threshold, appears to be limited.

3.3. *The Prohibition against Excessive Collateral Damage to the Environment under Customary International Law*

That does not mean that there is no additional protection to the environment during international armed conflict in addition to Articles 35 and 55 AP I. As mentioned in section 1, it is arguable that since the early 1990s three rules of customary international law have emerged, including a specific prohibition against excessive collateral damage to the environment during international armed conflict.[76] This rule follows from the general principles of proportionality and ambituity and complements the conventional and customary prohibitions against excessive collateral damage to civilian objects.

---

75 Heintschel von Heinegg and Donner, *supra* note 65, p. 289.

76 The other two rules are the prohibition against wanton destruction to the natural environment and a general duty of care for the natural environment during international armed conflict. *See* Koppe, *supra* note 4, pp. 246–278.

The emergence of this specific prohibition is evidenced in State practice, such as the drafting of Article 8(2)(b)(iv) of the Rome Statute, which provides for individual responsibility for causing excessive environmental damage during international armed conflict. Pursuant to Article 8(2)(b)(iv) an intentional attack "in the knowledge that such attack will cause incidental loss of life or injury to civilians or damage to civilian objects or widespread, long-term and severe damage to the environment which would be clearly excessive in relation to the concrete and direct overall military advantage anticipated" qualifies as a war crime. Although inspired by Articles 35(3) and 55 AP I, the text of Article 8(2)(b)(iv) clearly joins in with the customary prohibition to cause excessive collateral damage to civilian objects and the civilian population as reflected in Articles 51(5)(b) AP I. Article 8(2)(b)(iv) introduces a similar balancing test which is absent in the text of Articles 35(3) and 55 AP I. According to the drafters of the Rome Statute, this particular war crime qualifies as "a serious [violation] of the laws and customs applicable in international armed conflict, within the established framework of international law" (*chapeau* Article 8(2)(b) Rome Statute), which suggests the existence of a customary prohibition against causing excessive collateral damage to the environment.

Further evidence and inferences can be found in the United States *Commander's Handbook on the Law of Naval Operations*,[77] and public statements made by State representatives in public memorandums or within the framework of the General Assembly or before the International Court of Justice (usually referring to both the prohibition of wanton destruction of the environment and the prohibition against excessive collateral damage together). Canada, for example, stated in 1992:

> An important evolution was thus taking place which reflected the importance of the ecological point of view and which should be brought to bear on other questions, such as that of proportionality (the need to strike a balance between the protection of the environment and the needs of war) or that of the distinction between military and non-military objectives. Under the same principle, the environment as such should not be the object of direct attack, and his delegation would like to see that point reflected in the resolution to be adopted after discussion of the item.[78]

---

77 NWP 1-14M, *The Commander's Handbook on the Law of Naval Operations, Department of the Navy* (Newport, RI, 2007), para. 8.4, available at <www.nwc.navy.mil>.

78 A/C.6/47/SR.8, Summary Record of the 8th meeting of the Sixth Committee of the General Assembly on 1 October 1992, p. 6, para. 20. For more references, *see* Koppe, *supra* note 4, pp. 264–268.

Additionally, the 1994 *San Remo Manual on International Law Applicable to Armed Conflicts at Sea*,[79] the 1993 *ICRC Guidelines*[80] and the 1999 *ICRC Model Manual on the Law of Armed Conflict*,[81] each include, in so many words, a prohibition against causing excessive collateral damage to the environment.

Finally, the existence (or emergence) of a customary prohibition against causing excessive collateral damage to the environment has been acknowledged in literature[82] and confirmed by the ICRC in 2005 in its *Study on Customary International Humanitarian Law*. Customary Rule 43C comprehensively provides: "Launching an attack against a military objective which may be expected to cause incidental damage to the environment which would be excessive in relation to the concrete and direct military advantage anticipated is prohibited."

It is submitted that this relatively new rule of customary international law complements Articles 35 and 55 AP I (*i.e.* for States parties to AP I). The customary prohibition emerged later in time (arguably in the 1990s) and States were fully aware of the existence of Articles 35 and 55 AP I at that time. Further, the customary rule appears to provide relative protection to the environment (depending on the military interests involved) whereas Articles 35(3) and 55 provide absolute protection, even if the customary prohibition against excessive collateral damage would not be breached. This would mean that any military action which causes damage to the environment would first have to be assessed under this relatively new customary prohibition; and subsequently, if no breach can be established and if applicable, by reference to Articles 35(3) and 55 AP I.

Schematically, an *ex post facto* assessment of the legality of an attack would then look as follows:

1. Qualification of the damaged object as (elements of) the environment.

---

79 San Remo Manual on International Law Applicable to Armed Conflicts at Sea, in *International Review of the Red Cross* (1995), No. 309, para. 46(d) and 13(c).

80 A/48/269, Report of the Secretary-General to the General Assembly on the Protection of the Environment in the Environment in Times of Armed Conflict, of 29 July 1993, with Annexed the ICRC Guidelines for Military Manuals and Instructions on the Protection of the Environment in Times of Armed Conflict, principle 4.

81 A. P. V. Rogers and P. Malherbe, *Fight it Right; Model Manual on the Law of Armed Conflict for Armed Forces* (International Committee of the Red Cross, ICRC, Geneva, 1999) para. 702(e) and (f).

82 Heintschel von Heinegg, and Donner, *supra* note 65, p. 294; J.-M. Henckaerts, 'Towards Better Protection for the Environment in Armed Conflict: Recent Developments in International Humanitarian Law', 9 *Review of European Community and international environmental law*(2000) p. 18; L. Lijnzaad and G. J. Tanja, 'Protection of the Environment in Times of Armed Conflict: The Iraq-Kuwait War', 40 *Netherlands International Law Review* (1993) p. 184; M. Bothe, 'Protection of the Environment in Times of Armed Conflict', in N. Al-Nauimi and R. Meese (eds.), *International Legal Issues Arising Under the United Nations Decade of International Law; Proceedings of the Qatar International Law Conference '94* (Martinus Nijhoff Publishers, The Hague, 1995) p. 98.

2. If the damaged object qualifies as (elements of) the environment, then the attack was unlawful as a matter of principle provided that:
   a. the damage to the environment was collateral;[83] and
   b. the damage to the environment was excessive in relation to the concrete and direct military advantage anticipated (customary prohibition against excessive collateral damage to the environment).
3. In the alternative (in case the damaged object qualifies as (elements of) the environment and the damage to the environment is not excessive in relation to the concrete and direct military advantage anticipated), the attack was unlawful as a matter of principle provided that:
   a. the attack caused widespread, long-term and severe damage to the environment thereby prejudicing the health or survival of the population; and
   b. the attack was intended or expected to cause such damage (Article 55 AP I).

The result of such *ex post facto* assessment of the legality of an attack causing damage to the environment will be similar to an assessment on the basis of the method advocated by those who argue that the environment is also protected by Articles 51 and 52 AP I as discussed above. However, the methodology and approach are different (reliance on the relatively new customary prohibition against excessive collateral damage to the environment rather than on Articles 51 and 52 AP I) and based on a more persuasive interpretation of Additional Protocol I.

3.4. *The Scope of the Prohibition against Excessive Collateral Damage to the Environment*

Finally, the scope of the prohibition against excessive collateral damage to the environment and therefore the responsibility for breach of this prohibition will depend on two factors. First, responsibility for breach of this prohibition will depend on the assessment of the damage to the environment. Second, responsibility for breach will depend on the foreseeability (and thus the expectation) of this damage to those who decide to launch an attack. Only then will it be possible to establish whether or not the damage to the environment was excessive in relation to the military advantage obtained.

As to the assessment of the damage to the environment, it is necessary that the damage to the environment has actually materialised. Contrary to damage

---

83 As was mentioned above, willful or wanton destruction of the natural environment during armed conflict is also prohibited under customary international law. This rule of customary international law arguably emerged in the 1990s and its existence has been confirmed by the ICRC in its CIHL Study (Rule 43). Koppe, *supra* note 4, pp. 256–278. This contribution deals with the prohibition of excessive collateral damage to the natural environment.

to civilians and civilian objects, which is generally immediately visible, damage to the environment may only materialise after some time. Indeed, Verwey recognised that

> many interactive natural processes have not yet been (fully) understood, resulting in the fact that harmful effects which are not (yet) recognized or expected may occur now or in the future. Only quite recently, science has become able to demonstrate that even apparently restricted, relatively short-term and seemingly insignificant forms of environmental impact may subsequently turn out to have triggered serious or significant ecological disruption.[84]

Therefore, the assessment of any damage to the environment may take time and thus it may also take time before the responsibility of a wrongdoer can be established. This phenomenon is not uncommon in domestic law, where health damage resulting from smoking, asbestos or other toxic substances may materialise years after the wrongful act was committed. Although this may be undesirable for belligerents who wish to settle any responsibilities and damages after a conflict as soon as possible, it is inevitable due to the nature of the damage. It therefore follows that there may be circumstances under which the responsibility for causing excessive collateral damage to the environment (or widespread, long-term and severe damage under Articles 35 and 55 AP I) may be established years after the conflict has ended.

As to the foreseeability of possible damage to the environment, it appears that such would have to be assessed on the basis of objective criteria and on the basis of the information available to the relevant commander at the time of the attack.[85] This means that it must be established that the relevant commander knew or should have known that the attack and the means and methods used would cause excessive collateral damage to the environment. If it cannot be established that the relevant commander could reasonably have known that the attack and the means and methods used would cause such damage to the environment, the damage was not foreseeable and responsibility cannot be established.[86]

---

84 Verwey, *supra* note 71, p. 12.

85 Both the United Kingdom and France made such declaration upon ratification of Additional Protocol I on 28 January 1998 and 11 April 2001 respectively. As to the scope of Articles 35(3) and 55 AP I they stated that the risk of environmental damage would have to be assessed objectively and on the basis of the information available at the time. Declarations and reservations of States Parties to Additional Protocol I available in the ICRC International Humanitarian Law database at <www.icrc.org>.

86 Similar standards are generally accepted for foreseeability of damage in relation to Articles 35(3) and 55 AP I. *See* M. Bothe, 'War and Environment', in R. Bernhardt (ed.), *Encyclopaedia of Public International Law; Volume Four; Quirin, Ex Parte to Zones of Peace* (Elsevier, Amsterdam, 2000) p. 1344; Dinstein, *supra* note 64, p. 183.

It follows that increasing knowledge about natural process and the impact of military activities on ecological processes in the long term will therefore increase the scope of this prohibition.[87] It is therefore suggested that environmental experts and biologists should further investigate the consequences of warfare on the environment and make this knowledge publicly available. Furthermore it is suggested that environmental experts and biologists assume the responsibility to further explain to the military the nature of environmental processes and the sensitivities of ecological systems. While it appears that there is a fruitful dialogue between the military and humanitarian organisations, in particular the ICRC, such dialogue appears to be absent between the military and environmental organisations. The more people know about the environment, the higher the standards of what is expected of the military, and the better the protection of the environment against collateral damage, will be. There is still a world to gain in that respect.

4. Summary and Conclusions

The need to protect the environment during armed conflict has generally been recognised by the international community. Prior to 2012, the various United Nations conferences on the environment and sustainable development repeatedly expressed concern for the environment and the General Assembly even proceeded, in 2001, to declare 6 November of each year the 'International Day for Preventing the Exploitation of the Environment in War and Armed Conflict'. The need to protect the environment has further become evident in practice after the use of Agent Orange in Vietnam, the burning of oil wells in Kuwait and massive oil spills in the Persian Gulf and the Mediterranean Sea.

Although the consequences of warfare have proven to be disastrous, attention on the relevant rules protecting the environment during armed conflict has been relatively modest. Furthermore, and in the absence of judicial decisions in this area, opinions differ as to the scope and the adequacy of the existing legal framework. It is therefore significant that the ILC decided in 2011 to include the protection of the environment in relation to armed conflicts in its long-term programme of work. As suggested by Marie Jacobsson, the aim of the ILC's work in this area should include the identification of "new developments in case law or in customary law"; the clarification of "the relation between existing treaty law and new legal developments (including legal reasoning)"; "the formulation of ap-

87 It is even arguable that – in view of the above-mentioned conventional (first sentence Article 55 AP I) and customary duty of care of belligerents for the natural environment during armed conflict – states are required to do active research and obtain information on the likely consequences for the environment of military activities.

plicable rules and … principles of general international law of relevance for the topic"; and suggestions "to achieve a uniform and coherent system" in this area.[88]

This study has attempted to contribute to the ILCs work in this area. First it clarified the foundations of the existing legal framework in relation to the protection of the environment during armed conflict. Second it clarified the basis for and scope of the prohibition against excessive collateral damage to the environment during armed conflict.

As to the foundations of the existing legal framework, it is submitted that current conventional and customary rules of armed conflict (entailing specific obligations for belligerent States) which protect the intrinsic value of the environment during armed conflict cannot be deduced from the four fundamental principles of the law of armed conflict: the principles of military necessity, distinction, proportionality and humanity. In order to explain the existence of specific obligations in this area, it is therefore submitted that they follow from a new *fundamental* principle of the law of armed conflict: the principle of ambituity. Similar to the principle of humanity, the principle of ambituity provides for an absolute limitation to the necessities of war. Article 35(3) AP I is a pure reflection of the principle of ambituity, as is the customary duty of care which belligerent States must observe during armed conflict which arguably emerged in the 1990s. Other rules which aim to protect the environment during armed conflict, such as the prohibition of wanton or excessive collateral damage to the environment, are reflections of a compromise between the principle of ambituity and the principles of distinction or proportionality.

It is further submitted that the fundamental principles of the law of armed conflict, including the principle of ambituity, qualify as general principles of law in the sense of Article 38(1)(c) Statute. Although the general principles of law were traditionally understood as referring to general principles of domestic law common to all legal systems, there is increasing recognition that the general principles of law also include general principles of international law, including principles of specific areas of international law. As such, the fundamental principles of the law of armed conflict would also qualify as general principles of law.

As an autonomous source of international law, the general principle of ambituity and the other fundamental principles of the law of armed conflict may be used to interpret existing conventional or customary rules of international law (perhaps by (cross) reference to related principles of international environmental law) or to fill any *lacunae* within the law and thereby supplement the rights and obligations of States during armed conflict. Further it is not impossible that, under specific circumstances, the principle of ambituity may be applied in deviation of conventional or customary rules of international law. This could mean that, under exceptional circumstances, the application of this principle could in

88 A/66/10, Report of the International Law Commission; Sixty-third session (26 April – 3 June and 4 July – 12 August 2011); Annex E – Protection of the environment in relation to armed conflicts (Ms. Marie G. Jacobsson), para. 31.

itself determine the rights and obligations of belligerents during armed conflict, including those articulated in Articles 35(3) and 55 AP I, and the customary prohibitions of wanton and excessive collateral damage to the environment and the customary duty of care for the environment during armed conflict.

As to the basis and scope of the specific prohibition against excessive collateral damage to the environment during armed conflict, it is submitted that this prohibition cannot be based on Articles 51 and 52 AP I. On the basis of a contextual interpretation of Article 55 AP I and in light of the legislative history of Article 55 AP I and 35(3) AP I, it is submitted that Article 55 AP I was intended to be a stand-alone provision, providing for specific protection to the environment, and specifying the general protection of the environment as a civilian object under Articles 51 and 52 AP I. It follows that the legality of any (intended) attack under Additional Protocol I must therefore be assessed by reference to this provision first and by reference to this provision alone. This holds true even though, in hindsight, Articles 51 and 52 AP I could have been a more effective basis for protecting the environment during armed conflict than Article 55 (and 35(3)) AP I.

Instead the prohibition against excessive collateral damage follows from a relatively new rule of customary international law, which arguably emerged in the 1990s. It is submitted that this relatively new rule of customary international law complements Articles 35 and 55 AP I (*i.e.* for States parties to AP I). Further, in view of the scope of this prohibition, and since it emerged later in time, it is submitted that any military action which causes collateral damage to the environment would first have to be assessed under this relatively new customary prohibition, and subsequently if no breach can be established and if applicable by reference to Articles 35(3) and 55 AP I.

Finally, it has been explained that environmental damage may materialise long after the conflict has ended and that the prohibition against excessive collateral damage to the environment essentially depends on the knowledge of military commanders and decision-makers of environmental processes. It is therefore suggested to further investigate the consequences of warfare on the environment and that environmental experts and biologists make this knowledge publicly available and explain their findings to the military. The more people know about the environment, the higher the standards of what is expected of the military, and the better the protection of the environment against collateral damage, will be.

In relation to the above-mentioned aims of a possible study of the ILC on the protection of the environment in relation to armed conflict, it is suggested that the ILC should include and consider in its discussions the meaning and scope of the fundamental principles of the law of armed conflict, in particular the emergence of the principle of ambituity. It is further suggested that the ILC should clarify the relationship between these fundamental principles and the conventional and customary rules which protect the environment during armed conflict and consider the argument made here that these fundamental principles qualify as general principles of law in the meaning of Article 38(1)(c) Statute. Finally, it is suggested that the ILC should clarify the relationship between the rules which specifically protect the environment during armed conflict – both conventional and customary – and the general rules of *ius in bello* which protect civilian objects during armed conflict.

4 The Ethics, Principles and Objectives of Protection of the Environment in Times of Armed Conflict

Michael Bothe*

1. Introduction: The Question

Is war the end of ethics or ethical behaviour? Are killing and devastation, as they occur in war, unethical *per se*? If one looks at the ethical discourses over the centuries[1] this is a position which can certainly be found, although if one takes the discourse as a whole, it is an extreme position. Nevertheless, regardless of whether war is or is not unethical *per se*, as the rich literature on war and ethics proves war does not lead to an abdication of ethics.[2] Rather, in relation to war, ethical considerations go in two different, albeit not necessarily mutually exclusive directions. On the one hand there is the virtue of courage in fighting. Courage in fighting for the defence of the soldier's country is also an ethical postulate which can be related to the concept of chivalry. This, on the other hand, brings into play the second direction of ethical considerations, that of ethical demands as a restraint in warfare. Restraint in the ways and means of waging war is a demand of the just war theory which holds that just wars are only those which are, *inter alia*, conducted by just means.[3]

What are the consequences of ethical approaches for the protection of the environment in armed conflict? The just war theory seems to implicate reference to the law of armed conflict in that unlawful warfare is also unethical. While this reasoning may appear to lead to a vicious circle, as will be demonstrated, this

---

* Professor emeritus, Faculty of Law, J.W. Goethe University, Frankfurt/Main

1 *See* A. Biehler, 'Pacifism', in particular MN 2 and 4, in R. Wolfrum (ed.), *Max Planck Encyclopedia of Public International Law* (MPEPIL), available at <www.mpepil.com> (last visited 30 September 2013).

2 A. J. Coates, *The ethics of war* (Manchester University Press, Manchester, 1997); R. Sorabji (ed.), *The ethics of war – shared problems in different traditions*, (Ashgate, Aldershot *et al.*, 2006).

3 P. P. Christopher, *Just War Theory: an historical and philosophical analysis* (University of Massachusetts Amherst, 1990).

Rosemary Rayfuse (ed.), War and the Environment: New Approaches to Protecting the Environment in Relation to Armed Conflict
Copyright 2014 Koninklijke Brill NV. Printed in The Netherlands. ISBN 978-90-04-27064-0 pp. 91-234

is not necessarily the case. In addition, the specific discourse on environmental ethics may also be relevant. The principal demand of environmental ethics is conduct that respects the need to preserve the natural environment of the planet.[4] Different approaches exist concerning the way in which this goal is to be reached: the ecocentric and the anthropocentric approach.[5] The former demands the preservation of nature for its own sake, while the latter requires this preservation for the benefit of humankind. In the international discourse on environmental policy, the pure ecocentric approach is largely set aside. Rather, an anthropocentric approach which requires the preservation of the environment in order not to jeopardise the living conditions of present and future generations is the prevailing and generally recognised policy principle.[6] In this way, the preservation of the environment is a demand of intergenerational equity.[7]

The purpose of this study is to attempt to clarify the ethical requirements concerning the legal protection of the environment in armed conflict. It takes as its starting point a number of assumptions. The first is that there is an ethical underpinning for the law relating to the protection of the environment in armed conflict. The second assumption is that certain principles can be derived from these underpinnings. Finally, the third assumption is that such principles have inspired and continue to inspire the objectives of designing and applying a legal regime. The point of this study is to demonstrate whether, and if so why, these assumptions are correct.

2. The Ethics of the Laws of War and of Environmental Law

In attempting to answer the question of the protection of the environment in armed conflicts, one immediately encounters the phenomenon of the fragmentation of international law, or the notion that different areas of international law develop in a quasi-autonomous way. The fact of fragmentation can be observed simply by looking at the reality of the international order.[8] Nevertheless, some theorists of international law oppose this view, insisting, instead, on the unity

---

4 The first author to advocate this approach was R. Carson, *Silent Spring* (New York, 1962). For a more recent analysis, *see in particular* H. Rolston, *A New Environmental Ethics: The Next Millenium for Life on Earth* (Routledge, New York/London, 2012).

5 Rolston, *ibid.*, in particular pp. 33 *et seq.*

6 Principle 1 of the Rio Declaration of Environment and Development 1992: "Human beings are at the center of concern for sustainable development."

7 Principle 3 of the Rio Declaration: "The right to development must be fulfilled so as to equitably meet developmental and environmental needs of present and future generations."

8 *See* G. Hafner, 'Pros and Cons Ensuing from Fragmentation of International Law', 25 *Michigan Journal of International Law* (2004) pp. 849–864; A. Fischer-Lescano, 'Regime Collisions: The Vain Search for the Legal Unity in the Fragmentation of Global Law', 25 *Michigan Journal of International Law* (2004) pp. 999–1046.

of the legal order[9] as an important consideration in counterbalancing the fact of fragmentation. Indeed, the fragmented areas of international law are not watertight compartments. In the reality of the international system, an addressee of international law is most often subject to various legal regimes in dealing with a single set of facts. This can, but does not necessarily have to, and indeed should not, lead to conflicting legal demands. The international legal order must therefore provide ways and means to accommodate possibly diverging demands coming from different areas of the law.[10]

Two of the areas or fields of the fragmented system of international law are the law of armed conflict and international environmental law.[11] Both these areas owe their very existence to philosophical and ethical considerations, which have already been referred to and are relevant for the present inquiry.

2.1. *The Law of Armed Conflict*

The essentials of the modern law of armed conflict derive from philosophical concepts developed by Jean-Jacques Rousseau, the great philosopher of the Age of Enlightenment. We owe to him the concept that war is limited to a confrontation between the military organisations of sovereigns, a concept which logically leads to the principle of distinction between civilians and combatants. The ultimate source of the concept is the rule of reason: unnecessary violence is unreasonable and therefore a sin against human nature. The reasoning of Rousseau is still worth quoting:[12]

> War then is a relation, not between man and man, but between State and State, and individuals are enemies only accidentally, not as men, nor even as citizens, but as soldiers, not as members of their country, but as its defenders. Finally, each State can have for enemies only other States, and not men; for between things disparate in nature there can be no real relation.
>
> Furthermore, this principle is in conformity with the established rules of all times and constant practice of all civilized peoples. … The foreigner, whether King, individual, or people, who robs, kills, or detains the subjects, without declaring war on the prince, is not an enemy, but a brigand. Even in real war, a just prince, while laying hands, in the enemy's country, on all that belongs to the public, respects the

9 P.-M. Dupuy, 'L'unité de l'ordre juridique international', 297 *RdC* (2002) pp. 9–489.

10 Hafner, *supra* note 8, p. 856.

11 M. Tignino, 'Droit international de l'environnment', in R. van Steenberghe (ed.), *Droit international humanitaire: un régime spécial de droit international?* (Bruylant, Brussels, 2013) pp. 267–299; *see also* M. Bothe, 'Conclusion générale', in R. van Steenberghe (ed.), *Droit international humanitaire: un régime spécial de droit international?* pp. 321–331, in particular at pp. 329 *et seq.*

12 J.-J. Rousseau, *The Social Contract*, Book I ch. 2, 1762, translated 1782 by G.D.H. Cole, available at <www.constitution.org/jjr/socon.htm> (last visited 24 August 2012).

> lives and goods of individuals: he respects rights on which his own are founded. The object of the war being the destruction of the hostile State, the other side has a right to kill its defenders, while they are bearing arms; but as soon as they lay them down and surrender, they cease to be enemies or instruments of the enemy, and become once more merely men, whose life no one has any right to take. Sometimes it is possible to kill the State without killing a single one of its members; and war gives no right which is not necessary to the gaining of its object. These principles are not those of Grotius; they are not based on the authority of poets, but derived from the nature of reality and based on reason.

This philosophical concept is the *fons et origo* of two fundamental principles of the modern law of armed conflict: the principle of distinction and the principle of necessity. The latter principle is often understood or misunderstood as an over-broad justification of the use of military force. But it also constitutes a restraint on the use of force in that only that amount of force is justified which is necessary to achieve a legitimate military purpose.

At the time of Rousseau, this philosophical concept of war corresponded to the realities of warfare, the so-called cabinet wars of the 18th century.[13] That type of warfare soon disappeared, and the wars of our time make the wars of the 18th century look like folklore (although the blood toll of some of them was considerable). Despite this change, however, the rules of the law of war developed pursuant to the philosophical concept of the Enlightenment have withstood the pressure of military facts. The reason lies in the phenomenon of 'public conscience', to use the term of the Martens clause of the Hague Conventions.[14] Public conscience stands in the way of killing innocent civilians and taking their property. To use a term of legal sociology,[15] the resilience of the principle of distinction and the prohibition of unnecessary suffering can also be explained by the fact of "scandalisation". Related concepts are those of a *colère publique*[16] or indignation.[17] The meaning of these terms is that certain facts are considered to be unacceptable to public conscience and are therefore to be rejected and opposed.

Scandalisation of public opinion is a driving force for maintaining and developing reasonable restraints on military force. The scandalisation of public opinion as a result of the human suffering caused by war thus accounts for both

---

13 S. C. Neff, *War and the Law of Nations* (CUP, Cambridge, 2005) pp. 163 *et seq.*

14 Hague Convention IV, Preamble: "... the inhabitants and the belligerents remain under the protection and the rule of the principles of the law of nations, as they result from the usages established among civilised peoples, from the laws of humanity, and the dictates of the public conscience."

15 N. Luhmann, *Das Recht der Gesellschaft* (Suhrkamp, Frankfurt/Main, 1993) p. 581; A. Fischer-Lescano, *Globalverfassung* (Velbrück, Weilerswist, 2005) pp. 67 *et seq.*

16 Luhmann, *ibid.*, referring to the expression coined by E. Durkheim, *Über soziale Arbeitsteilung*, 1930, 3rd edition (Frankfurt/Main, 1999), at pp. 118 *et seq.*

17 S. Hessel, *Indignez vous* (Indigènes éditions, Paris, 2010).

the maintenance of the fundamental principles of the laws of war and for the continuous improvement of this law.[18] The first example of this process was the initiative taken by Henry Dunant who, after being scandalised by the sufferings of the battle of Solferino, appealed to the conscience of European rulers of his time who, in 1864, negotiated the first Geneva Convention.[19] The scandalisation over the use of chemical weapons in the World War I led to their legal prohibition in 1925.[20] This same mechanism led to the adaptations of the Geneva Conventions to new developments after World War I and II by the Geneva Conventions of 1929 and 1949 as well as after the first three decades of post-World War II conflicts by the Additional Protocols of 1977.[21]

The idea that legal restraints on the methods and means of warfare are based on the rule of reason leads to another ethical underpinning of the law of armed conflict. Respect of these rules serves the re-establishment of peace after the war.[22] To put it in more general terms: these legal restraints are needed for the sake of the future existence of the population affected by the war. This is an important point to which we will revert further below.

The rule of reason and the concern for the future have from very early times introduced an element of environmental conservation into ethical rules on the conduct of hostilities:[23] In *Deuteronomy* 20: 19, we find the admonition:

> When you are at war, and lay siege to a city … do not destroy its trees by taking the axe to them, for they provide you with food …

---

18 M. Bothe, 'The Historical Evolution of International Humanitarian Law, International Human Rights Law, Refugee Law and International Criminal Law', in H. Fischer *et al.* (eds.), *Crisis Management and Humanitarian Protection, Festschrift für Dieter Fleck* (Berliner Wissenschaftsverlag, Berlin, 2004) pp. 37–45, in particular at pp. 38 *et seq.*

19 R. Kolb, *Ius in bello. Le droit international des conflits armés*, 2nd edition (Helbing & Lichtenhahn, Basel, 2009) pp. 39 *et seq.*

20 M. Bothe, *Das völkerrechtliche Verbot des Einsatzes chemischer und bakteriologischer Waffen* (Carl Heymanns, Cologne *et al.*, 1973) pp. 21 *et seq.*, 99 *et seq.*

21 For a brief summary of the history, *see* M. Bothe and K. J. Partsch, in M. Bothe, K. J. Partsch and W. A. Solf, *New Rules for Victims of Armed Conflicts. Commentary on the Two 1977 Protocols Additional to the Geneva Conventions of 1949* (Martinus Nijhoff, The Hague et al., 1982) at pp. 1 *et seq.*

22 Coates, *supra* note 2, p. 273. *See also* B. Orend, '*Jus post bellum*: The Perspective of a Just-War Theorist', 20 *Leiden Journal of International Law* (2007) pp. 571–591, in particular at p. 584.

23 N. Solomon, 'The ethics of war: Judaism', in Sorabji, *supra* note 2, pp. 108–137, at p. 113.

A caveat must, however, be added concerning the use of moral arguments relating to the rules of warfare. Generally, ethical principles are not absolute.[24] As general principles, they do not provide easy solutions for every concrete situation. Countervailing principles may limit the scope of one or the other principle. In the context of armed conflict, the will to defend one's country is often considered as an ethical requirement. This approach might give legitimacy to measures which are otherwise problematic from an ethical point of view. The best known example of the resulting tension between various ethical demands is the attempt to justify torture for the sake of a country's security. This is an ethical underpinning of security interests and 'military necessity', in this case not understood as a restraint, but as a circumstance justifying military force. It can be shown, for instance, in the use of ethical language to justify resort to war. As an example, one can quote the National Security Strategy published by President Bush in 2002:

> In the war against global terrorism, we will never forget that we are ultimately fighting *for our democratic values.*[25]

Thus, democratic values are used to give legitimacy to wars which otherwise would be considered as illegal. Seen in this light, legal restraints on the use of military force can be situated in a tension between the ethical requirement of humanity and that of democracy. This tension is in a way related to the perennial question of freedom of opinion and expression on the one hand and the need to defend democracy against internal enemies.

In conflicts where a spirit of exclusion based on religious or ethnic criteria reigns, such as conflicts involving ethnic cleansing, the language of morality leads to more bitterness in conflict. Historic experience shows that a spirit of exclusion leads to a disregard of legal restraints[26] and a degeneration of armed conflicts to butchery. In such a situation, the language of morality may even be used to justify war crimes. Thus, extreme caution is necessary where morality is used to justify violence. Otherwise, there can be no adequate balance between "humanity" and "military necessity"[27] which is the basis for a realistic law of armed conflicts, a law which is acceptable and accepted because it adequately takes into account both

---

24 H. Spencer, 'Absolute and Relative Ethics', in *The Principles of Ethics* (1897, new edition, Liberty Classics, Indianapolis, 1978) vol. I, pp. 99 *et seq.*

25 National Security Strategy 2002, p. 7 (emphasis added), available at <http://merln.ndu.edu/whitepapers/USnss2002.pdf> (last visited 30 August 2012).

26 M. Bothe 'Multiculturalism and the Development of International Humanitarian Law', in S. Yee and J.-I. Morin (eds.), *Multiculturalism and International Law* (The Hague, 2009) pp. 617–628.

27 H. P. Gasser and N. Melzer, *Humanitäres Völkerrecht*, 2nd edition (Nomos/Schulthess, Zürich *et al.*, 2012) pp. 27 *et seq.*

principles. A duty to conserve nature in warfare may become the victim of such tensions or imbalances.[28]

2.2. *Environmental Law*

Some elements of what today is called international environmental law have a long history, originating, particularly, in the need to regulate the use of certain shared resources (fisheries, waters).[29] A somewhat more idealistic concern for nature appeared around 1900 as a source of inspiration for law making, both nationally and internationally. However, it is the full awareness of the finite character of the resources of the Earth that has triggered the development of modern environmental law, both national and international, that has taken place since the end of the 1960s.[30] This awareness has led to restraints on human activities, in particular restraints on the exploitation of natural resources, in order to ensure the living conditions of both present and future generations.[31] Care for the next generation is a fundamental principle of human morality.[32] In the environmental context this concern is now embodied in the principle of intergenerational equity which forms one of the ethical bases of environmental law.[33]

Like the law of armed conflict, the principle of intergenerational equity amounts to respecting a rule of reason: moderation for the sake of human survival. It is simply unreasonable to use resources in a way that nothing is left for users in the future. It should be noted that this is essentially an anthropocentric

---

28 Solomon, *supra* note 23.

29 P. H. Sand, 'The Evolution of International Environmental Law', in D. Bodansky, J. Brunnée, and E. Hey (eds.), *The Oxford Handbook of International Environmental Law* (OUP, Oxford, 2007) pp. 29–43, at pp. 31 *et seq.*; P. Sands and J. Peel, *Principles of International Environmental Law*, 3rd edition (CUP, Cambridge, 2012) pp. 23 *et seq.*; J. Wyatt, 'Law-making at the intersection of international environmental, humanitarian and criminal law: the issue of damage to the environment in international armed conflict', 92:879 *International Review of the Red Cross* (2010) pp. 583–646, at pp. 599 *et seq.*

30 M. Bothe, 'Environment, Development, Resources', 318 *RdC* (2005) pp. 333–516, at pp. 410 *et seq.*

31 E. Brown Weiss, *In Fairness to Future Generations: International Law, Common Patrimony, and Intergenerational Equity* (United Nations University, Tokyo/New York, 1988) *passim.*

32 R. Attfield, 'Environmental ethics and global sustainability', in H. A. M. J. Ten Have (ed.), *Environmental Ethics and International Policy* (UNESCO, Paris, 2006) pp. 69–87, at pp. 80 *et seq.*

33 C. D. Stone, 'Ethics and International Environmental Law', in Bodansky *et al.*, *supra* note 29, pp. 292–312, at pp. 304 *et seq.*; T. B. Adams, 'Rawls' Theory of Justice and International Environmental Law', 20 *Global Business and Development Law Journal* (2007) pp. 1–13; E. Agius, 'Environmental ethics: Towards an intergenerational perspective', in Ten Have, *supra* note 32, pp. 89–115.

approach. The purely ecocentric approach, or respect for nature for its own sake, cannot with the same degree of plausibility rely on the rule of reasonable moderation.[34] For this reason, the ecocentric approach remains controversial.

Scientific reflection has certainly played a role in the development of environmental law. The warnings of scientist have triggered political initiatives and as a consequence legal developments as a response to environmental risks and dangers highlighted by the scientific community. The first and probably most influential scientific document was the study by the Club of Rome entitled *The Limits of Growth*, which stirred awareness of the finite character of the Earth's resources[35] and inspired legal developments providing for their more parsimonious use. However, scandalisation, or learning from disasters, has also played a major role. Disasters like oil spills and heavy pollution incidents have been major factors driving the development of environmental law.[36]

Nevertheless, countervailing considerations slowing down or sometimes preventing the development of environmental law also exist. These considerations have mainly been based on economic interests, including, in particular, interests in short term gain. A common method of giving an appearance of legitimacy to such interests has been the invocation of an alleged need to maintain employment.[37] Put in this way, there is a conflict between intragenerational equity, in the example expressed as a just concern for the welfare of the workers, and intergenerational equity, expressed as concern for the living conditions of future generations. The notion of "sustainable development" seems to provide a compromise solution for this conflict.[38] As formulated by the Brundtland Report, the principle of sustainable development serves as a guidance for policy and behaviour that "meets the needs of the present generation without compromising the ability of future generations to meet their own needs".[39]

2.3. The Law of Armed Conflict and International Environmental Law

In the beginning of the 1970s, the moral factors driving the development of the law of armed conflict and of environmental law met. When the two Protocols additional to the Geneva Conventions were negotiated, the awareness of the finite character of the Earth's resources could not be left aside.[40] A provision on

34 But see H. Rolston, 'Intrinsic values on Earth: nature and nations', in Ten Have (ed.), *supra* note 32, pp. 47–67, at p. 63.

35 D. H. Meadows *et al.*, *The Limits of Growth. A Report to the Club of Rome* (Macmillan, New York, 1972).

36 Sand, *supra* note 29, p. 34.

37 Bothe, *supra* note 30, p. 414.

38 Bothe, *supra* note 30, pp. 479 *et seq.*

39 World Commission on Environment and Development, *Our Common Future* (1987) p. 43.

40 Wyatt, *supra* note 29, pp. 610 *et seq.*

the protection of the environment in times of armed conflict had to be inserted. The negotiations were in particular driven by a scandalisation which related both to the law of armed conflict and environmental law, namely the use of chemical weapons, in particular the use of herbicides during the Vietnam War with their disastrous environmental and health consequences. However, countervailing military interests proved to be strong. The result has been an ongoing debate of several decades between perceived military requirements and the need to preserve the environment even in times of armed conflict.[41] In this battle, the cause of the environment has gained some ground, but the situation still far from satisfactory. While a compromise formula between long-term environmental interest and short-term economic interest has arguably been found in the notions of sustainable development and more recently in that of a green economy,[42] this compromise has not seemed possible in the case of environmental restraints on warfare. There still is no such notion as sustainable or green warfare.

3. Principles

3.1. The Law of Armed Conflict

The important principles of the law of armed conflict derived from Rousseau's concept of war are the principle of distinction and the prohibition of 'unnecessary suffering'. The principle of distinction means that attacks may only be directed against military objectives, not against civilian objects or the civilian population.[43] Where attacks against military objectives entail incidental civilian damage, the attack is permissible only if the incidental damage is not excessive in relation to the military advantage anticipated (principle of proportionality).[44] Those who decide on an attack must take 'precautionary measures' to make sure that the attack does not violate these principles.[45] These rules are anchored not only in treaty law, they also constitute customary law.

---

41 For an analysis of the historic development *see* M. Bothe, 'Military Activities and the Protection of the Environment', 37 *Environmental Policy and Law* (2007) pp. 232–238.

42 UNEP, *Towards a Green Economy. Pathways to Sustainable Development and Poverty Eradication* (2011) (known as "Green Economy Report"); S. Dröge and N. Simon, 'The Green Economy: An Economic Concepts for Everyone?', in M. Beisheim and Susanne Dröge (eds.), *UNSCD Rio 2012. Twenty Years of Sustainability Policies – Now Put into Practice* (Stiftung Wissenschaft und Politik Research Paper 8, Berlin, 2012) pp. 17–30.

43 API: Articles 51 and 52. These rules constitute customary law. *See* ICRC, J.-M. Henckaerts, L. Doswald-Beck, *Customary International Humanitarian Law* (ICRC/CUP, Cambridge, 2005), Rules 1–24, Vol. 1, pp. 3–77.

44 AP I: Article 51

45 AP I: Article 57.

The prohibition of unnecessary suffering[46] means that acts causing damage to the enemy must be limited to those which are necessary to achieve a military advantage. That prohibition is formulated in a general way in Article 23(e) of the Hague Regulations and in Article 34 of Additional Protocol I (AP I). It is also a leading principle which is the basis for the prohibition of particular weapons as indicated, for example, by the very name of the UN Weapons Convention, formally entitled the Convention on Prohibitions … of Certain Conventional Weapons Which May be *Deemed to be Excessively Injurious.*[47]

Both principles are important for the protection of the environment in times of armed conflict. Attacks against elements of the environment which are civilian objects are, as such, prohibited. The definition of civilian objects is a negative one, encompassing all those objects which are not military objectives. That definition is therefore formulated by turning the two elements of the definition of the military objective according to Article 52 AP I into a negative phrase. Civilian objects are objects which do not contribute to the military effort of a party to the conflict and whose destruction does not yield a military advantage.[48] The essential weakness of this principle of 'civilian immunity' as a means of environmental protection lies in the fact that it is relatively easy to turn an element of the environment into a military objective.[49] If a military unit is present, or is about to be present, in a protected area, this area becomes a military objective because the use of the area yields a military advantage.

The proportionality principle relating to incidental or 'collateral' damage entails the question of the respective weight of environmental concerns and military gains in what is called the proportionality equation. The decision whether civilian casualties or damages are 'excessive in relation to the military advantage anticipated' requires a balancing of assets or values. On one side of this 'equation' is the military advantage, on the other the civilian damage. It is generally recognised that this is a rule which, theoretically, is impossible to apply as it requires a quantitative comparison of things which cannot be compared, in particular not quantitatively. Nevertheless, proportionality is a principle which is applied in many fields of the law.[50] This is so because its practical attraction lies in the fact that it establishes reasonable limits for action taken in the furtherance of one particular interest for the sake of safeguarding other interests. Seen in this light,

46 Hague Regulations: Article 23(e); AP I: Article 35(2).

47 Emphasis added.

48 Article 52.

49 M. Bothe, C. Bruch, J. Diamond and D. Jensen, 'International law protecting the environment during armed conflict: gaps and opportunities', 92:879 *International Review of the Red Cross* (2010) pp. 569–592, at pp. 576 *et seq.*

50 E. Crawford, 'Proportionality', in R. Wolfrum (ed.), *Max Planck Encyclopedia of Public International Law*, available at <www.mpepil.com> (last visited 16 October 2012).

it is a development of Rousseau's idea of reasonable limits of warfare.[51] What is new is the recognition of the need to include environmental damage in the civilian damage to be considered.

This equation determines both the legality and the illegality of attacks and the scope of precautionary measures to be taken. Those who decide upon an attack have to make sure, in particular by seeking appropriate information on the civilian consequences of an attack, that the civilian (including environmental) damage is not excessive in relation to the military advantage anticipated. The decider is required to take 'feasible' measures for this purpose. What is feasible in relation to the prognostication, and consequently prevention, of environmental damage is a difficult question which remains to be clarified.

Where an element of the environment is a military objective, attacking, destroying or otherwise damaging it is, as a matter of principle, permissible. It has, however, to be asked whether long-term damage to the environment nevertheless affects the legality of an attack. Articles 35(3) and 55 AP I provide just that restraint.[52] It is submitted, however, that the requirements in these provisions are inadequate as the threshold of impermissible damage is both unclear and too high.[53]

The principle forbidding unnecessary suffering renders unlawful any attack which destroys elements of the environment without yielding a significant military advantage. The prohibition of 'wanton destruction' is an expression of the same principle, formulated as the prohibition of destruction not "imperatively demanded by the necessities of war"[54] or of "destruction … of property not justified by military necessity and carried out unlawfully and wantonly"[55] which constitutes a grave breach. This is also a rule of customary law.[56]

Finally, the guiding principle formulated in the Martens clause[57] that the victims of armed conflicts are protected by the rules based on the "dictates of public conscience" is now also considered to cover environmental concerns.[58]

---

51 *See* above text accompanying *supra* note 12.

52 W. A. Solf, in Bothe, Partsch and Solf, *supra* note 21, pp. 344 *et seq.*

53 Bothe *et al.*, *supra* note 49, pp. 575 *et seq. See* below text accompanying *infra* note 65.

54 Article 22(g) Hague Regulations.

55 Article 147 Geneva Convention IV.

56 *Customary International Humanitarian Law*, *supra* note 43, Rule 50, pp. 175 *et seq.*

57 *See supra* note 14.

58 A. Afriansyah, 'Environmental Protection and State Responsibility in International Humanitarian Law', 7 *Indonesian Journal of International Law* (2010) pp. 242–299, at p. 264.

3.2. International Environmental Law

One of the fundamental principles underlying many rules of international environmental law, as already stated, is intergenerational equity. As articulated in Principles 1 and 2 of the Stockholm Declaration[59] and Principle 3 the Rio Declaration,[60] the principle requires concern for the living conditions of future generations.[61] There is a plethora of rules of environmental law imposing restraints on human behaviour for the sake of preserving the necessary living resources for future generations. Nevertheless, the concrete application of the principle is difficult to determine. The principle provides no hard and fast yardstick for the restraint on the use of resources which the present generation must accept in order to save them for future generations.[62] The notion of sustainable use or management of specific resources may be helpful, but it does not provide a complete answer to the concrete problems of sustainable development of a whole economy. The latter is much more complex. For instance, the principle of intergenerational equity does not exclude substitution. If a specific resource is exhausted, but others may take its place, intergenerational equity is not (necessarily) jeopardised.[63] If one takes a broader approach through the notion of sustainable development, one is back to the problem of uncertainty of yardstick for what is permissible and what not.

A legal principle which serves to implement the principle of intergenerational equity is the precautionary principle.[64] This principle requires relevant actors to take measures for the preservation of the environment even in the absence of scientific certainty as to the risk of environmental damage. The rationale of the

---

59 Declaration adopted by the United Nations conference on the Human Environment, 1971:

> Principle 1: "Man ... bears a solemn responsibility to protect and improve the environment for present and future generations. ..."
>
> Principle 2: "The natural resource of the earth, including air, water, land, flora and fauna and especially representative samples of natural ecosystems, must be safeguarded for the benefit of present and future generations."

60 Rio Declaration on Environment and Development, 1992:

> Principle 3: "The right to development must be fulfilled so as to equitably meet developmental and environmental needs of present and future generations."

61 Bothe, *supra* note 30, pp. 485 *et seq.*

62 *Ibid.*

63 *See* F. Ferrand, 'Le développement soutenable est-il une notion de droit international public?', in M. Bothe and P. H. Sand (eds.), *Environmental Policy. From Regulation to Economic Instruments* (Martinus Nijhoff, The Hague *et al.*, 2003) pp. 245–295, at pp. 260–265.

64 Sand and Peel, *supra* note 29, pp. 219 *et seq.*; Bothe, *supra* note 30, pp. 487 *et seq.*; M. D. Young, 'Intergenerational equity, the precautionary principle and ecologically sustainable development', 31 *Nature & Resources* (1995) pp. 16–27.

precautionary principle is twofold: it ensures that in case of uncertainty about possible damage the decision-maker errs on the safe side, and it reserves space for a future use of resources. It is mainly this latter aspect which makes the precautionary principle a tool for intergenerational equity.[65]

If interpreted in the light of the preceding reasoning, Articles 35 and 55 AP I have the potential to serve as a tool of intergenerational equity. These two provisions restrain attacks not only on civilian objects, but also on military objectives. They constitute, at least potentially, a comprehensive protection against environmental damage caused by military activities. As the prohibition of attacks is not limited to the traditional immunity of civilian objects, it provides the opportunity to take the needs of environmental conservation into account regardless of the current use, military or not, of that object. In this respect, it provides a better opportunity for environmental preservation than the traditional rule of distinction. However, as the threshold of impermissible damage provided for in these articles is much too high from the point of view of environmental concerns, at least if interpreted according to their negotiating history,[66] they fail to meet this goal. Conventional battlefield damage, for instance, is held not to be covered.[67] Nevertheless, if interpreted in a dynamic way, the criteria contained in the two articles could serve as a tool of intergenerational equity in restraining the conduct of warfare. For that purpose, it would be necessary to base the interpretation of the three criteria on an increased knowledge about the long-term character of war damage. This could not happen without a more thorough analysis of the effects of warfare on the environment. A careful analysis of causation chains triggered by hostilities, in particular of their impact on life supporting systems is necessary. This would provide new answers as to whether the effect of an attack is 'widespread' and 'long-lasting'. It would also be necessary to take account of ecological values in determining what is 'severe'.

Another fundamental principle of international environmental law, well enshrined in customary law, is the prohibition of significant transboundary harm.[68] As articulated in Principle 2 of the Rio Declaration and Principle 21 of the Stockholm Declaration, the no harm principle requires states to ensure that "activities within their jurisdiction or control do not cause damage to the environment of other States or of areas beyond the limits of national jurisdiction". This includes damage caused by war. This is illustrated, for instance, in the reaction to the long range air pollution caused by the burning oil wells towards the

65 Bothe, *supra* note 30, at p. 488.

66 *See* above text accompanying *supra* note 53.

67 W. A. Solf, in Bothe, Partsch and Solf, *supra* note 21, p. 348.

68 Wyatt, *supra* note 29, pp. 599 *et seq.*; A. Douhan, 'Liability for Environmental Damage', in R. Wolfrum (ed.), *Max Planck Encyclopedia of Public International Law*, available at<www.mpepil.com>; U. Beyerlin and T. Marauhn, *International Environmental Law* (Hart *et al.*, Oxford, 2011) pp. 41 *et seq.*; the leading case still is the *Trail Smelter Arbitration* (1941), 3 *RIAA* 1907.

end of the second Gulf War and the long distance maritime oil pollution caused by their destruction.[69] The United Nations Compensation Commission awarded the sum of USD 252 million as compensation for this damage.[70] In terms of the law of armed conflict, the prohibition of causing 'transfrontier' damage is also a part of the law of neutrality, an important rule of which is that the territory of the neutral state is inviolable.[71]

Prevention is, of course, the best means to protect the environment against damage. However, where damage has already occurred, restoration and rehabilitation is necessary. The response of international law to that need is found in the principle of cooperation. Formulated in Principle 7 of the Rio Declaration, it requires states to "cooperate in a spirit of global partnership to conserve, protect and *restore* the health and integrity of the Earth's ecosystem".[72] This cooperation, which includes, for example, technical cooperation, can also be based on the principle of solidarity.[73] In two relevant General Assembly resolutions,[74] solidarity is defined as "a fundamental value, by virtue of which global challenges must be managed in a way that distributes costs and burdens fairly, in accordance with basic principles of equity and social justice, and ensures that those who suffer or [who] benefit the least receive help from those who benefit most". Based on this idea of equity, environmental rehabilitation has become part of post-conflict peace building. It has been an important focus of UNEP's Disasters and Conflicts Programme.[75] There is a vast international practice of bilateral (*e.g.* by such agencies as USAID) and multilateral assistance in post-conflict environmental management. International actors engaged in these efforts are peacekeeping operations, UNDP, UNEP or the World Bank.[76]

69 *See* K. Hirschmann, *The Kuwaiti Oil Fires* (Facts on file, New York, 2005) pp. 29 *et seq.*

70 UNCC, Governing Council, *Report and Recommendation made by the Panel of Commissioners concerning the Fifth Installment of "F4" Claims*, UN Doc. S/AC.26/2005/10, 30 June 2005.

71 *Legality of the Threat or Use of Nuclear Weapons*, ICJ Advisory Opinion of 8 July 1996, paras. 88 *et seq. See also* M. Bothe, 'The Law of Neutrality', in D. Fleck (ed.), *The Handbook of International Humanitarian Law*, 3rd edition (OUP, Oxford, 2013) pp. 549–580, at MN 1108.

72 Emphasis added.

73 D. Campanelli, *Solidarity, Principle of*, MN 6, in R. Wolfrum (ed.), *Max Planck Encyclopedia of Public International Law*, available at<www.mpepil.com>.

74 GA resolution 56/151 of 19 December 2001 and 57/213 of 18 December 2002.

75 *See* <www.unep.org/disastersandconflicts/> (last visited 31 August 2012). *See From Conflict to Peacebuilding: The Role of Natural Resources and the Environment*, UNEP Policy Paper, 2009.

76 This practice is now extensively documented by a research project undertaken by the Environmental Law Institute (Washington, D.C.), UNEP, the University of To-

3.3. *The Law of Armed Conflict and International Environmental Law*

The fragmentation of international law entails the problem of a possible conflict between two or more areas of law where both or more areas appear to be relevant for one single situation, for the decision of one actor.[77] In the relationship between the law of armed conflict and environmental law, one aspect of this question is the continued validity of treaties (including environmental agreements) in times of armed conflict. This subject has been dealt with by the ILC.[78] If, as the ILC maintains, environmental agreements continue to be applicable in times of war, both the environmental treaty and IHL have to be applied in parallel. This requires a solution of conflicts between the two sets of rules which allows respect for the norms of both areas of law. That principle is already widely recognised and called principle called mutual supportiveness.[79]

As a consequence, the core principles of international environmental law, namely the concern for future generations (intergenerational equity) and the prohibition of causing transboundary damage (intragenerational equity), have to be inserted in the application of the law of armed conflict. This has a number of concrete consequences.

The first consequence is that environmental concerns have to be included to a sufficient degree on the civilian side of the proportionality equation.[80] If and to the extent that elements of the environment constitute civilian objects, damage caused to them by attacks against military objectives has to be balanced against the military advantage anticipated. However, what is the respective weight of that environmental damage in comparison to the military advantage? Can only immediate harmful effects be considered or also long-term and indirect effects? Only if the latter approach is adopted can the protection of elements of the environment, being civilian objects, effectively safeguard the living conditions of future generations.

Second, environmental concerns have to be included in precautionary measures to be taken by persons deciding upon launching attacks, applying where necessary the precautionary principle as it is defined in environmental law.[81] The military commander is not a biologist or a specialist in any other environmental

kyo and McGill University (Montreal), *see* <www.environmentalpeacebuilding.org> (last visited 16 October 2012).

77 *See* above text accompanying *supra* notes 8–11.

78 Draft Articles on the effects of armed conflicts on treaties, ILC, *Report on the work of its 63rd session*, 2011, UN Doc. A/66/10.

79 R. Pavoni, 'Mutual Supportiveness as a Principle of Interpretation and Law-Making: a Watershed for the "WTO and Competing Regimes" Debate?', 21 *European Journal of International Law* (2010) pp. 649–679 .

80 *See* above text accompanying note 44; Bothe, Bruch, Diamond and Jensen, *supra* note 49, p. 578.

81 *See* Bothe *et al.*, *supra* note 49, p. 578.

science. Thus it can rightly be asked: how will he be able to weigh the environmental consequences of an attack? The usual instruments of evaluating the environmental consequences of a human activity, such as environmental impact assessments, are not available to the military commander. Nevertheless, ways and means must be found to integrate that knowledge into military decision-making. The recent ICRC Study on customary international humanitarian law suggests that the precautionary principle in the sense of environmental law must indeed be applied in assessing the environmental consequences of an attack which is about to be launched.[82]

Third, the interpretation of the triple qualification of environmental damage contained in Articles 35(3) and 55 AP I has to be revisited.[83] If interpreted according to the negotiating history, the two provisions are without real value for environmental protection. However, it is both possible and even necessary to adopt a dynamic interpretation which corresponds to changing attitudes in the international community.

Fourth, the interpretation of the rule prohibiting unnecessary suffering, or of military necessity, has to take account of environmental concerns. There are different degrees of necessity. The judgment that a certain act is necessary implies a judgment that a certain goal must be obtained at the expense of other interests. If environmental concerns are introduced into the notion of military necessity, it means that countervailing environmental interests my render a certain military action 'less necessary'.

Fifth, a rule of customary international law has developed that methods and means of warfare must be employed with 'due regard' for the environment. This rule is now articulated in Article 44 of the *San Remo Manual on Naval Warfare*, Article 89 of the *Manual of Air and Missile Warfare*,[84] and Rule 44 of the *Customary International Law Study*.[85] The interpretation of the 'due regard' principle involves interpretation problems similar to those related to the proportionality principle.

Sixth, hostilities must be conducted in such a way that no significant damage is caused to states not parties to the conflict.[86] This rule derives from two fundamental rules of both environmental law and the law of neutrality, namely the prohibition of transboundary harm enshrined in customary environmental law, on the one hand, and the rule that neutral territory is inviolable, on the other. This rule needs to be reconfirmed.

---

82 ICRC, Henckaerts, and Doswald-Beck, *supra* note 43, pp. 150 *et seq.*

83 *See* section 3.2.

84 HPCR (Program on Humanitarian Policy and Conflict Research at Harvard University) (ed.), *Manual on International Law Applicable to Air and Missile Warfare* (Bern, 2009).

85 ICRC, Henckaerts, and Doswald-Beck, *supra* note 43.

86 *See* above text accompanying *supra* note 67.

Seventh, and finally, it is suggested that there is a usage, indeed even an emerging legal duty, to cooperate in post-conflict restoration of elements of the environment that have been damaged by armed conflict.[87] Environmental rehabilitation is certainly becoming (albeit too slowly) an established principle of post conflict peace-building. In this respect, more detailed models for practical procedures need to be elaborated.

4. Objectives

Towards the end of the 1960s, awareness of global environmental problems emerged triggering the recognition of the need to address these problems through law. It was also recognised that these developments could not ignore the environmental consequences of war. Thus appeared the meeting, or should one say collision, between the laws of war and environmental law in the 1970s. This encounter has since triggered further developments which have not, however, occurred without setbacks. When attempts have been made to develop IHL in the sense of a better protection of the environment, military interests have several times prevailed over environmental concerns. The legal situation as it stands is not satisfactory.[88] This is why the ICRC, when it launched an initiative to further develop international humanitarian law in particular areas where this was most needed, singled out the protection of the environment in relation to armed conflicts as one of the relevant themes.[89] In the ensuing consultation process states have chosen different problems as priorities. However, the fact that the ILC is planning to work on the problem[90] is encouraging and gives hope for future developments.

The objectives of the further development of the law must be that the ethical and legal principles explained in this paper are clarified and concretised, and that doubt concerning their validity and application is removed. This applies to rules imposing restraints on military operations as well as to obligations to promote and ensure post-conflict rehabilitation. In short, in order to ensure that the living basis for future generations is not jeopardised by warfare, the relevant rules of international law must be strengthened and developed on the basis of the ethical and legal principles.

---

87 *See* above text accompanying *supra* notes 74 and 75.

88 Bothe *et al.*, *supra* note 49, in particular pp. 578 *et seq.*

89 *See* the address of the President of the ICRC, 21 September 2010: J. Kellenberger, 'Strengthening Legal Protection for Victims of Armed Conflicts. The ICRC Study on the Current State of International Humanitarian Law', 92:879 *International Review of the Red Cross* (2010) pp. 799–804, at pp. 802 *et seq.*

90 International Law Commission, *Report on the work of its 63rd session* (2011), UN Doc. A/66/10, pp. 288 and 347 *et seq.*

5. Conclusion

It has been shown that the ethical foundations of international humanitarian law and of environmental law have some points in common. Both regimes are based on the rule of reason which leads to a concern for the future. Peace is an ultimate goal of legal restraints on methods and means of warfare. Securing peace means safeguarding the possibilities of a decent existence in the future. This is also a major goal of environmental law. The impact that this latter goal has had on the development of positive law is based on the recognition, resulting from scientific analysis of the life supporting systems on Earth, that restraints on human activities are not only necessary to prevent current damage to persons and elements of the environment, but also in order to safeguard the carrying capacity of the Earth. This has led to a new evaluation of legal regulation concerning economic activities, in particular through the growing application of the precautionary principle.

The recognition of the fact that this need of restraint for the sake of future generations must apply to all human activities has been somewhat slower to arrive in military thinking. However, this has happened, albeit still not to a sufficient degree. Nevertheless, various ways and means exist to ensure that concern for future generations or, in a more short-term perspective concern for the life after the war, finds its way into military decision-making. The adoption of two environmental provisions in the first 1977 Protocol additional to the Geneva Conventions was a first step. However, these provisions need new interpretation. Given that customary international law has developed the 'due regard' principle and that environmental rehabilitation has become a general practice in post conflict peace-building, it is clear that environmental values must now be recognised in the balancing of values required by the proportionality principle.

All these developments are certainly laudable from an environmental point of view, particularly in the light of the ethical principles elaborated in this study. Nevertheless, this general recognition of principles still is too abstract. The principles now need concretisation through appropriate procedures. In this process, the epistemic community of international lawyers has a role to play.

5 Advancing the Legal Protection of the Environment in Relation to Armed Conflict: Protocol I's Threshold of Impermissible Environmental Damage and Alternatives

Carson Thomas

> When thou shalt besiege a city a long time, in making war against it to take it, thou shalt not destroy the trees thereof by forcing an axe against them: for thou mayest eat of them, and thou shalt not cut them down (for the tree of the field is man's life) to employ them in the siege:
>
> Only the trees which thou knowest that they be not trees for meat, thou shalt destroy and cut them down; and thou shalt build bulwarks against the city that maketh war with thee, until it be subdued.
>
> *Deuteronomy 20: 19-20*[1]

1. Introduction

When the United Nations Environment Programme (UNEP) published its 2009 report, *Protecting the Environment During Armed Conflict*, its first finding was that Articles 35 and 55 of Additional Protocol I to the Geneva Conventions "do not effectively protect the environment during armed conflict due to the stringent and imprecise threshold required to demonstrate damage".[2] It is not surprising that UNEP begins its discussion of legal protection for the environment in relation to armed conflict with Articles 35 and 55, and that Protocol I's protections are found inadequate.

Additional Protocol I was the first treaty to provide direct protection to the environment in international armed conflict,[3] and at first glance seems to provide extensive environmental protection from intentional and collateral harm. Article

1 *Deuteronomy* 20:19-20, King James Version.

2 United Nations Environment Programme, *Protecting the Environment during Armed Conflict: An Inventory and Analysis of International Law* (UNEP, Nairobi, 2009) p. 4.

3 M. Schmitt, 'Humanitarian Law and the Environment', 28 *Denver Journal of International Law and Policy* (2000) p. 273.

Rosemary Rayfuse (ed.), War and the Environment: New Approaches to Protecting the Environment in Relation to Armed Conflict
 ISBN 978-90-04-27064-0 pp. 109-234

35, which concerns basic rules on the means and methods of warfare, prohibits "methods or means of warfare which are intended, or may be expected, to cause widespread, long-term and severe damage to the natural environment".[4] Article 55 protects the environment within the context of civilian objects and imposes the obligation to take care to "protect the natural environment against widespread, long-term and severe damage".[5] The operative core of these provisions is the triple and cumulative standard of 'widespread', 'long-term' *and* 'severe' that must be reached before environmental damage is prohibited. These terms are not defined in the Protocol, but they are generally interpreted as setting a very high threshold.[6] The result is an elevated, uncertain and imprecise threshold that significantly narrows the scope of the prohibition.[7]

This study presents both conceptual and practical considerations for increasing the level of environmental protection in wartime within the legal context created by Articles 35 and 55. Articles 35(3) and 55 represent a point of agreement between States parties that there is a threshold beyond which environmental damage is prohibited regardless of the military situation.[8] These provisions bifurcate the legal protection of the environment in armed conflict. Above the threshold, environmental damage is prohibited. Beneath the threshold, other international humanitarian law (IHL) instruments and customary principles apply and may offer environmental protection, usually by balancing environmental

4 Protocol Additional to the Geneva Conventions of 12 August 1949, and relating to the Protection of Victims of International Armed Conflicts (Protocol I) of 8 June 1977, Article 35(3).

5 *Ibid.*, Article 55.

6 M. Bothe *et al.*, 'International Law Protecting the Environment During Armed Conflict: Gaps and Opportunities', 92 *International Review of the Red Cross* (2010) p. 575. *See also* W. A. Solf, 'Article 55: protection of the natural environment', in M. Bothe *et al* (eds.), *New Rules for Victims of Armed Conflict: Commentaries on the Two 1977 Protocols Additional to the Geneva Conventions of 1949* (Martinus Nijhoff, The Hague, 1982) p. 347; *Diplomatic Conference on the Reaffirmation and Development of International Humanitarian Law Applicable in Armed Conflicts, 1974–1977,*CDDH/215/Rev. 1, para. 27.

7 L. Lijnzaad and G. Tanja, 'Protection of the Environment in Times of Armed Conflict: The Iraq-Kuwait War', 40 *Netherlands International Law Review* (1993) p. 180; W. Verwey, 'Observation on the Legal Protection of the Environment in Times of International Armed Conflict', 7 *Hague Yearbook of International Law* (1994) p. 36.

8 This is presented as a conceptual framework for conventional warfare. In its commentary to the Draft Protocols, the ICRC disclaimed an intention to "broach" the problems of atomic, bacteriological and chemical warfare. International Committee of the Red Cross, *Draft Additional Protocols to the Geneva Conventions of Aug 12, 1949; Commentary* (ICRC, Geneva, 1973) p. 2. The issue of Protocol I's applicability to nuclear warfare is particularly controversial. *See* E. V. Koppe, *The Use of Nuclear Weapons and the Protection of the Environment during International Armed Conflict* (Hart, Portland, 2008) pp. 366–372.

damage against military necessity. Article 55 can then be interpreted as imposing the obligation to determine where the contemplated environmental damage will fall in relation to the threshold and what legal rules therefore apply.

Given that the threshold is set at a high level, and State parties have not demonstrated sufficient political will to officially revise it,[9] significant attention must be devoted to limiting environmental damage beneath the threshold. The text of *Deuteronomy*, which is often cited as an early source for strictures on environmental damage in wartime, offers guidance in the search for more flexible and environmentally favourable frameworks. The text's mandate may be interpreted as early versions of the prohibition of 'wanton' destruction and the 'due regard' principle, articulated more recently in the *Customary International Humanitarian Law Study* published by the International Committee of the Red Cross.[10] The author of *Deuteronomy* also demonstrates that legal and practical arguments should be addressed to those individuals actually considering environmentally harmful military action, *e.g.* a besieging army.

The objective of this study is to propose legal and strategic frameworks to be addressed to military decision-makers considering environmentally harmful actions. It argues that the principle of military necessity that underlies the laws of armed conflict can be found compatible with enhanced environmental protections. The ultimate goal is not only to develop operational guidelines for military decision-makers, but also to avoid the false dilemma between environmental harm and failing to achieve war aims and risking soldiers.

2. History of Legal Protection for the Environment in Armed Conflict

Wartime damage to the environment, both deliberate and unintentional, has a history at least as long as that of large-scale armed conflict. Wars from classical times through the modern era offer numerous examples of the destruction of the environment as a weapon of war and as collateral harm: from salting enemy fields and poisoning wells to massive defoliation campaigns and destruction of petroleum and chemical facilities.[11] However, there is also an ancient tradition

9 *See* R. Falk, 'The Inadequacy of the Existing Legal Approach to Environmental Protection in Wartime', in J. Austin and C. Bruch (eds.), *The Environmental Consequences of War: Legal, Economic, and Scientific Perspectives* (Cambridge UP, Cambridge, 2000) pp. 143–144.

10 J.-M. Henckaerts and L. Doswald-Beck, *Customary International Humanitarian Law* (ICRC and Cambridge University Press, Cambridge, 2005) Rule 44.

11 *See* J. Austin and C. Bruch, 'Introduction', in J. Austin and C. Bruch (eds.), *The Environmental Consequences of War: Legal, Economic, and Scientific Perspectives* (Cambridge University Press, Cambridge, 2000) p. 1.

of efforts to ameliorate this harm on religious,[12] philosophical,[13] ethical[14] and, increasingly during the late-20th century, legal grounds.

During the 1960s and 1970s, the rise to prominence of the international environmental movement concurrent with public concern over the means and methods of warfare utilised in Vietnam led to the creation of international humanitarian legal instruments that explicitly address the protection of the environment. Since the Vietnam War, environmental damage in wartime has continued, but so have legal efforts to prevent and punish it, most dramatically during and after the Gulf War of 1990–1991.[15] In particular, significant international legal attention was paid to the issue in the early 1990s.[16] The International Committee of the Red Cross included several environmental provisions in its 2005 *Customary International Humanitarian Law Study.*[17] However, the customary nature of these environmental protections is debated, especially by the United States.[18] The continuing damage and the lack of definitive legal standards led the United Nations Environmental Programme (UNEP) to conclude in its 2009 report, *Protecting the Environment During Armed Conflict*, that "the environment continues to be the silent victim of armed conflicts worldwide".[19]

In 2011, the United Nations International Law Commission decided to include the topic of the Protection of the Environment in Relation to Armed Conflict in its future programme of work.[20] The study will consider treaty law, customary international law, soft law and case law from the legal regimes of international humanitarian law, international criminal law, international environ-

12 *See Deuteronomy*, *supra* note 1.

13 *See* H. Grotius, 'On Moderation in Despoiling an Enemy's Country', in *On the Law of War and Peace*, trans. A.C. Campbell (London, 1814), <www.constitution.org/gro/djbp_312.htm>, visited on 12 March 2012.

14 *E.g.*, G. Reichberg and H. Syse, 'Protecting the Natural Environment in Wartime: Ethical Considerations from the Just War Tradition', 37 *Journal of Peace Research* (2000)pp. 449–468.

15 Austin and Bruch, *supra* note 11, p. 2.

16 *See* A. Roberts, 'The Law of War and Environmental Damage', in J. Austin and C. Bruch (eds.), *The Environmental Consequences of War: Legal, Economic, and Scientific Perspectives* (Cambridge University Press, Cambridge, 2000) p. 49.

17 Henckaerts and Doswald-Beck, *supra* note 10, Rules 44–45.

18 *See* J. Marsh, 'Lex Lata or Lex Ferenda? Rule 45 of the ICRC Study on Customary International Humanitarian Law', 198 *Military Law Review* (2008) pp. 131–133 (discussion of the letter written by US State Department Legal Advisor John Bellinger and U.S. Defence Department General Counsel William Haynes which provided the U.S. government's "initial reactions" to the ICRC Study).

19 United Nations Environment Programme, *supra* note 2.

20 *Report of the International Law Commission Sixty-third Session (26 April–3 June and 4 July–12 August 2011)* (A/66/10) Annex E, p. 347.

mental law and human rights law.[21] There is no doubt that efforts to develop the legal protections for the environment in relation to armed conflict should and will be based on a consideration of all potentially applicable regimes. However, given the traditional view of international humanitarian law as the *lex specialis* of armed conflict,[22] any approach that attempts to broaden the scope of legal protection for the environment in wartime will need to consider the relevant provisions and principles of IHL.[23]

3. Protocol I's Legal Threshold and Its Difficulties

Before 1976, the word 'environment' could not be found in any treaty on the law of war.[24] The actions of the United States during the Vietnam War prompted the creation and adoption of the first international legal instruments that specifically address protection of the environment in wartime.[25] The United States utilised chemical herbicides, most notoriously Agent Orange, in a massive defoliation campaign and experimented with weather alteration techniques.[26] The scale, severity and apparent longevity of the environmental damage led to the adoption of the 1976 Environmental Modification Convention (ENMOD) and the inclusion of environment provisions in the 1977 Additional Protocol I to the 1949 Geneva Conventions (Protocol I).

3.1. *Protocol I*

Article 35(3) of Protocol I provides:

21 *See e.g.* S. Vöneky, 'Peacetime Environmental Law as a Basis of State Responsibility for Environmental Damage Caused by War', in J. Austin and C. Bruch (eds.), *The Environmental Consequences of War: Legal, Economic, and Scientific Perspectives* (Cambridge UP, Cambridge, 2000); S. A. J. Boelart-Suominen, 'International Environmental Law and Naval War: The Effect of Marine Safety and Pollution Conventions During International Armed Conflict', in *Newport Paper No. 15* (Naval War College, Newport, 2000). A. Crawford and J. Bernstein, *MEAs, Conservation and Conflict – A Case Study of Virunga National Park, DRC* (International Institute for Sustainable Development, Winnipeg, 2008); J. Wyatt, 'Law-Making at the Intersection of International Environmental, Humanitarian and Criminal Law: The Issue of Damage to the Environment in International Armed Conflict', 92 *International Review of the Red Cross* (2010) pp. 593–646.

22 *E.g. Legal Consequences of a Wall in the Occupied Palestinian Territory*, 9 July 2004, ICJ, Advisory Opinion, para. 106, <www.icj-cij.org/docket/files/131/1671.pdf>, visited on 29 September 2012.

23 Roberts, *supra* note 16, p. 47.

24 *Ibid.*, p. 50.

25 Austin and Bruch, *supra* note 11, pp. 1–2.

26 *Ibid.*

> It is prohibited to employ methods or means of warfare which are intended, or may be expected, to cause widespread, long-term and severe damage to the natural environment.

According to Article 55:

> 1. Care shall be taken in warfare to protect the natural environment against widespread, long-term and severe damage. This protection includes a prohibition of the use of methods or means of warfare which are intended or may be expected to cause such damage to the natural environment and thereby to prejudice the health or survival of the population.
> 2. Attacks against the natural environment by way of reprisals are prohibited.[27]

The key terms 'widespread', 'long-term' and 'severe' are not defined in Protocol I, its commentaries or its negotiating history.[28] During the negotiations, some delegates stated that they understood 'long-term' to be a period measured in decades,[29] but no official position was adopted. There is nothing in the records defining 'widespread' or 'severe'. This lack is especially acute in Protocol I because damage must be 'widespread, long-term *and* severe' before it is prohibited, which sets a high threshold of harm. Damage could satisfy one or two of the criteria without being prohibited.

In addition to the high and uncertain threshold of harm, the effectiveness of Protocol I's environmental provisions is undermined by the fact that a number of militarily-important States remain non-parties, including the United States, Iran, Pakistan, India, Turkey and Israel.[30] The United States has historically opposed the environmental articles of Protocol I on the ground that they are excessively broad.[31] The United States also opposes categorising Articles 35(3) and 55

27 Protocol I, *supra* note 4.

28 M. Schmitt, 'Humanitarian Law and the Environment', 28 *Denver Journal of International Law and Policy* (2000) p. 277.

29 *See Official Records of the Diplomatic Conference on the Reaffirmation and Development of International Law Applicable in Armed Conflicts*, Vol. 15, p. 360.

30 *See* ICRC list of State Parties to Protocol Additional to the Geneva Conventions of 12 August 1949, and relating to the Protection of Victims of International Armed Conflicts (Protocol I), 8 June 1977, <www.icrc.org/ihl.nsf/WebSign?ReadForm&id=470&ps=P>, visited on 12 March 2012.

31 Schmitt, *supra* note 28. *See also* M. Matheson, 'Session One: The United States Position on the Relation of Customary International Law to the 1977 Protocols Additional to the 1949 Geneva Conventions', 2 *American University Journal of International Law and Policy* (1987) p. 419; A. Sofaer, 'Agora: The US Decision Not to Ratify Protocol I to the Geneva Conventions on the Protection of War Victims', 82 *American Journal of International Law* (1988) p. 784.

as customary international law, as is clear from the United States' comments on Article 45 of the ICRC *Customary International Humanitarian Law Study*.[32]

The negotiation of Protocol I and ENMOD was roughly contemporaneous, and the drafters of each were aware of the other instrument.[33] It is therefore no coincidence that the thresholds of impermissible environmental harm in ENMOD and Protocol I use very similar language. However, the States negotiating Protocol I made it very clear that the interpretation was not to be the same as that applied to ENMOD. The consensus was that Protocol I's threshold of impermissible environmental damage is higher.[34] ENMOD nonetheless serves as a useful contrast for interpreting Protocol I's use of the operative terms, 'widespread', 'long-lasting' and 'severe'.

3.2. *ENMOD*

ENMOD[35] specifically deals with the use of the environment as a weapon and prohibits "military or any other hostile use of environmental modification techniques having widespread, long-lasting or severe effects as the means of destruction, damage or injury to any other State Party".[36] Environmental modification techniques are defined as "any technique for changing – through the deliberate manipulation of natural processes – the dynamics, composition or structure of the Earth, including its biota, lithosphere, hydrosphere and atmosphere, or of outer space",[37] which an authoritative UN Understanding stated could include "an upset in the ecological balance of a region".[38]

The key operative phrase 'widespread, long-lasting or severe' was also the subject of a 1976 Understanding of the Committee of the Conference of Disarmament:

> It is the understanding of the Committee that, for the purposes of this Convention, the terms "widespread," "long-lasting" and "severe" shall be interpreted as follows:
> (a) "widespread": encompassing an area on the scale of several hundred square kilometres;
> (b) "long-lasting": lasting for a period of months, or approximately a season;

32 *See* Marsh, *supra* note 18.

33 *See* Solf, *supra* note 6.

34 K. Hulme, *War Torn Environment: Interpreting the Legal Threshold* (Martinus Nijhoff, Leiden,2004) p. 90.

35 Convention on the Prohibition of Military or Any Other Hostile Use of Environmental Modification Techniques, 10 December 1976, (ENMOD).

36 *Ibid.*, Article I.

37 *Ibid.*, Article II.

38 *Ibid.*, Annex to the Convention, Understanding Relating to Art. II. The ENMOD Convention Understandings were transmitted by the Committee on the Conference on Disarmament to the UN General Assembly on 2 September 1976.

(c) "severe": involving serious or significant disruption or harm to human life, natural and economic resources or other assets.

It is further understood that the interpretation set forth above is intended exclusively for this Convention and is not intended to prejudice the interpretation of the same or similar terms ifused in connexion with any other international agreement.[39]

It is important to note the disjunction of the terms 'widespread, long-term *or* severe' in the ENMOD Convention as opposed to their conjunction in Protocol I. ENMOD sets a lower threshold for the prohibited damage than that set by Protocol I; however, the scope of ENMOD is severely circumscribed by its limitation to environmental modification techniques. Moreover, the modification must be 'deliberate',[40] thus ruling out its application to unintended, collateral damage. The Understanding attached to ENMOD gives the following examples of prohibited deliberate modification: "earthquakes; tsunamis; an upset in the ecological balance of a region; changes in weather patterns (clouds, precipitation, cyclones of various types and tornadic storms); changes in climate patterns; changes in ocean currents; changes in the state of the ozone layer; and changes in the states of the ionosphere".[41] Thus, ENMOD, by its terms, has very limited application to the conduct of conventional warfare, and its interpretive guidance specifically disclaims equivalence with Protocol I.

The lack of application in conventional warfare has also been a criticism of Protocol I with scholars suggesting that "Arts. 35(3) and 55 will not impose any significant limitation on combatants waging conventional warfare. It seems primarily directed to high level policy decision makers and would affect such unconventional means of warfare as the massive use of herbicides or chemical agents which could produce widespread, long-term and severe damage to the natural environment."[42] Some have even questioned whether the threshold was reached by the means and methods of warfare employed in Vietnam, which the provisions were intended to prohibit, as the damage to nature caused during that conflict may not have lasted for several decades.[43]

Therefore, if the threshold is interpreted in the light of its negotiating history, Protocol I's protections may be nearly as limited in scope as those afforded by

---

39 *Ibid.*, Annex to the Convention, Understandings Regarding the Convention.

40 *Ibid.*, Article II.

41 *Ibid.*, Annex to the Convention, Understanding Relating to Art. II.

42 M. Bothe *et al.*, *New Rules for Victims of Armed Conflict: Commentary on the Two 1977 Protocols Additional to the Geneva Conventions of 1949* (Martinus Nijhoff, The Hague, 1982) p. 348.

43 M. Bothe *et al.*, 'International Law Protecting the Environment During Armed Conflict: Gaps and Opportunities', 92:879 *International Review of the Red Cross* (2010) p. 576.

ENMOD.[44] This presents the additional danger that an overly restrictive and ambiguous definition of impermissible damage will serve to legitimate, rather than limit, environmental harm when that damage is clearly beneath the threshold.

In defining impermissible environmental damage in the context of armed conflict, Protocol I's threshold cannot be ignored as Articles 35(3) and 55 continue to be the most specific express treaty provisions on environmental damage. In fact, the tripartite threshold has been given new life by its incorporation into the 1998 Rome Statute of the International Criminal Court.[45] Scholars have attempted to use the international legal tools of treaty interpretation to obviate the difficulties of this threshold.[46] The difficulties of the threshold have proven to be challenging if not intractable for those seeking greater environmental protections. Some commentators have proposed alternative standards found in traditional law of war principles, other IHL treaty provisions and international environmental law.[47] These alternatives seem to necessitate that either Protocol I's threshold has fallen into desuetude;[48] or that the most explicit treaty provisions do not always, or exclusively, apply;[49] or that other standards govern environmental damage up to the threshold.

4. Other IHL Instruments and Customary Principles

Apart from the express environmental provisions of Protocol I and ENMOD, a number of IHL instruments and customary principles may offer protection for the environment in relation to armed conflict. The provisions that provide protection for civilians and civilian property and those that limit the means and methods of warfare provide indirect protection to the environment.[50] Also important are the customary law of war principles of proportionality, which demands a proportional relationship between collateral damage and direct expected military value, and discrimination, which provides criteria for distinguishing permissible military targets from non-combatants.[51] These customary principles

44 *Ibid.*

45 Rome Statute of the International Criminal Court (ICC) of 17 July 1998, A/CONF.138/9, Article 8(2)(b)(iv) (the Article adds elements of scienter and proportionality).

46 *See e.g.* Hulme, *supra* note 34.

47 *See e.g.* Bothe, *supra* note 43, pp. 569–750.

48 *Ibid*, p. 576 (defining 'desuetude' as the principle that a legal provision loses its binding force as the result of non-use for a sufficiently long period of time).

49 *Contra* the principle of *lex specialis derogat legi generali.*

50 M. Schmitt, 'War and the Environment: Fault Lines in the Prescriptive Landscape', in J. Austin and C. Bruch (eds.), *The Environmental Consequences of War: Legal, Economic, and Scientific Perspectives* (Cambridge UP, Cambridge, 2000) p. 94.

51 Roberts, *supra* note 16, pp. 50–51.

arguably provide protection against wanton and excessive environmental damage even in cases not addressed by explicit environmental protection provisions.[52]

Applicable treaty provisions, many of which are considered customary law, are found in the 1907 Hague and 1949 Geneva Conventions, Protocol I and the Chemical and Conventional Weapons Conventions.[53] For example, the 1907 Hague Convention's Article 23(g) forbids destruction and seizure of enemy property unless "imperatively demanded by the necessities of war".[54] Article 53 of the Fourth Geneva Convention of 1949 similarly protects property with reference to military necessity: "[a]ny destruction by the Occupying Power of real or personal property ... is prohibited, except where such destruction is rendered absolutely necessary by military operations".[55] In the absence of legitimate and imperative military necessity, these articles would likely prohibit actions like Iraq's destruction of Kuwaiti oil fields in the Gulf War.[56]

Protocol I also contains provisions that protect civilian populations and objects. Article 48, on Basic Rules, mandates that, at all times, parties to a conflict must distinguish between civilians and combatants and between civilian objects and military objectives. Operations may only be directed against military objectives.[57] Article 52 also prohibits targeting civilian objects and strictly limits attacks to military objectives, defined as "those objects which by their nature, location, purpose or use make an effective contribution to military action and whose total or partial destruction, capture or neutralization, in the circumstances ruling at the time, offers a definite military advantage".[58]

Civilian objects are defined negatively as everything that is not a military object. At least one commentator advocates an interpretation that includes "all components of the environment – land, air, flora, fauna, atmosphere, high seas, etc. – that do not present an advantage ... to a military operation".[59] According to the terms of Article 52, the advantage must be definite, military and current to

---

52 *See* M. Schmitt, 'Green War: An Assessment of the Environmental Law of International Armed Conflict', 22 *Yale Journal of International Law* (1997) pp. 52–62.

53 Schmitt, *supra* note 50.

54 Convention (IV) Respecting the Laws and Customs of War on Land and its Annex: Regulations Concerning the Laws and Customs of War on Land, The Hague, 18 October 1907, Article 23(g).

55 Convention (IV) Relative to the Protection of Civilian Persons in Time of War, Geneva, 12 August 1949, Article 53.

56 *See* US Department of Defence, *Conduct of the Persian Gulf War: Final Report to Congress* (US Government Printing Office, Washington, D.C., 1992) pp. 623–624.

57 Protocol I, *supra* note 4, Article 48.

58 *Ibid.*, Article 52.

59 Schmitt, *supra* note 50, p. 97.

the circumstances, which rules out speculative advantages. Both Article 48 and 52 are considered to reflect customary international law.[60]

Articles 51(5)(b) and 57(2)(a)(iii) codify the customary law principle of proportionality. Indiscriminate attacks are those "which may be expected to cause incidental loss of civilian life, injury to civilians, damage to civilian objects ... which would be excessive in relation to the concrete and direct military advantage anticipated".[61] Article 57 on precautions in attack requires military planners and decision-makers to refrain from indiscriminate attacks.[62]

Article 54 prohibits attacks for any motive on objects indispensable to the survival of the civilian population, including foodstuffs, agricultural areas, crops, livestock, drinking water installations and irrigation works.[63] However, paragraph three of the article provides an exception when these objects are used as "sustenance solely for the members of its armed forces; or ... if not as sustenance, then in direct support of military action".[64]

Article 56 provides protection for works and installations containing dangerous forces, namely dams, dykes and nuclear electrical generating stations.[65] These protections do not apply if the works or installations are used in "regular, significant and direct support of military operations and if such attack is the only feasible way to terminate such support".[66] The official commentary also makes clear that the list of protected works is exhaustive and specifically does not include petroleum storage facilities or refineries, despite their potential for causing severe civilian losses.[67]

While these treaty provisions may provide indirect protection for the natural environment, they were not originally drafted with that intent.[68] Reliance on such indirect protection is not ideal for ensuring protection of the environment. The provisions and principles are widely dispersed throughout different sources of customary and treaty law. They may not be specific enough to provide practical guidance without further authoritative elaboration. They arguably do not reflect

---

60 C. Greenwood, 'Customary Law Status of the 1977 Geneva Protocols', in A. Delissen and G. Tanja (eds.), *Humanitarian Law of Armed Conflict: Challenges Ahead* (Martinus Nijhoff, Dordrecht, 1991).

61 Protocol I, *supra* note 4, Article 51(5)(b).

62 Protocol I, *supra* note 4, Article 57(2)(a)(iii).

63 Protocol I, *supra* note 4, Article 54(1).

64 Protocol I, *supra* note 4, Article 54(3).

65 Protocol I, *supra* note 4, Article 56.

66 *Ibid.*, Article 56(2).

67 *Commentaries to Protocol Additional to the Geneva Conventions of 12 August 1949, and Relating to the Protection of Victims of International Armed Conflicts (Protocol I), 8 June 1977*, paras. 2147–2150, <www.icrc.org/ihl.nsf/COM/470-750071?OpenDocument>, visited 12 March 2012.

68 Roberts, *supra* note 16, pp. 66–67.

the scope and depth of contemporary environmental concerns. Investigation and enforcement are infrequent and often appear to be arbitrary victor's justice.[69]

In addition to the practical problem of anticipatory measurement of environmental harm, there is the question of determining the weight of environmental considerations in the proportionality calculus. Is environmental harm only a proxy for civilian harm? Can environmental damage be excessive even if the full extent and nature of the damage are uncertain?[70] These questions give rise to more basic philosophical issues of anthropocentrism and culturally-contingent environmental valuations.[71]

The most direct challenge to the adequacy of protection is the fact that almost all of the IHL provisions described above expressly allow for deviation on the grounds of military necessity. The US Navy's *The Commander's Handbook on the Law of Naval Operations* contains a characteristic formulation of the principles applicable to environmental damage in wartime as they are implemented in modern military manuals:

> It is not unlawful to cause collateral damage to the natural environment during an attack upon a legitimate military objective. However, the commander has an affirmative obligation to avoid unnecessary damage to the environment to the extent that it is practicable to do so consistent with mission accomplishment. To that end, and as far as military requirements permit, methods or means of warfare should be employed with due regard to the protection and preservation of the natural environment. Destruction of the natural environment not necessitated by mission accomplishment and carried out wantonly is prohibited. Therefore, a commander should consider the environmental damage that will result from an attack on a legitimate military objective as one of the factors during targeting analysis.[72]

The key referents in this formulation are 'mission accomplishment' and 'military requirements', *i.e.* military necessity. The parameters of mission accomplishment are the baseline against which to measure collateral environmental damage. A recent publication on the gaps and opportunities in the protection of the environment notes that it is necessary to prevent the transformation of environmental elements into military objectives,[73] a transformation accomplished on the basis ofmilitary necessity.

Protection of the environment therefore depends on military commanders balancing military necessity against environmental and humanitarian norms. As

69 *Ibid.*

70 Bothe, *supra* note 43, p. 578.

71 Schmitt, *supra* note 50, p. 127.

72 *The Commander's Handbook on the Law of Naval Operations*, 8.4 Environmental Considerations, Naval Warfare Publication NWP 1-14m/FMFM 1-10/ COMDTPUB P5800.7.

73 Bothe, *supra* note 43, p. 577.

Professor Richard Falk puts it, "from the perspective of a military actor, almost any environmentally harmful initiative can be given a subjectively acceptable legal rationale".[74] The challenging task is to make effective arguments for environmental protection that incorporate this balance and to prevent unreflective subordination of environmental restraints to mission objectives and prevention of risk to soldiers.

5. Interpreting the Balance between Military Necessity and Humanity in Protocol I's Threshold

Before turning to an interpretation of what Protocol I's threshold can accomplish, it is important to explore what the threshold itself represents. In his article on the balance between the principles of military necessity and humanity inherent in rules of IHL, Professor Michael Schmitt claims that "[e]xtant treaty law … reflects an agreed-upon balance between military necessity and humanity, such that neither independently justifies departure from its provisions, unless otherwise specifically provided for in the law".[75] Schmitt goes on to assert that the principle of military necessity is not a limitation on military operations but instead represents the State's legitimate interest in not unduly restricting its own freedom of military action in armed conflict.[76] States must balance this interest against the equally valid obligation to protect its population and their property.[77]

Some IHL provisions, including many of those discussed above, expressly allow for deviation from a rule that protects civilians and civilian objects on the basis of military necessity.[78] This can be seen in Article 53 of the Fourth Geneva Convention on the protection of property in occupied territory "except where such destruction is rendered absolutely necessary by military operations".[79] Similarly, Protocol I's Article 54(5) allows for derogation from the ban on "scorched earth" tactics "where required by imperative military necessity".[80] More often, the balance between military necessity and humanity operates implicitly, underlying the principles of proportionality and distinction.[81] Indeed, Schmitt cites the United States Department of Defence's *Law of War Manual* in support of this position:

---

74 Falk, *supra* note 9, pp. 143–144.

75 M. Schmitt, 'Military Necessity and Humanity in International Humanitarian Law: Preserving the Delicate Balance', 50 *Virginia Journal of International Law* (2010) p. 799.

76 *Ibid.*

77 *Ibid.*

78 *Ibid.*, p. 802.

79 Convention (IV) Relative to the Protection of Civilian Persons in Time of War, Geneva, 12 August 1949, Article 53.

80 Protocol I, *supra* note 4, Article 54(5).

81 Schmitt, *supra* note 74, pp. 803–805.

"Where an express prohibition has been stated, neither military necessity nor any other rationale of necessity may override that prohibition. Military necessity was weighed by nations as each express prohibition was promulgated, and again at the time each State Party ratified or acceded to each treaty."[82] The outcome of this State-centric positivism is a requirement to adhere closely to the existing law without seeking to supplement the express rules with additional obligations to reconsider the balance of military necessity and humanity. In this way, normative clarity will be maintained.[83]

Under this understanding of humanitarian law, the legal threshold in Protocol I represents a point of agreement between State parties that there is a point beyond which environmental damage is prohibited regardless of the military necessity. Article 35(3) is clear in its prohibition of "methods and means of warfare which are intended, or may be expected, to cause widespread, long-term and severe damage to the natural environment". While the threshold may practically set too high a bar, as a theoretical matter any damage that exceeds the threshold is prohibited. Therefore, at a certain level of environmental harm, there is no longer any need to conduct proportionality or targeting analyses. This plays a normative role as it signifies the importance of the environment within humanitarian considerations.

The norm-announcing aspect of the threshold may not be particularly encouraging for proponents of environmental protection given the difficulty of actually reaching the threshold. However, the obligation to 'take care' to protect the natural environment in Article 55(1) combines with Article 35(3)'s strict prohibition to produce more immediate functional consequences. As Dr. Karen Hulme argues, "the obligation to 'take care' requires states to, at least, contemplate what environmental damage might be caused by their military operations and just how serious a level of harm is foreseeable".[84] If States take this obligation seriously, they will have to undertake some sort of environmental impact assessment when there is a danger of exceeding the threshold, a process likely to have protective value even if the action's consequences are ultimately deemed to lie beneath the threshold.[85]

Importantly, this interpretation of Protocol I's threshold does not preclude the application of other IHL instruments and customary provisions to limit damage that is beneath the threshold. In fact, the existence of a strict prohibition based on the environment's humanitarian importance should encourage a substantial increase in the valuation of the environment in proportionality analyses. This should result in a robust application of the other laws that offer protection to the environment up to the threshold of prohibited damage. The next section

82 *Ibid*, p. 801, fn. 19.

83 *Ibid*, p. 839.

84 K. Hulme, 'Taking Care to Protect the Environment Against Damage: A Meaningless Obligation?', 92 *International Review of the Red Cross* (2010) p. 689.

85 *Ibid.*

of this study proposes that arguments for protecting the environment should be addressed to those military decision makers who are actually in the position to make environmentally harmful decisions. Furthermore, framing the need for environmental protection in terms of traditional law of war principles and current political and military strategic realities may make decision makers more receptive to increasing the level of protection.

6. Strategies for Implementing IHL Protection for the Environment below the Threshold of Protocol I

Legal rules and general guidelines necessarily involve some degree of abstraction. Their adequacy is then often judged by how well they have or would have prevented harm in particular historical instances or will prevent harm in current or hypothetical future scenarios. An overemphasis on consequences can be misleading, at least in this case where the rules are addressed to decision-making processes. While the ultimate goal may be to prevent significant environmental harm in wartime, the intermediate goal, or the means to the ultimate goal, is to guide the military decision-making process in such a manner that environmental harm is less likely.

The following observations are intended to provide practical and strategic guidance to those considering environmentally harmful military decisions with regard to several salient factors. They are also intended to expand the temporal and conceptual scope of the issue to emphasise the importance of choices made prior to environmental damage as opposed to *ex post* determinations of legal violations. Indeed, the very use of the nomenclature 'protection of the environment *in relation to* armed conflict', instead of *during* armed conflict, highlights the fact that the deleterious effects of armed conflict on the environment can occur before, during and long after the actual conflict violence. This expansion of the temporal scope of the issue emphasises choices made prior to as well as subsequent to environmental damage occurring, rather than focusing merely on findings of liability. As Paul Szasz remarks, "the measures that can be taken before a particular conflict arises, and in any event before an actual combat operation has begun, and especially those that can be taken after the end of the conflict, appear to have been somewhat neglected even though they may well be less controversial and more effective".[86]

6.1. Strategic Arguments for Environmental Protection

The most obvious strategic argument is that excessive environmental damage undermines long-term peace, as natural resources and the environment are instru-

86 P. Szasz, 'Comment: The Existing Legal Framework, Protecting the Environment During Armed Conflict', in R. Grunawalt *et al.* (eds.), *Protection of the Environment During Armed Conflict* (Naval War College, Newport, R.I., 1996) p. 284.

mental in post-conflict peace building and economic and societal recovery.[87] It can, of course, be argued that not destroying strategic resources, like oil refineries or chemical plants, will unnecessarily prolong the conflict and lead to greater loss of life, both civilian and military. This would seem to be a regression to the problematic balancing of environmental harm and military necessity. However, framing military necessity in terms of strategic goals, instead of tactical operational aims, opens up important new arguments, including the effect of environmental damage on the prospects for long-term peace.

Military victory has traditionally been defined as "the destruction of the enemy's main forces on the battlefield" which leads to the achievement of campaign objectives likely to include deterrence of future aggression and the substantial reduction of the enemy's future war-making capability.[88] At the tactical battlefield level, military victory can be seen as the withdrawal, retreat or surrender of enemy forces and frustration of their objectives while achieving one's own.[89]

Both political leaders and military commanders should be able to recognise that the "classic error in warfare is 'to mistake military victory for political victory'".[90] Battlefield victories are neither necessary nor sufficient to achieve political aims. While military victories may provide the opportunity for strategic victory, means and methods that serve the former may be detrimental to the latter.

Strategic victory entails achieving a complex series of interrelated objectives. One scholar defines the parameters for strategic victory, at least for Western nations in the post-Cold War security setting, as: 1) information control; 2) military deterrence; 3) political self-determination with policies favourable to the victor's core national interests; 4) economic reconstruction; 5) domestic security and social justice; 6) diplomatic respect, international and domestic support and approval for the victor from the domestic public, foreign allies, international organisations and others.[91] When incorporated into this framework, environmental protection arguably becomes a positive strategic goal, especially for the last three criteria, instead of an impediment to military expediency.

---

87 C. Bruch *et al.*, 'Post-conflict Peace Building and Natural Resources', 19 *Yearbook of International Environmental Law* (2008) pp. 58–96.

88 R. Mandel, 'Defining Postwar Victory', in J. Angstrom and I. Duyvesteyn (eds.), *Understanding Victory and Defeat in Contemporary War* (Routledge, Oxford, UK, 2007) p. 21.

89 *Ibid.*, pp. 20–21.

90 *Ibid.*, p. 19.

91 *Ibid.*, pp. 20–21.

6.2. *Factors Affecting Strategic Arguments for Environmental Protection*

Cleary, the viability of certain strategic arguments for environmental protection depends on the circumstances of a particular conflict, particularly the relationship between military success and strategic victory. In some cases, military success and strategic victory may be functionally identical. These include instances of existential self-defence wherein a State must achieve military victory in order to survive, and given the extreme circumstances seeks nothing more in the short term than immediate survival. The International Court of Justice (ICJ) in its *Nuclear Weapons* Advisory Opinion reaffirmed "the fundamental right of every State to survival, and thus its right to resort to self-defence ... when its survival is at stake".[92] It then acknowledged that "extreme circumstances of self-defence, in which [the State's] very survival would be at stake", necessitate a different set of legal and ethical considerations.[93]

As the ICJ recognised, there are significant legal, moral and practical differences between conflicts where the survival of a State is at stake and conflicts where the goals are geo-political, humanitarian or economic. Placing a conflict along the spectrum between existential threats and wars of policy may give strategic decision-makers guidance in defining the necessity to be weighed against environmental damage.

Other features of conflicts are also relevant to the inquiry. In many contemporary conflicts, there are clear asymmetries in the tactics available to each party. There is often a party that enjoys clear superiority in conventional armaments and technology, especially air power. In the absence of some sort of restraint, like legal protections for the environmental, this technological superiority may lead strategic decision-makers to actively seek out opportunities to use their advantage even after exhaustion of militarily-significant targets.

Another factor that may often be relevant is whether the military engagements take place on foreign soil. An army operating on distant soil may be less likely to be overly concerned as to whether their actions cause environmental harm. At least 19 States have domestic laws that mandate some degree of institutional responsibility for their militaries in regard to the domestic environment.[94] These States, including the United States, require their militaries to comply with

92 *Legality of the Threat or Use of Nuclear Weapons*, 8 July 1996, ICJ, Advisory Opinion, para. 96,<www.icj-cij.org/icjwww/icases/iunan/iunanframe.htm>, visited on 12 March 2012.

93 *Ibid.*, para. 97.

94 A. Westing, 'In Furtherance of Environmental Guidelines for Armed Forces During Peace and War', in J. Austin and C. Bruch (eds.), *The Environmental Consequences of War: Legal, Economic, and Scientific Perspectives* (Cambridge University Press, Cambridge, 2000).

environmental laws, at least domestically, in peacetime.[95] However, this institutional responsibility does not necessarily carry over into the sphere of international armed conflict, except insofar as mandated by international humanitarian law.

There is also the realpolitik factor that politically powerful States, like the United States, are unlikely to face international sanctions for environmental damage while internationally-isolated States can be subjected to unified Security Council action. In the aftermath of the Gulf War, Security Council Resolution 687 declared Iraq "liable under international law for any direct loss, damage, including environmental damage and the depletion of natural resources, or injury to foreign Governments, nationals and corporations, as a result of Iraq's unlawful invasion and occupation of Kuwait".[96] There were no similar actions taken in response to US actions in Vietnam or the North Atlantic Treaty Organization's Kosovo campaign.

The lessons learned by Western military powers in contemporary conflicts may translate into greater environmental protection. If the goal of guerrilla warfare or insurgency is to "place the onus of indiscriminate warfare on the opposing army" in order to mobilise the population,[97] then the perception of excessive environmental damage disserves strategic interests. This sort of argumentation appeals to the current US counterinsurgency doctrine, which recognises "the military utility of limits on the use of force".[98] It is hard to win the hearts and minds of people whose lands have been despoiled and livelihoods destroyed by wartime pollution, especially if that pollution was caused by attacks designed to destroy infrastructure with civilian utility.

Strategic decision-makers must also recognise the circumstances in which damage is likely to have effects beyond the boundaries of the States which are party to the conflict. In the *Nuclear Weapons* Advisory Opinion, the ICJ considered the argument that the customary principle of neutrality serves to prohibit environmental damage that affects neutral States:

> The principle of neutrality, in its classic sense, was aimed at preventing the incursion of belligerent forces into neutral territory, or attacks on the persons'or ships of neutrals. Thus: 'the territory of neutral powers is inviolable' (Article 1 of the Hague Convention (V) Respecting the Rights and Duties of Neutral Powers and Persons in Case of War on Land, concluded on 18 October 1907); 'belligerents are bound to

---

95 *Ibid.*

96 United Nations Security Council, United Nations Security Council Resolution 687 (1991), UN SCOR, 46th Session, 2981st meeting, UN Doc. S/RES/687, para. 16.

97 M. Walzer, *Just and Unjust Wars: A Moral Argument with Historical Illustrations* (Basic Books, New York, 2006) pp. 179–180.

98 Schmitt, *supra* note 39, p. 837 (referring to the approach taken in the *U.S. COIN Manual*. Headquarters, Department of The Army & Headquarters, Marine Corps Combat Dev. Command, Counterinsurgency, FM 3-24, MCWP 3-33.5 (2006)).

> respect the sovereign rights of neutral powers . . .' (Article 1 to the Hague Convention (XIII) Respecting the Rights and Duties of Neutral Powers in Naval War. concluded on 18 October 1907), 'neutral states have equal interest in having their rights respected by belligerents . . .' (Preamble to Convention on Maritime Neutrality, concluded on 20 February 1928) It is clear, however, that the principle of neutrality applies with equal force to trans-border incursions of armed forces and to the transborder damage caused to a neutral State by the use of a weapon in a belligerent State.[99]

While the Court did not rule on the specific application of the principle in the context of nuclear weapons, it did affirm that "the principle of neutrality ... is of a fundamental character ... applicable ... to all international armed conflict, whatever type of weapons might be used".[100] The principle of neutrality then provides an additional argument against attacks on targets that may cause trans-boundary harm, *e.g.* attacks on petrochemical facilities near international waterways.[101]

7. Conclusion: Relevance of Alternative Frameworks to Interpretations of the Legal Threshold Set by Articles 35(3) and 55

This study accepts that Articles 35(3) and 55 represent a point of agreement between State parties that there is a point beyond which environmental damage is prohibited regardless of the military situation. As noted at the outset, in addition to signalling the importance of considering environmental harm in military decisions, the threshold requirement of 'widespread, long-lasting and severe' damage bifurcates the legal protection of the environment in armed conflict. Above the threshold, environmental damage is prohibited. Beneath the threshold, other IHL instruments and customary principles apply and serve to limit environmental harm, usually as a function of the balancing of potential harm against military necessity. In this context, it has been argued that determinations of military necessity should be refocused by emphasising strategic considerations. Furthermore, strategic decision-makers should reformulate military necessity in terms of strategic necessity when deciding what may or may not constitute acceptable environmental damage. This argument is particularly important for addressing States that dispute the applicability of specific treaty obligations that provide environmental protection. This could help to establish the content and

99 *Nuclear Weapons* Advisory Opinion, *supra* note 87, para. 88 (quoting Nauru, Written Statement (1), p. 35, IV E).

100 *Ibid.*, para. 89.

101 Transboundary environmental harm may also involve the application of customary and treaty-based international environmental law. *See e.g.* International Law Commission, Draft Articles on Prevention of Transboundary Harm from Hazardous Activities (UN Doc. A/56/10).

scope of the obligation to protect the environment in relation to armed conflict in customary international law.

Other possible avenues to achieve the progressive development of the law also exist. For example, adoption of an effective and acceptable framework for environmental protection in situations falling short of the high threshold of impermissible damage might establish a similarly effective and acceptable interpretation of the direct protection provided by Articles 35(3) and 55. In other words, if 'widespread, long-lasting and severe' can be divorced from the currently understood interpretations, this threshold could possibly serve as a useful decision-making tool.[102] Finally, it must be asked, what is the most effective way to inculcate environmental protection into strategic considerations and thus into the culture of military decision-making? As the author of *Deuteronomy* understood long ago, arguments for environmental regard and against wanton destruction must acknowledge military realities without sacrificing legal or ethical clarity.

---

102 *E.g.*, a military commander could conduct an analysis wherein he or she compares a proposed attack with a baseline standard, *e.g.* the explosion of conventional munitions. He then asks if attacking this target with these weapons (the attack) will damage an area greater than the blast radius, *i.e.* is the attack widespread? Will the attack lead to continuing effects after the battle ends, *i.e.* is the attack long-lasting? Lastly, will the attack seriously impair strategic goals by endangering or alienating the local population, *i.e.* is the attack severe?

6 Environmental Protection in Armed Conflict: Filling the Gaps with Sustainable Development

Onita Das*

1. Introduction

Armed conflict, whatever its justification or cause, poses considerable challenges to the environment and, in turn, places considerable strain on the war-affected human population. Armed conflict inevitably has an impact on the environment whether due to the environment being a military target or part of collateral damage. As the United Nations Environment Programme (UNEP) recently reported, the environment "continues to be a silent victim of armed conflicts worldwide".[1] This is regrettable because damage done in times of conflict can be irreversible, and the restoration of peace may represent a greater challenge if the supporting physical environment has been seriously impaired.

Conflict-related environmental damage is nothing new. However, as is evident from the experiences of the Vietnam War, the 1991 Gulf War, Kosovo, Afghanistan, and the on-going conflict in Sudan, damage to and destruction of the environment as a result of warfare impacts not only the environment but also the war-torn population, having a negative effect on their security, livelihoods and well-being. This negative exposure can disrupt sustainable development. As set out in Principle 24 of the Rio Declaration:

> Warfare is inherently destructive of sustainable development. States shall therefore respect international law providing protection for the environment in times of armed conflict and cooperate in its further development, as necessary.[2]

---

* Lecturer in Law, University of the West of England, Bristol, UK Research Officer, Global Network for the Study of Human Rights and the Environment

1 UNEP, *Protecting the Environment During Armed Conflict: An Inventory and Analysis of International Law* (UNEP, Switzerland 2009) p. 4.

2 UN, *Declaration on Environment and Development*, Rio de Janeiro, 12 August 1992, UN Doc. A/ CONF.151/26/REV.1.

Rosemary Rayfuse (ed.), War and the Environment: New Approaches to Protecting the Environment in Relation to Armed Conflict
Copyright 2014 Koninklijke Brill NV. Printed in The Netherlands. ISBN 978-90-04-27064-0 pp. 129-234

This study examines the legal nexus between conflict-related environmental damage and sustainable development. It begins with a brief explanation of why the protection of the environment during armed conflict within the existing legal framework is considered inadequate, and explores the possibility of utilising the overarching concept of sustainable development and its relevant substantive principles to fill the gaps of environmental protection provided by international humanitarian law (IHL). Section 2 sketches the impact of armed conflict on sustainable development in practice. Section 3 reviews the theoretical concept of sustainable development and the 'sub-principles' that are integral to the overarching concept. Section 4 briefly discusses the existing legal framework for environmental protection in armed conflict and reflects on the principal limitations of the legal status quo. The final section introduces an argument for integrating the concept of sustainable development and its sub-principles to better protect the environment during times of armed conflict based on the 'Berlin Rules' approach.

2. Impact of Armed Conflict on Sustainable Development

Armed conflict is the antithesis of sustainable development which is most commonly defined as "development that meets the needs of the present without compromising the ability of future generations to meet their own needs".[3]

The devastating effects of armed conflict often go against the notion that "[t]he world has a responsibility to future generations".[4] Armed conflict, be it international or internal, has various impacts, both short and long-term, on the environment, development and human well-being. As UNEP notes, "[t]he affects [sic], even of internal conflicts, are felt at various spatial levels, within the immediate area of conflict, and often in neighbouring countries. Conflict undercuts or destroys environmental, physical, human and social capital, diminishing available opportunities for sustainable development."[5] This is evident from the various wars and armed conflicts that have occurred in the recent past.

During the Vietnam War American forces deliberately destroyed the Vietnamese environment as part of their military tactics. US military operations included a massive deforestation campaign using millions of tons of herbicide as well as bombarding agricultural zones as part of their food denial strategy.[6]

---

3 World Commission on Environment and Development (WCED), *Our Common Future* (also known as the "Brundtland Report), 'Chairman's Foreword' (1987), <www.un-documents.net/ wced-ocf.htm>, visited on 30 June 2012.

4 A-M. Sacquet, *World Atlas of Sustainable Development* (Anthem, London, 2005) p. 30.

5 C. Huggins *et al.*, 'Environment for Peace and Regional Cooperation', in UNEP, *Africa Environment Outlook 2* (DEWA/UNEP, Nairobi, 2006) p. 324.

6 Stanford Biology Study Group, 'The Destruction of Indochina', 27 *Bulletin of the Atomic Scientists* (1971) p. 36.

This included, for example, destroying 30 per cent of Vietnam's ecologically vital coastal mangrove forests[7] which, in addition to their crucial role in protecting the soil, water and surrounding plant life, were also "a vital nursery for the nation's fish stocks, a primary source of protein in the region".[8] This illustrates, in part, the obstruction of sustainable development; the destruction of the Vietnamese countryside resulting in inadequate access to natural resources and land, thus affecting the livelihoods of the population, the extensive loss of biodiversity, and the various short and long-term health problems caused by the chemicals used during US military operations.[9] Such negative war effects forced the rural population to migrate towards the cities,[10] severely disrupting sustainable development in the Vietnamese countryside and adding pressure to the cities.[11] Furthermore, studies indicate that the debilitating effects of the intensive herbicide-destroyed areas of vegetation are still being felt decades later.[12]

The 1991 Gulf War also caused serious challenges to sustainable development in the region. In this case, the Iraqi army sabotaged and set ablaze more than 700 oil-wells during their retreat from Kuwait in the last stages of the war.[13] Iraq's actions caused smoke from burning oil-wells to pollute the air[14] and spillage from the oil-wells to contaminate the soil as well as underground aquifers in Kuwait.[15] The negative effects of such pollution were not only felt by Kuwait but also its neighbouring countries.[16] From air pollution to damage to desalination plants, the conflict-related environmental destruction had an environmental, economic

---

7 A. H. Westing, 'Assault on the Environment', in *Environmental Conference on Cambodia, Laos, and Vietnam, Long-Term Consequences of the Vietnam War: Ecosystems* (Föreningen Levande Framtid, Stockholm, 2002) p. 3, <www.nnn.se/environ/ecology.pdf>, visited on 22 September 2012.

8 P. J. Cooper and C. M. Vargas, *Sustainable Development in Crisis Conditions: Challenges of War, Terrorism, and Civil Disorder* (Rowman & Littlefield, Lanham, MD, 2008) p. 91.

9 *Ibid.*, p. 90.

10 D. Keane, 'The Environmental Causes and Consequences of Migration: A Search for the Meaning of "Environmental Refugees"', 16 *Georgetown International Environmental Law Review* (2004) p. 213 (footnote omitted).

11 M. Parnwell, *Population Movements and the Third World* (Routledge, London, 1993) p. 143.

12 *See e.g.* Cooper and Vargas, *supra* note 8, pp. 89–92 (on the long-lasting effects of the Vietnam War).

13 K. Hulme, *War Torn Environment: Interpreting the Legal Threshold* (Martinus Nijhoff, Leiden,2004) p. 164.

14 *Ibid.*, pp. 164–165.

15 *Ibid.*, p. 171.

16 S. A. Earle, 'Persian Gulf Pollution: Assessing the Damage One Year Later', *National Geographic*, February 1992, p. 129.

and social impact on the Gulf States.[17] In addition to the impact on the health and livelihoods of the Gulf population,[18] the damage itself and the substantial costs incurred, as well as the destroyed oil resources and forgone revenues,[19] had a negative effect on the development of the Gulf States.[20] For example, as a direct result of the war, the Gulf States suffered a loss in GDP amounting to USD 710.4 billion.[21] This illustrates the loss and diversion of a vital resource that could have been used for the positive and sustainable development of the State and region as a whole.

While the damage to the environment was intentional in both the Vietnam and Gulf conflicts, the North Atlantic Treaty Organization's (NATO) 78-day aerial bombing campaign in the 1999 Kosovo conflict caused significant collateral environmental damage.[22] Factories, power and chemical plants, for example, were included in NATO military strategy and tactical targets.[23] NATO operations that included the destruction of industrial sites and infrastructures caused hazardous substances to pollute the soil, water and air of the Federal Republic of Yugoslavia (FRY) and several neighbouring countries.[24] This had a negative impact on sustainable development in the affected areas. The damage to the environment had serious effects not only on the natural environment, which until the conflict remained relatively unpolluted,[25] but also had serious impacts on the health and quality of life of the population of the FRY and the other affected

---

17 On effects of the conflict-related damage *see* UNEP, *Desk Study on the Environment in Iraq* (UNEP, Nairobi, 2003) pp. 56–69.

18 *Ibid.*

19 H. Askari, *Middle East Oil Exporters: What Happened to Economic Development?* (Edward Elgar, UK, 2006) p. 300 (*e.g.* the burning of more than 60 per cent of Kuwait's oil-wells cost the country approximately USD 5.8 billion in damages for its oil installations. This excludes "the cost of any foregone oil revenues and lost oil reserves").

20 *Ibid. See also* A. Alnasrawi, 'Iraq: Economic Consequences of the 1991 Gulf War and Future Outlook', 13 *Third World Quarterly* (1992) p. 335.

21 Askari, *supra* note 19, p. 300.

22 A. H. Cordesman, *The Lessons and Non-Lessons of the Air and Missile Campaign in Kosovo* (Praeger, USA, 2001) pp. 95–190.

23 International Criminal Tribunal for the former Yugoslavia (ICTY), *Final Report to the Prosecutor by the Committee Established to Review the NATO Bombing Campaign against the Federal Republic of Yugoslavia*, 13 June 2000, para. 14, <www.icty.org/sid/10052>, visited on 22 September 2012.

24 Council of Europe, *Environmental Impact of the War in Yugoslavia on South-East Europe*, Report by Committee on the Environment, Regional Planning and Local Authorities, Doc. 8925, 10 January 2001, paras. 18–42. *See also* Hulme, *supra* note 13, pp. 187–204.

25 Council of Europe, *supra* note 24, para. 35.

countries of Southeast Europe[26] including, for example, the pollution of drinking water sources for more than ten million people.[27]

Each conflict, as seen above, presents different consequences and challenges to sustainable development. The questions that arise are: do the laws of IHL protect the environment sufficiently to avoid or mitigate such negative consequences (both environmentally and to the disruption to sustainable development as a whole), and, if not, can the concept of sustainable development be used to fill the gaps in the existing legal regime? To explore these questions, the following sections review the concept of sustainable development and the existing laws that protect (or not) the environment during times of armed conflict.

3. Sustainable Development – An Overarching Concept

Sustainable development is an evolving concept,[28] having developed from the 1972 Stockholm Conference on the Human Environment[29] to the recent 2012 UN Conference on Sustainable Development (Rio + 20).[30] It is a widely accepted concept,[31] being cited and used globally as an objective to achieve or as a guideline to govern both domestic and international issues.

The concept of sustainable development requires that for development to be sustainable, the three pillars of economic, social and environmental interests must be integrated.[32] As Dernbach points out in an argument central to present concerns, "[s]ustainable development redefines progress to include environmental protection or restoration as something to be achieved along with other goals, not something to be sacrificed in order to reach these goals".[33] Thus, sustainable development and protecting the environment should not be sacrificed in times of armed conflict.

26 *Ibid.*, *see* summary.

27 *Ibid.*, para. 21.

28 *See e.g.* N. Schrijver, *The Evolution of Sustainable Development in International Law: Inception, Meaning and Status* (Martinus Nijhoff, Leiden, 2008). *See also* Eartsummit2012, 'SustainableDevelopment Timeline', <www.earthsummit2012.org/about-us/sd-timeline>, visited on 21 June 2012.

29 UNEP, *Report of the UN Conference on the Human Environment*, Stockholm, 5–16 June 1972, UN Doc. A/CONF.48/14/Rev.1.

30 UNSCD, *Rio + 20 UN Conference on Sustainable Development*, 20–22 June 2012, UN Doc. A/CONF.216/L.1.

31 M. W. Gehring and M.-C. Cordonier Segger (eds.), *Sustainable Development in World Trade Law* (Kluwer Law, The Netherlands, 2005) p. 4.

32 *See e.g.* World Bank, *Inclusive Green Growth: The Pathway to Sustainable Development* (World Bank, Washington, DC, 2012) p. 2.

33 J.C. Dernbach, 'Achieving Sustainable Development: The Centrality and Multiple Facets of Integrated Decision-making', 10 *Indiana Journal of Global Legal Studies* (2003) p. 247.

3.1. *Concept of Sustainable Development: Definition and Elements*

There has been considerable debate about the definition of sustainable development. However there is still no general agreement as to its exact meaning because "[f]inding one accepted, universal definition of sustainable development that is appropriate for all cultures and regions of the world is not straightforward".[34] Nevertheless, to reiterate, the Brundtland Commission's definition that sustainable development is "development that meets the needs of the present without compromising the ability of future generations to meet their own needs"[35] is the most generally accepted and widely used. The Brundtland definition has, however, been criticised as being too vague and lacking in substantive meaning.[36] Nevertheless, as Reid argues, "despite its vagueness – indeed perhaps because of it – the Brundtland definition makes an important statement ... [I]t has more of the character of a moral principle than a precise definition."[37] It is argued that its vagueness in itself enables this definition to be used as a guiding principle for sustainable development in differing circumstances, without it being so hopelessly vague that it cannot guide decision-making in these various contexts.

Scholars have varying views on the components or principles that make up the concept of sustainable development. Sands, for example, argues that as a principle of international law, sustainable development requires recognition of inter- and intra-generational equity; sustainable use of natural resources; common but differentiated environmental responsibilities; and the integration of environmental decision-making.[38] Magraw and Hawke indicate four components of sustainable development: intergenerational equity; intragenerational equity; environmental protection; and the integration of economic, social and environmental interests.[39] The 2002 New Delhi Declaration of Principles of International

---

34 M-C. Cordonier Segger, 'The Role of International Forums in the Advancement of Sustainable Development', 10 *Sustainable Development Law & Policy* (2009) p. 4.

35 Our Common Future, *supra* note 3.

36 *See e.g.* K. Morgan, 'The Green State: Sustainability and the power of purchase', in A. Pike *et al.* (eds.), *Handbook of Local and Regional Development* (Routledge, Oxon, 2011) p. 88; D. French, *International Law and Policy of Sustainable Development* (MUP, Manchester, 2005) p. 16.

37 D. Reid, *Sustainable Development – An Introductory Guide* (Earthscan, London, 1995) p. xvi. *See also* Morgan, *ibid.* (referencing Meadowcroft, argues that the Brundtland definition is in essence "a normative standard that serves as a meta-objective for policy").

38 P. Sands, 'Environmental Protection in the Twenty-First Century: Sustainable Development and International Law', in R. L. Revesz *et al.* (eds.), *Environmental Law, the Economy and Sustainable Development* (CUP, Cambridge, 2000) pp. 369–379.

39 D. B. Magraw and L. D. Hawke, 'Sustainable Development', in D. Bodansky *et al.* (eds.), *Oxford Handbook of International Environmental Law* (OUP, Oxford, 2007) pp. 613–638.

Law Relating to Sustainable Development[40] (New Delhi Declaration) formulated seven core principles[41] that come under the overarching concept of sustainable development: duty of states to ensure sustainable use of natural resources; equity and the eradication of poverty; common but differentiated responsibilities; precautionary approach to human health, natural resources and ecosystems; participation and access to information and justice; good governance; and integration and interrelationship.

It is argued that the New Delhi Declaration still remains one of the high watermarks in the general development of the concept of sustainable development as it provides a framework of principles which could be used as a set of guidelines with which to pursue sustainable development. As the preamble to the New Delhi Declaration states, "the application and, where relevant, consolidation and further development of the [New Delhi] principles of international law relevant to the activities of all actors involved would be instrumental in pursuing the objective of sustainable development in an effective way".[42] The relevant principles within the structure of the concept provided by the New Delhi Declaration thus provide the framework for the present discussion.

3.2. *Sustainable Development: Legal Significance*

The concept and principle of sustainable development is reflected and endorsed in various international instruments:[43] from the 1987 Brundtland Report,[44] 1992 Rio Declaration[45] including its programme of action, Agenda 21, the 2002 World

40 International Law Association (ILA), 'New Delhi Declaration of Principles of International Law Relating to Sustainable Development, 2 April 2002', 2 *International Environmental Agreements: Politics, Law and Economics* (2002) p. 211: (Preamble).

41 ILA, *Report of the Seventieth Conference, New Delhi* (New Delhi, 2002) pp. 861–862 (citing Schrijver: "The body of the Declaration contained in the Report did not claim to be exhaustive").

42 Preamble, New Delhi Declaration, *supra* note 40. The ILA's International Law on Sustainable Development Committee's work continues, *see* ILA website <www.ila-hq.org/en/committees/ index.cfm/cid/1017>, visited on 28 June 2012.

43 *See* Schrijver, *supra* note 28, pp. 102–141: referencing *e.g.* UN Framework Convention on Climate Change (UNFCCC) (1992) 31 *ILM* 851; UN Convention on Biological Diversity (UNCBD) (1992) 31 *ILM* 822; UN Convention to Combat Desertification in Those Countries Experiencing Serious Drought and/or Desertification, particularly in Africa (UNCCD) (1994) 33 *ILM* 1328. *See also* P. Sands *et al.*, *Principles of International Environmental Law*, 3rd edition (CUP, Cambridge, 2012) p. 207: referencing *e.g.* 2002 North-East Pacific Convention; 2006 International Tropical Timber Agreement; 2009 Agreement on Port State Measures to Prevent, Deter and Eliminate Illegal, Unreported and Unregulated Fishing.

44 Our Common Future, *supra* note 3.

45 Rio Declaration, *supra* note 2.

Summit on Sustainable Development's (WSSD) Johannesburg Declaration[46] and its associated Plan of Implementation,[47] to the most recent outcome of the Rio + 20 Summit: "The Future We Want".[48] As Schrijver notes, "[n]owadays, the concept of sustainable development can be found in international instruments covering various issue-areas and is solidly embedded in treaty practice".[49]

The concept and principle of sustainable development has also been supported, directly and indirectly, by international courts and tribunals.[50] In *Gabčikovo Nagymaros*[51] the International Court of Justice (ICJ) acknowledged that "[t]his need to reconcile development with protection of the environment is aptly expressed in the concept of sustainable development".[52] The General Agreement on Tariffs and Trade (GATT)/World Trade Organization (WTO) Panel in *Shrimp/Turtle*[53] noted that the Preamble of the WTO Agreement expressly recognises the "objective of sustainable development".[54] The Panel also concluded that sustainable development integrates economic, social development and environmental protection issues.[55] Further examples of cases that reference sustainable development are the 2005 *Iron Rhine* case[56] and the more recent *Pulp Mills* case.[57]

Although sustainable development is reflected in various international documents and jurisprudence, its legal status remains uncertain.[58] Despite its indeterminate legal status, it is argued that sustainable development is a concept

46 UN, *Report of the World Summit on Sustainable Development*, Johannesburg, South Africa, 26 August–4 September 2002, UN Doc. A/CONF.199/20.

47 *Ibid.*, p. 6.

48 Rio + 20, *supra* note 30.

49 Schrijver, *supra* note 28, p. 104.

50 *Ibid.*, pp. 141–153 (on sustainable development in international jurisprudence).

51 *Case Concerning the Gabčikovo-Nagymaros Project (Hungary/Slovakia)*, 25 September 1997, ICJ, Judgment, *I.C. J. Reports 1997*, p. 7, <www.icj-cij.org/docket/files/92/7375.pdf>, visited on 2 July 2012.

52 *Ibid.*, p. 78, para. 140.

53 *United States – Import Prohibition of Certain Shrimp and Shrimp Products*, 12 October 1998, WTO, Appellate Body Report, <www.wto.org/english/tratop_e/dispu_e/cases_e/ds58_e.htm>, visited on 2 July 2012.

54 *Ibid.*, para. 129.

55 *Ibid.*

56 *Iron Rhine ("Ijzeren Rihn") Railway Arbitration (Belgium* v. *Netherlands)*, 24 May 2005, Award of the Arbitral Tribunal, pp. 28–29, <www.pca-cpa.org/showpage.asp?pag_id=1155>, visited on 2 July 2012.

57 *Case Concerning Pulp Mills on the River Uruguay* (*Argentina* v. *Uruguay*), 20 April 2010, I.C.J. Judgment, *ICJ Reports 2010*, p. 52, para. 171; p. 52, paras. 175–177; and pp. 55–56, paras. 184–189, <www.icj-cij.org/docket/files/135/15877.pdf/>, visited on 2 July 2012.

58 French, *supra* note 36, p. 36.

with significant legal effect.[59] The concept or term 'sustainable development' continues to be widely used, categorised as a 'soft-law'[60] principle and concept that has gained "worldwide currency as a desirable objective for the management of global natural resources".[61]

3.3. Sustainable Development – An Overarching Concept: A Framework of Guiding Principles

It is submitted that the principles best used as a framework of guidance in which to achieve or contribute to sustainable development are the core principles stemming from the New Delhi Declaration.[62] As the concern here is protection of the environment in armed conflict, this study makes reference only to those principles which are most pertinent to the present topic: equity, precaution and integration.

The principle of equity "refers to both *inter-generational equity* (the right of future generations to enjoy a fair level of common patrimony) and *intra-generational equity* (the right of all peoples within the current generation of fair access to the current generation's entitlement to the Earth's natural resources)".[63] Simply put, this principle calls for States to endorse fair and equitable utilisation of resources amongst the population of the present generation as well as taking into account the rights of future generations in relation to those resources. This principle, or elements of it, can be seen in various international documents relevant to sustainable development,[64] as well as in case-law.[65] At present this principle is

59 *Ibid.*

60 J. Stanton, 'Sustainable Development of Genetically Modified Organisms', 10 *New Zealand Journal of Environmental Law* (2006) p. 7.

61 V. Nanda, 'International Environmental Protection and Developing Countries' Interests: The Role of International Law', 26 *Texas International Law Journal* (1991) p. 498.

62 New Delhi Declaration, *supra* note 40.

63 Principle 2.1, *ibid.*

64 *See e.g.* Articles 3 and 5, Rio Declaration, *supra* note 2; Preamble and Article 3(1), UNFCCC, *supra* note 43; Article 2(1), UNCCD, *supra* note 43; Preamble and Article 15(7), UNCBD, *supra* note 43.

65 *See e.g. Minors Oposa v. Secretary of the Department of Environment and Natural Resources (DENR)*, 30 July 1993, Supreme Court of the Philippines, (1994) 33 *ILM* 173, p. 185; *Request for an Examination of the Situation in Accordance with Paragraph 63 of the Court's Judgement of 20 December 1974 in the Nuclear Tests (New Zealand v. France)*, 22 September 1995, ICJ, Order, p. 341 (Dissenting Opinion of Judge Weeramantry), <www.icj-cij.org/docket/files/97/7567.pdf>, visited on 2 July 2012; *Legality of the Threat or Use of Nuclear Weapons*, 8 July 1996, ICJ, Advisory Opinion, General List No. 95, para. 29, <www.icj-cij.org/docket/files/95/7495.pdf>, visited on 2 July 2012 (ICJ recognised that 'quality of life' in relation to the environment also affected 'generations unborn').

not yet entrenched within customary international law "due in part to difficulties in identifying with certainty the needs of future generations, and the lack of consensus between States on the obligation to ensure distributional justice between States".[66] Nevertheless, regardless of its normative status, the equity principle is being increasingly reflected in multilateral declarations, treaties and judicial decisions relevant to sustainable development. This is evidence of not only the international community's growing commitment to it but also that this principle is an important objective or guidance tool for States and the international community in striving for sustainable development.[67]

The precautionary principle is based on the idea that it is preferable to prevent damage or destruction to the environment even in light of scientific uncertainty, rather than dealing with the damage or pollution after it has occurred.[68] Various international environmental instruments[69] have increasingly begun to refer to the 'precautionary principle,'[70] 'precautionary approach'[71] or 'principle of precautionary action'[72] when faced with various national, regional and international environmental problems. The precautionary principle is also reflected in case-law.[73] With regard to its legal status, opinion in the field is divided. Some scholars consider there to be sufficient evidence that the precautionary principle is part of customary international law.[74] Others argue that, at the very least, this principle is an emerging or evolving norm of customary international law.[75] Schrijver, for example, doubts whether it has reached customary status due to divided academic opinion and lack of judicial declaration as to the principle's legal

66 M.-C. Cordonier Segger and A. Khalfan, *Sustainable Development and Law: Principles and Practices & Prospects* (OUP, Oxford, 2004) p. 132.

67 *See e.g.* Schrijver, *supra* note 28, pp. 175–178; French, *supra* note 36, pp. 59–67 (on this principle relevant to sustainable development).

68 Principle 4, New Delhi Declaration, *supra* note 40.

69 *See e.g.* Article 3(3), UNFCCC, *supra* note 43; Preamble, Article 8(g) and Article 14, UNCBD, *supra* note 43.

70 Article 2(5)(a), Convention on the Protection and Use of Transboundary Watercourses and International Lakes, (1992) 31 *ILM* 1312.

71 Principle 15, Rio Declaration, *supra* note 2.

72 *See* UNEP, *Report of the Governing Council on the Work of Its Fifteenth Session*, 25 May 1989, UN Doc. A/44/25.

73 *See e.g. Nuclear Tests* case, *supra* note 65, p. 290, para. 5; *Gabćikovo-Nagymaros* case, *supra* note 51, p. 68, para. 97; *The Mox Plant Case (Ireland* v. *UK)*, 2 December 2001, ITLOS, Request for Provisional Measures (Order), (2002) 41 *ILM* p. 405. For review of cases, *see* Sands, *supra* note 43, pp. 224–228.

74 *See* A. Trouwborst, 'The Precautionary Principle in General International Law: Combating the Babylonian Confusion', 16 *Review of European Community & International Environmental Law* (2007) p. 185 (on precautionary principle as a customary norm).

75 Cordonier Segger and Khalfan, *supra* note 66, p. 155.

status.[76] Ultimately however, the exact legal status of this principle is less relevant as it continues to be widely used in treaty law.[77] Thus, as such the precautionary principle is a crucial and operational tool for the achievement of sustainable development, particularly to avoid undue damage to the environment as a result of unknown scientific risks.

The principle of integration, according to Cordonier Segger and Newcombe, "is a bedrock principle of sustainable development".[78] It reflects the interdependence of and interrelationship between various aspects (*e.g.* economic, financial, social, environmental, and human rights) of rules and principles of international law relating to sustainable development including consideration of the needs of current and future generations.[79] The integration of environmental protection with economic and social development makes this principle a crucial aspect of sustainable development, notwithstanding the considerable *prima facie* relevance to issues relating to armed conflict. This salient principle is reflected in a myriad of declarations, treaties and conventions[80] as well as being referred to in case-law.[81] Although the integration principle is not a customary norm, it "remains both the principle tool to achieve sustainable development"[82] as well as being "the most practicable legal principle in the area".[83]

Cordonier Segger and Khalfan conclude that the New Delhi Declaration principles in most cases "are as yet emerging principles of international law".[84] Nevertheless, these principles (equity, precaution and integration) have gained some degree of international recognition. Regardless of their legal status, these three principles are an important part of the concept of sustainable development and provide helpful objectives in order to achieve it. It is thus submitted that these principles could also be used in the context of protecting the environment during

76 Schrijver, *supra* note 28, p. 194. *See also* P. Birnie and A. Boyle, *International Law and the Environment*, 2nd ed. (OUP, Oxford, 2002) pp. 119–120.

77 *See e.g.* Sands, *supra* note 43, pp. 217–223 (on its reflection in treaty law).

78 M.-C. Cordonier Segger and A. Newcombe, 'An Integrated Agenda for Sustainable Development in International Investment Law', in M.-C. Cordonier Segger *et al.* (eds.), *Sustainable Development in World Investment Law* (Kluwer Law, The Netherlands, 2011) p. 124.

79 *See* Principle 7.1, New Delhi Declaration, *supra* note 40.

80 *See e.g.* Principle 4, Rio Declaration, *supra* note 2: "to achieve sustainable development, environmental protection shall constitute an integral part of the development process and cannot be considered in isolation for it"; Preamble, UNFCCC, *supra* note 43; Article 6(b), UNCBD, *supra* note 43; Articles 2(1) and 2(2), UNCCD, *supra* note 43.

81 *See e.g. Gabčíkovo-Nagymaros*, *supra* note 51, p. 90 (Separate Opinion of Vice-President Weeramantry); *Iron Rhine*, *supra* note 56, p. 59.

82 French, *supra* note 36, p. 57.

83 *Ibid. See also* Sands, *supra* note 43, pp. 215–217.

84 Cordonier Segger and Khalfan, *supra* note 66, p. 171.

armed conflict. In practical terms, this would mean that belligerents would have to use or keep some element of these principles in mind when planning their military strategy or weighing targeting decisions in order to avoid environmental damage that could unduly obstruct sustainable development. How and where these principles of sustainable development could be integrated into protecting the environment during armed conflict is discussed further in section 5 below. Prior to that the following section briefly reviews the existing laws of IHL that provide protection to the environment during armed conflict.

4. Environmental Protection during Armed Conflict – Relevant Rules and Principles of International Humanitarian Law

There is little specific legal protection for the environment during times of warfare.[85] However, a number of treaty provisions and customary principles converge in this field, and it is argued that these embrace a broad range of threats to the environment arising from armed conflict. This section thus briefly explores the adequacy (or not) of the relevant rules and principles of IHL that afford, direct or indirect, protection to the environment during armed conflict.

4.1. *Laws Relating to Environmental Protection in Times of Armed Conflict: An Overview*

4.1.1. International Armed Conflict (IAC)

With regard to IACs, the Convention on the Prohibition of Military or Any Other Hostile Use of Environmental Modification Techniques (ENMOD)[86] and two provisions within the 1977 Protocol Additional to the Geneva Conventions of 12 August 1949 relating to the Protection of Victims of International Armed Conflicts (AP I)[87] were expressly formulated to protect the environment during armed conflict.

ENMOD does not specifically deal with damage to the environment during armed conflict, but with protecting the environment from being used as a weapon by prohibiting military or any other hostile use of "environmental modi-

85 M. N. Schmitt, 'War and the Environment: Fault Lines in the Prescriptive Landscape', in J. E. Austin and C. E. Bruch (eds.), *The Environmental Consequences of War: Legal, Economic, and Scientific Perspectives* (CUP, Cambridge, 2000) p. 92. However, the International Law Commission (ILC) has formulated draft articles and an annex indicating that peacetime treaties may continue to operate during armed conflict, including treaties protecting the environment. *See* UN, *Report of the International Law Commission*, Sixty-Third Session, 26 April–3 June and 4 July–12 August 2011, UN Doc. A /66/10, pp. 173–217 and pp. 351–368.

86 (1976) 167 *ILM* 88.

87 (1977) 1125 *UNTS* 3.

fication techniques[88] having widespread, long-lasting or severe effects as a means of destruction, damage or injury to any other State Party".[89] Thus, ENMOD has a threshold, becoming applicable only if the environment is manipulated causing either widespread, long-lasting *or* severe effects, in the alternative.[90] This means that acts manipulating the environment can only be considered unlawful if the environmental damage encompasses several hundred square kilometres, lasts over a period of months (approximately a season) or involves "serious or significant disruption or harm to human life, natural and economic resources or other assets".[91]

By contrast, Articles 35(3) and 55[92] of AP I deal specifically with damage to the natural environment. Article 35(3) prohibits the employment of "methods and means of warfare which are intended, or may be expected, to cause widespread, long-term and severe damage to the natural environment". The prohibition in Article 35(3) is absolute and "continues to apply in the absence of any direct threat to the population or to the flora and fauna of the enemy State. It is the natural environment itself that is protected."[93]

Similarly, Article 55 refers specifically to environmental damage but with a further anthropocentric link. Article 55(1) provides that "[c]are shall be taken in warfare to protect the natural environment against widespread, long-term and severe damage. This protection includes a prohibition of the use of methods or means of warfare which are intended or may be expected, to cause such damage to the natural environment and thereby to prejudice the health or survival of the population". Article 55(2) goes on to prohibit "[a]ttacks against the natural environment by way of reprisals".

Although these AP I provisions theoretically afford specific protection to the environment during armed conflict, environmental protection and ultimately sustainable development are obstructed by the stringent criteria set out in Articles 35(3) and 55. Unfortunately, for any environmental damage to be prohibited, the damage must reach the high triple threshold criteria of AP I: 'wide-

---

88 Techniques that change "through the deliberate manipulation of natural processes – the dynamics, composition or structure of the Earth, including its biota, lithosphere, hydrosphere and atmosphere, or of outer space". *See* Article II, ENMOD, *supra* note 86. For types of phenomena that could be caused by environmental modification techniques, *see* Understanding to Article II, ENMOD.

89 Article 1, ENMOD, *ibid.*

90 *Ibid.*

91 *See* Understanding to ENMOD, *ibid.*

92 These two provisions are complementary. *See* Y. Sandoz *et al.* (eds.), *Commentary on the Protocol Additional to the Geneva Conventions of 12 August 1949, and relating to the Protection of Victims of International Armed Conflicts (Protocol I)* (Martinus Nijhoff, Geneva, 1987) pp. 389–420 (Article 35 commentary) and pp. 661–664 (Article 55 commentary).

93 *Ibid.*, p. 420.

spread, long-term *and* severe' cumulatively,[94] thus making these provisions difficult to apply in practice.[95]

It is also worth noting that despite ENMOD and AP I providing the most direct environmental protection in armed conflict, not all States are contracting parties. It is therefore necessary to consider other means to bind those parties, either via other warfare conventions or via provisions which may be used to indirectly protect the environment during armed conflict. This is where the relevant provisions within the Hague Regulations of 1899[96] and 1907[97] and the fourth Geneva Convention (GC) of 1949[98] and customary IHL come in. Both the Hague and Geneva Conventions are part of customary international law and, accordingly, binding on all States.[99]

The Hague Regulations do not expressly protect the environment in armed conflict. However, they contain provisions that limit the means and methods of warfare,[100] resulting in indirect environmental protection. Article 23(g) of Hague IV, for example, prohibits the destruction or seizure of enemy property "unless such destruction or seizure be imperatively demanded by the necessities of war".[101] This limits the damage to property of the conflict-State and could further prevent or minimise potential environmental harm that may be caused by such destruction or seizure.[102] Article 55 of Hague IV provides that the occupying State may use and benefit from public property as well as reasonably exploit natural resources in the occupied territory. This provision thus requires the occupier to act

94 Scholars maintain this threshold criteria is open to interpretation. 'Long-term' is interpreted as a period of decades but thus far, there is no agreement on the interpretation of 'widespread' and 'severe'. *See* Sandoz, *supra* note 92, p. 417.

95 It appears the authors of AP I did not intend "acts of warfare which cause short-term damage to the natural environment" and "battlefield damage incidental to conventional warfare" to be normally prohibited by these provisions. The Article "is primarily directed to … such damage as would be likely to prejudice, over a long term, the continued survival ofthe civilian population or would risk causing major health problems". *See* Sandoz, *supra* note 92, p. 417.

96 Hague Convention (II) with Respect to the Laws and Customs of War on Land (29 July 1899) 32 Stat 1803.

97 Hague Convention (IV) Respecting the Laws and Customs of War on Land (18 October 1907) 36 Stat 2277.

98 Geneva Convention (IV) Relative to the Protection of Civilian Persons in Time of War (12 August 1949) 75 *UNTS* 287.

99 M. N. Schmitt, *Essays on Law and War at the Fault Lines* (TMC Asser, The Netherlands, 2012) pp. 303 and 430.

100 Article 22, Hague II; Article 22, Hague IV.

101 Article 23(g), Hague IV.

102 UNEP, *supra* note 1, p. 16 (enemy property "could include protected areas, environmental goods and natural resources").

as administrator and safeguard these resources but prohibits the occupier from permanently destroying or altering them.[103]

One of the key provisions of GC IV that provide some form of environmental protection is Article 53, which prohibits the occupying power from destroying real or personal property except when militarily necessary.[104] Although this provision is limited to destruction by an occupying State subject to military necessity, it does offer some scope for environmental protection particularly since environmental damage often occurs in such circumstances.[105]

Provisions that indirectly touch on the protection of the environment in times of armed conflict are also provided by API. In particular, Article 54 prohibits combatants from destroying the civilian population's means of survival, namely foodstuffs, agricultural areas and irrigation works, subject to these objects being used in direct support of the enemy forces. Article 56 deals with the danger to the environment as a consequence of destroying dams, dykes or nuclear power stations. Article 52 provides general protection of civilian objects and Article 57 requires precaution in attacks during military operations, both of which have an indirect bearing on environmental protection. Ultimately, these provisions that afford some protection for the human population and the environment may contribute to alleviating the impact of warfare on the environment and mitigating the obstruction to sustainable development.

Limits to the means and methods of warfare and as a result some form of environmental protection are also provided by the customary principles of warfare: humanity, discrimination, distinction, proportionality and military necessity.[106] These principles are applicable throughout an armed conflict whether it be international or non-international.

The principle of humanity dictates that the infliction of superfluous and unnecessary suffering, injury or destruction causing harm not actually necessary for the achievement of legitimate military objectives should be avoided.[107] This could also be interpreted to include a duty to ensure that war-related envi-

---

103 Article 55, Hague II; Article 55, Hague IV. *See also* 2000 Schmitt, *supra* note 85, p. 95.

104 Provides similar scope of protection to property as Article 55, Hague IV.

105 This can occur when an occupying army retreats from the occupied territory. *See* e.g. *US* v. *List* (*The 'Hostages Case'*) (1949) 11 CCL No. 10 Trials 1230, pp. 1295–1297 (retreating German army adopted scorched earth tactics in Norway and Finland). *See* 'ICRC Commentary (Art. 53, GC IV)', <www.icrc.org/ihl.nsf/1a13044f3bbb5b8ec12563fb0066f226/a13817cda3424c3cc12563cd0042c6e6!OpenDocument>, visited on 2 July 2012 (on scope of property protected by Article 53).

106 For affirmation of their customary status, *see* J.-M. Henckaerts and L. Doswald-Beck, *Customary International Humanitarian Law: Volume I: Rules* (CUP, New York, 2005).

107 Principle of humanity is set out as the 'laws of humanity' within the 1899 Martens Clause.

ronmental damage should not be caused to the extent that it causes unnecessary suffering to the human population.[108]

The principle of distinction imposes upon combatants the legal obligation to distinguish between combatants and civilians and between military objectives and civilian objects.[109] This principle also incorporates the principle of discrimination which specifies that only legitimate military objectives[110] must be targeted.[111] In an environmental context, this would include civilian targets that are environmental in nature or civilian targets (*e.g.* chemical factory) which, if damaged or destroyed, could cause harm to the environment. In essence, the principle of discrimination provides that care must be taken in selecting means and methods of warfare and military targets.[112]

The principle of proportionality sets crucial limits on warfare, requiring that the level of force employed by combatants in armed conflict be proportionate and not excessive to the military objective for which use of force is necessary.[113] This principle could equally apply to any environmentally-related military objective or any military objective where the use of force may cause disproportionate damage to the environment.[114] All four customary principles are of course subject to the principle of military necessity.

Military necessity is a subjective doctrine which provides that a combatant is justified in applying any force necessary to secure the complete surrender of an adversary as soon as possible, as long as the means are not prohibited by the law of war provisions.[115] In an environmental context, any military target or means and methods of warfare, whether it is an environmental target or means and

108 M. N. Schmitt, 'Green War: An Assessment of the Environmental Law of International Armed Conflict', 22 *Yale Journal of International Law* (1997) pp. 61–62 (on applicability of this principle to the environment).

109 This customary principle is reaffirmed in Article 48, AP I and in *Nuclear Weapons* case, *supra* note 65, p. 257, para. 78.

110 Article 52(2), AP I: "military objectives are limited to those objects which by their nature, location, purpose or use make an effective contribution to military action and whose total or partial destruction, capture or neutralization, in the circumstances ruling at the time, offers a definite military advantage".

111 Article 48, AP I.

112 A. Roberts, 'The Law of War and Environmental Damage', in Austin and Bruch, *supra* note 85, p. 50.

113 Although the term 'proportionality' does not expressly appear in any IHL treaty, it has an established place within the laws of war. The essence of this principle can be found in Articles 51(5)(b) and 57(2), AP I.

114 *See* Schmitt, *supra* note 108, pp. 55–61 (on applicability of this principle to the environment).

115 M. J. T. Caggiano, 'The Legitimacy of Environmental Destruction in Modern Warfare: Customary Substance Over Conventional Form', 20 *Boston College Environmental Affairs Law Review* (1993) p. 485.

methods that may affect the environment, will be subject to this principle.[116] As military necessity is the reasonable assessment or judgement of a military strategist or commander in the heat of battle,[117] reliance on this provision for protection of the environment is subjective.[118]

4.1.2. Non-International Armed Conflict (NIAC)

Although there are few IHL laws that protect the environment during IACs, there are even fewer IHL rules that do so in NIACs.[119] Protection afforded by Article 3 common to the four Geneva Conventions of 1949 is purely humanitarian and makes no mention of protecting specific objects or the environment during NIAC.[120] Indirect environmental protection in NIACs is only provided by the customary principles of humanity, discrimination, distinction, proportionality and military necessity which are applicable in IACs and NIACS, as well as a few provisions within 1977 Protocol Additional to the Geneva Conventions of 12 August 1949 relating to the Protection of Victims of Non-International Armed Conflicts (AP II).[121]

Articles 14 and 15 of AP II, being very similar in scope to Articles 52, 54 and 56 of AP I for example, anthropocentrically provide some form of protection to the environment during NIACs. Article 14, protecting objects indispensable to the survival of the civilian population (*e.g.* food, food-producing agricultural areas, crops, livestock, irrigation works, drinking water installations and supplies), indirectly protects water resources and the agricultural environment. Indirect environmental protection is also provided by Article 15 which protects "works and installations containing dangerous forces, namely dams, dykes and nuclear

---

116 Schmitt, *supra* note 108, pp. 52–55 (on applicability of this principle to the environment).

117 Caggiano, *supra* note 115, p. 497.

118 *See The Hostages* case, *supra* note 105, pp. 1295–1297: concluding that "although, in retrospect, [the German] General Rendulic may have erred in his assessment of military necessity, he was not guilty of a criminal act because the doctrine of military necessity may be justified by one's reasonable assessment of the situation".

119 UNEP, *supra* note 1, p. 28. *See also* International Committee of the Red Cross (ICRC), *Guidelines for Military Manuals and Instructions on the Protection of the Environment in Times of Armed Conflict* (ICRC, Geneva, 1993) paras. 4 and 6: parties to NIACs "are encouraged to apply the same rules that provide protection to the environment in international armed conflict and, accordingly, States are urged to incorporate such rules in their military manuals and instructions on the law of war".

120 ICRC, 'International Humanitarian Law and Sustainable Development' (26 August 2002), Information Paper prepared by the ICRC in the framework of the WSSD, Johannesburg, 26 August–4 September, 2001, <www.icrc.org/eng/resources/documents/misc/5dddem.htm>, visited on 3 July 2012.

121 (8 June 1977) 1125 *UNTS* 609.

electrical generating stations", by prohibiting attacks on these installations even where these are military objectives, if such attacks may cause the release of dangerous forces and consequently cause severe losses among the civilian population.

Thus, if respected by belligerents, these provisions within AP II and the relevant customary principles do afford some protection to the environment during NIACs. However, bearing in mind that most contemporary armed conflicts are internal in nature, the scope of protection for NIACs provided by the existing IHL regime is comparatively limited.[122]

4.2. Adequacy (or Not) of IHL Environmental Protection during Armed Conflict?

The relevant rules and principles within IHL as a whole do theoretically protect the environment during armed conflict to some extent and, from a sustainable development perspective, some of these laws do highlight the need to weigh the immediate and long-term effects[123] of any methods and means of warfare. Thus, such protection could, if respected, lessen the negative impact on the already vulnerable civilian population, the environment and the conflict-State as a whole. Nevertheless, there are flaws in the existing laws of warfare providing environmental protection.

First, the laws designed to specifically protect the environment, Articles 35(3) and 55 of AP I, are stringent and ambiguous in their scope for application, making them difficult to apply in practice.[124] Second, all relevant IHL laws protecting the environment have to be balanced with the subjective principle of military necessity.[125] Third, not all States are parties to the relevant conventions or protocols that protect the environment during armed conflict.[126] Fourth, as discussed above, most of the IHL environmental provisions only apply to IACs, leaving a gap in laws protecting the environment during NIACs[127] and, to complicate matters further, some modern conflicts have both international and non-international characteristics.[128] The clear divide of IHL protection during IACs and NIACs

122 UNEP, *supra* note 1, p. 28.

123 *See e.g.* ENMOD, *supra* note 86; Articles 35(3) and 55, API, *supra* note 87.

124 J.-M. Henckaerts and L. Doswald-Beck (eds.), *Customary International Humanitarian Law: Volume II: Practice* (CUP, Cambridge, 2005) p. 901.

125 K. Hulme, 'Environmental Protection in Armed Conflict', in M. Fitzmaurice *et al.* (eds.), *Research Handbook of International Environmental Law* (Edward Elgar, UK, 2010) p. 586.

126 Henckaerts, *supra* note 106, p. xxviii (for AP I and AP II); 2012 Schmitt, *supra* note 99, p. 448 (for ENMOD).

127 UNEP, *supra* note 1, p. 10.

128 J. K. Kleffner, 'Human Rights and International Humanitarian Law: General Issues', in T. D. Gill and D. Fleck (eds.), *The Handbook of The International Law of Military*

makes it difficult to ascertain which set of IHL rules apply to these contemporary 'hybrid' or transnational armed conflicts.[129] Finally, the existing laws of armed conflict protecting the environment do not have elements of or objectives relating to sustainable development within the relevant provisions. In light of increasing consciousness within the international community of the need to protect the environment as well as to achieve sustainable development, it is suggested that the existing laws of armed conflict should be updated to include sustainable development objectives (*e.g.* principles of equity, precaution and integration). Moreover, with weapons and tactics of warfare becoming ever more sophisticated, virulent and devastating, negatively affecting not only the human population but also the environment, there is a need to take a closer look at the existing laws protecting the environment in armed conflict.

5. The Way Forward: Sustainable Development and Environmental Protection during Armed Conflict

There is, as mentioned above, a body of treaty law which, whether directly or indirectly, provides protection to the environment during armed conflict. However, it is arguable that the existing laws have not kept pace with the times. As the world faces increasing environmental threats and challenges, from climate change and biodiversity loss to a rapidly growing population and rising scarcity in environmental resources, society cannot afford the added pressures of extensive environmental damage during armed conflict. The natural environment which has taken years to grow or accumulate and which is often sustained by peacetime conservation efforts can be destroyed within a matter of hours or days during warfare.

The key to the interrelationship between sustainable development and armed conflict is to ensure that any damage to the environment is not so extensive or severe that sustainable development is unduly obstructed or interrupted. This means efforts should be made to prevent or mitigate environmental risks as a result of war-related damage. Damage, which in combination with the breakdown of socio-economic, governance and development conditions, could threaten the livelihoods, health and security of the population and ultimately sustainable development of the war-torn State. Conflict-related environmental damage for example could have a direct impact on the livelihoods of a war-torn population by negatively affecting their access to the environment and natural resources as a result of pollution, loss of biodiversity and displacement of the population itself, thereby triggering the vicious cycle of environmental degradation and human vulnerability.[130]

Operations (OUP, New York, 2010) p. 58.

129 *Ibid.*, p. 59.

130 P. Saundry, 'Environmental Justice: Environmental and Socioeconomic Impacts of Armed Conflict in Africa', in C. J. Cleveland (ed.), *The Encyclopedia of Earth* (National Council for Science and the Environment, Washington, DC, 2008).

Therefore, in respect of these potential obstacles to sustainable development, the rules and principles of IHL which protect the environment during actual armed conflict play a crucial role. However, as noted above, the IHL laws protecting the environment in armed conflict are not easy to apply in practice; the specific or high thresholds and the convenient loophole of military necessity do not always protect the environment. It is thus argued that the existing body of IHL laws protecting the environment would benefit from the integration of sustainable development and its relevant substantive principles. The questions of why these sustainable development principles are relevant during armed conflict and how they could be possibly be used are discussed below.

5.1. Applicability of Sustainable Development Principles in Armed Conflict

As the UN Secretary-General comments,

> it is not easy to know in advance exactly what the scope and duration of some environmentally damaging acts will be; and there is a need to limit as far as possible environmental damage even in cases where it is not certain to meet a strict interpretation of the criteria of "widespread, long-term and severe".[131]

Thus, the precautionary principle for example is relevant during armed conflict because the risks and consequences of causing damage to the environment as a result of warfare tactics could include scientifically unknown long-term or irreversible harm. The uncertainty of the impact on the environment makes this principle crucial. In this context, the precautionary principle should not only be taken into account during times of armed conflict, but also in the application of the relevant rules and principles of IHL "since the duty to prevent environmental damage is not suspended by the outbreak of hostilities".[132] This argument is echoed by Henckaerts and Doswald-Beck that "[t]here is practice to the effect that lack of scientific certainty as to the effects on the environment of certain military operations does not absolve parties to a conflict from taking proper precautionary measures to prevent undue damage".[133] They thus argue that the precautionary principle is applicable to armed conflict.[134]

---

131 UN General Assembly, *Report of the Secretary-General on the Protection of the Environment in Times of Armed Conflict*, 29 July 1993, UN Doc. A/48/269, p. 7, para. 34.

132 R. Desgagné, 'The Prevention of Environmental Damage in Time of Armed Conflict: Proportionality and Precautionary Measures', 3 *Yearbook of International Humanitarian Law* (2000) p. 124.

133 Henckaerts, *supra* note 106, p. 150.

134 *Ibid.* (referencing *Nuclear Weapons* case, *supra* note 65 and *Nuclear Tests* case, *supra* note 65).

Taking note of the scientifically uncertain risks of increasingly sophisticated means and methods of warfare, it is submitted that the precautionary principle or approach should be taken into consideration during armed conflict. For example, military forces could perhaps integrate the precautionary principle or approach when considering the employment of new weaponry or tactics, being conscious of the possible uncertain scientific consequences to the environment and the human population if used. This principle should equally be taken into consideration when selecting military targets or objectives during conflict. Even though this would add an additional factor that has to be taken into account during warfare, taking note of lessons from previous wars, it would be regressive not to. This goes hand in hand with the equity principle, as seen from the examples of the Vietnam, Gulf and Kosovo conflicts, from extensive use of toxic chemicals on the environment, vast destruction of oil-wells, to high altitude aerial bombing targeting chemical factories, that the environment should not be destroyed to the point where present and future generations are unable to use it or that the environmental damage causes debilitating harm to them.[135]

The need to take into account the principle of intra- and inter-generational equity in armed conflict goes to the core of why we protect the environment in the first place, that is, for the most part, we protect the environment for the benefit of human beings. To reiterate, there is the notion or expectation of responsibility that the environment should not be damaged or destroyed to such an extent that it restricts both present and future generations from having access to it for their security, livelihoods and well-being.[136] This notion should equally apply during armed conflict.[137] Furthermore, such conflict-related environmental damage could not only have consequences for many generations to come, but it could also be an additional economic burden on the war-torn country that is already suffering from collapsed institutions and unstable socio-economic conditions, thereby adding further obstacles to sustainable development in the aftermath of conflict. Bearing this responsibility in mind when taking military action may contribute towards preventing decisions that may have devastating and irreparable consequences for the environment and human population of the conflict zone.

Finally, the principle of integration, as noted above, is one of the key principles of sustainable development.[138] The integration principle is equally important to armed conflict as it is the link that allows the integration of environmental considerations (including the overarching concept of sustainable development,

135 E. B. Weiss, 'Environmentally Sustainable Competitiveness: A Comment', 102 *Yale Law Journal* (1993) p. 2123 ("sustainable development implies that future generations have as much right as the present generation to a robust environment with which to meet their own needs and preferences").

136 *Ibid.*

137 *Ibid.*

138 Cordonier Segger and Newcombe, *supra* note 78, p. 124.

the precautionary principle and inter-and intra-generational equity) into the laws of war and warfare strategy. The question that follows is, however, how can these principles be integrated into the laws of warfare?

5.2. Environmental Protection in Armed Conflict – A 'Berlin Rules' Approach

There is no doubt that integrating sustainable development principles into the laws of war seems unlikely. Thus, it is not suggested that a new binding convention protecting the environment in armed conflict should be formulated.[139] As evidenced from previous relevant treaties, conventions and protocols, it is not easy for States to come to agreement on what is and is not acceptable regarding the environment during armed conflict. Indeed, even the 1977 Additional Protocols[140] have not been ratified by all States.[141] There is thus no compelling need for a binding new treaty as there is already a respectable body of rules. These are set out in the 1994 International Committee of the Red Cross (ICRC) Guidelines for Military Manuals and Instructions on the Protection of the Environment in Times of Armed Conflict[142] which constitutes a summary of the existing applicable IHL rules relating to the protection of the environment. These ICRC Guidelines "are intended as a tool to facilitate the instruction and training of armed forces in an often neglected area of international humanitarian law: the protection of the natural environment".[143] Though a very important step in summarising the relevant existing international rules on the protection of the environment during armed conflict and bringing these laws to the attention of States and its armed forces, these Guidelines were consolidated two decades ago and do not reflect recent development of the elements of sustainable development. More recently, in 2009, UNEP conducted a thorough report which "inventories and analyses the range of international laws that protect the environment during armed conflict."[144] The UNEP report reviews the current gaps and weaknesses in the existing framework and concludes with 12 recommendations to strengthen the current legal regime.[145] These include, for example, recommending clearer

139 For example, the possibility of a 'Fifth Geneva Convention' was debated in 1991 and received little support from the international community. *See* G. Plant (ed.), *Environmental Protection and the Law of War: A "Fifth Geneva" Convention on the Protection of the Environment in Time of Armed Conflict* (Belhaven, London, 1992).

140 AP I, *supra* note 87; AP II, *supra* note 121.

141 *The Law of Armed Conflict: Problems and Prospects*, 18–19 April 2005, Chatham House, London, p. 4, <www.chathamhouse.org.uk/files/3252_ilparmedconflict.pdf>, visited on 4 July 2012.

142 ICRC, *supra* note 119.

143 *Ibid.*, *see* 'Introduction' by H. P. Gasser.

144 UNEP, *supra* note 1.

145 *Ibid.*, pp. 52–54.

definitions of 'widespread, long-term and severe' as articulated in Articles 35 and 55 of API; updating the 1994 ICRC Guidelines; for the International Law Commission (ILC) to continue its work in the area of environmental protection in armed conflict; training for lawyers on enforcing international law protecting the environment in armed conflict; States integrating relevant international law protecting the environment during armed conflict into domestic legislation; creating a permanent UN body to monitor violations and address compensation for environmental damage in armed conflict; strengthening the Permanent Court of Arbitration (PCA) to mediate disputes of conflict-related environmental damage; to presenting an annual summary report on the environmental impacts of armed conflict to the UN General Assembly.[146]

Following on from the ICRC Guidelines and UNEP's report and recommendations, it is argued that there is a strong case for updating the existing laws relevant to the protection of the environment during war by setting them out clearly and comprehensively within a new non-binding text or code of rules. This task could perhaps be taken up by the International Law Association (ILA), building on their experience in formulating the 2004 Berlin Rules on Water Resources[147] (Berlin Rules) and their continuing work on sustainable development,[148] together with the ICRC who already have experience in consolidating the relevant rules for protecting the environment during armed conflict.[149] It is suggested that these new rules could take their cue from the ILA's Berlin Rules. The Berlin Rules made a major contribution to international law and international water law specifically by clearly and comprehensively setting out an up-to-date and non-binding assessment of environmental norms of international water law and management which includes a section on water protection in times of armed conflict. A new set of rules comprehensively and clearly prescribing rights and duties in respect of the ecological impact of armed conflict, bearing in mind the ever-increasing sophistication and technological advances in the means and methods of warfare, could not only mitigate the impact of conflict-related environmental damage on both the environment itself and the human population, it could further contrib-

146 *Ibid.*

147 *See* Berlin Rules on Water Resources (Berlin Rules), August 2004, (adopted, with dissenting views, by the ILA at the Seventy-First Conference, Berlin), <www.internationalwaterlaw.org/documents/intldocs/ILA_Berlin_Rules-2004.pdf>, visited on 3 July 2012. The Berlin Rules were adopted to replace the Helsinki Rules on the Uses of the Waters of International Rivers, adopted by the ILA at the Fifty-Second Conference, Helsinki, 1966. For further discussion on the Berlin and Helsinki Rules, *see* S. M. A. Salman, 'The Helsinki Rules, the UN Watercourses Convention and the Berlin Rules: Perspectives on International Water Law', 23 *Water Resources Development* (2007) pp. 629–631.

148 *See* ILA website, *supra* note 42.

149 ICRC, *supra* note 119.

ute to the development of international law and conflict-related environmental protection specifically.

The Berlin Rules cover not only international fresh surface waters and ground-waters (aquatic environment)[150] but also waters within the national boundaries of a State. They include the applicable sustainable development principles of international law such as public participation,[151] the precautionary approach,[152] the obligation for States to use their best efforts to manage such waters,[153] the obligation to take measures to manage waters sustainably[154] and to minimise environmental harm,[155] and identify the rights and duties of States[156] and individuals.[157] The Berlin Rules also require States to undertake the necessary environmental impact assessments,[158] including covering extreme situations (such as pollution accidents, floods and accidents),[159] and incorporate extended consideration of IHL rules relevant to the protection of water and water installations during times of armed conflict.[160] The Berlin Rules are, to reiterate, non-binding and are at present intended to provide a guidance framework in this area.[161] However, they have as their legally binding foundation the various treaty and customary provisions in the field of water law, which they flesh out in an accessible form. The Berlin Rules make no reference to any of the IHL provisions and conventions in Chapter X, which provides protection for waters and water installations during war or armed conflict.[162] Nevertheless, Chapter X set out rules prohibiting combatants from poisoning water indispensable for the

150 Article 3, Berlin Rules, *supra* note 147.

151 Articles 4, 10, 18, 30, *ibid.*

152 Article 23, *ibid.*

153 Articles 5 and 6, *ibid.*

154 Article 7, *ibid.*

155 Article 8, *ibid.*

156 *See e.g.* Article 68, *ibid.*

157 *See e.g.* Article 17, *ibid.*

158 Articles 29–31, *ibid.*

159 Articles 32–35, *ibid.*

160 Articles 50–55, *ibid.*

161 C. Staddon, *Managing Europe's Water Resources: Twenty-first Century Challenges* (Ashgate, England/USA, 2010) p. 51. *See also* ILA, *Water Resources Law*, Fourth Report of the Berlin Conference (ILA, Berlin, 2004) p. 4 (majority of the Committee conclude that these progressively developed Berlin Rules "will become settled customary international law in the near future, [and as such] all *Rules* are expressed as present legal obligations ('shall') …").

162 For commentary on Chapter X provisions, *see* Berlin Water Resources Report, *supra* note 161, pp. 43–45.

survival of civilians,[163] setting limits on targeting water or water installations[164] (including dams and dikes)[165] during conflict to prevent widespread, long-term and severe ecological harm prejudicial to the civilian population,[166] stipulating obligations of an occupying State regarding water resources,[167] and stating that peacetime water related treaties are still applicable during times of warfare subject to military necessity.[168]

Like the Berlin Rules, the proposed new Rules for Environmental Protection in Armed Conflict ('Environmental Rules') could set out the relevant principles and rules relating to the protection of the environment in armed conflict without specifically referring to any IHL laws. The reason for this is that, unlike the ICRC Guidelines which refer to and set out a summary of the existing IHL laws protecting the environment during armed conflict, the purpose of these proposed Environmental Rules is to suggest the addition of sustainable development principles or concepts. States may be less amenable to the implication that the existing IHL rules are to be amended or changed. Setting out these Environmental Rules without express reference to existing IHL laws in a non-binding setting may make them more palatable for States to accept. As a result, States may be more willing to include such Rules into their military manuals in order to train or develop a more environmentally conscious ethos amongst their soldiers. In any event, the existing IHL laws remain in force, and thus provide a 'backstop' and a legal foundation to these proposed Rules.

The proposed Environmental Rules could thus, for example, set out the scope of the Rules relating to the protection of the environment in armed conflict; set out how States should implement these Rules; provide a comprehensive and up-to-date section articulating the relevant definitions for terms within the Rules, including perhaps clear definitions for the terms 'widespread, long-term and severe' in the context of these Rules. This, of course, may be more difficult to achieve as such definitions may be contrary to the understandings of States as per the existing interpretations of the terms as used in Articles 35 and 55 of API.[169]

---

163 Article 50, Berlin Rules, *supra* note 147. The prohibition of poisoning drinking water is part of customary international law. This principle is also reflected in Article 23(a), Hague IV, *supra* note 97 and Article 54, AP I, *supra* note 87.

164 Article 51, Berlin Rules. This Article reflects the general principle of proportionality in armed conflict. *See* Berlin Water Resources Report, *supra* note 161, p. 43.

165 Article 53, Berlin Rules. This Article is reflected in Article 56, AP I.

166 Article 52, Berlin Rules. This Article is reflected in Articles 35 and 55, AP I.

167 Article 54, Berlin Rules. By requiring an occupying State to ensure sustainable use of water resources and to minimise environmental harm, this Article extends the duties set out in Article 55, GC IV, *supra* note 98, which stipulates obligations of an occupying power regarding food and medical supplies for the occupied population. *See* Berlin Water Resources Report, *supra* note 161, p. 45.

168 Article 55, Berlin Rules. *See* Berlin Water Resources Report, *supra* note 161, p. 45.

169 *See supra* notes 94 and 95 (on the intentions of AP I authors).

However, this may be overcome by specifying clearly that these 'new' definitions are to be read only in the context of the Rules. The Environmental Rules could also provide an opportunity to integrate sustainable development aims into the provisions on environmental protection in armed conflict, by calling for education and dissemination of these Rules, or for the inclusion of the precautionary approach in relation to the means and methods of warfare relevant to the environment. In addition, as in Chapter X of the Berlin Rules, and with reference to the precautionary and equity principles, the proposed Environmental Rules could include provisions prohibiting combatants from poisoning water or foodstuffs indispensable to the survival of civilians; set limits on targeting foodstuffs, agricultural areas and irrigation works (including dams and dikes or nuclear power stations) during conflict to prevent widespread, long-term and severe ecological harm prejudicial to the civilian population, and stipulate the obligations of an occupying State regarding the resources of the occupied State. Furthermore, bearing in mind the principle of sustainable development, the proposed Rules could also contain provisions protecting medical institutions and religious and cultural property as well as take the opportunity to clarify that peacetime environmental treaties are still applicable during times of warfare subject to military necessity.[170]

It is also suggested that in line with the requirements of sustainable development, and as recommended by the 2009 UNEP report,[171] the proposed Environmental Rules could contain a section on post-conflict actions dealing with conflict-related environmental damage. This section could include provisions regarding post-conflict international cooperation to deal with the aftermath of conflict-related environmental damage in the war-torn country (perhaps referring to the principle of common but differentiated responsibilities).[172] Using the UN Compensation Commission[173] as an example, the proposed Environmental Rules could set out criteria for the establishment of a permanent body to monitor conflict-related violations and environmental damage as well as deal with compensation and remedy mechanisms for environmental damage. The Rules could further provide for a compensation fund either through voluntary or mandatory State contributions and set out mechanisms for other legal remedies for conflict-related environmental damage and compliance reviews to ensure that these remedies are followed through. This would be particularly relevant where compensation alone may not be sufficient to ensuring that the war-torn country is back on track with regard to sustainable development. In that case, other mechanisms are needed to ensure that the damaged environment is remedied as much as possible to ensure that the present and future generations of the war-torn population are able to once again enjoy and utilise their environment.

---

170 *See* Sixty-Third ILC Report, *supra* note 85.

171 UNEP, *supra* note 1, pp. 54–55 (*see e.g.* recommendations 6 and 7).

172 *See e.g.* Sands, *supra* note 43, pp. 233–237.

173 *See e.g.* C. R. Payne and P. H. Sand (eds.), *Gulf War Reparations and the UN Compensation Commission: Environmental Liability* (OUP, USA, 2011).

It is not suggested that these proposed Environmental Rules should extend the primary norms applicable to the protection of the environment in armed conflict under the existing IHL regime. However, they could make an important contribution to raising awareness and add to the consciousness of the international community as to the level of environmental damage that is unacceptable in times of conflict. Indeed, clearly setting out both in-conflict and post-conflict provisions for environmental protection which embody sustainable development objectives where appropriate could result in the development of additional standards of protection for the environment in armed conflict. Moreover, limiting the damage permitted to the environment so that it does not threaten peoples' health and livelihoods as well as mitigating the negative impact on development and the environment itself could contribute to the cycle of sustainable development.

6. Conclusion

Warfare always occurs 'in' the environment and the environment therefore needs to be protected from its ravages. Moreover, conflict-related environmental damage not only impacts the environment but also the war-torn population, disrupting sustainable development by leaving behind a war-ravaged environment that may negatively affect their security, livelihoods and well-being well into the future. Various IHL rules and principles provide protection against unjustified environmental damage during armed conflict. However, the stringent thresholds of application of the specific laws of war formulated to protect the environment and the subjective balancing of the military necessity loophole render it very difficult to protect the environment adequately during an armed conflict. In addition, ever increasing sophistication in technology and weaponry means that damage done to the environment during armed conflict may be more devastating than ever before, even possibly irreversible.

Thus, this study argues for integrating salient principles of sustainable development, in particular the principles of precaution and intra- and inter-generational equity, into the means and methods of warfare when the environment is involved. This study further argues for the existing norms within IHL applicable to the environment to be clarified, consolidated and updated in a comprehensive new set of non-binding 'Environmental Rules' which integrate the relevant sustainable development principles. Such an approach could mean easier dissemination of obligations of environmental protection in warfare and also remind the international community of the level of environmental damage that is not acceptable in times of armed conflict.

7 Environment and War: Lessons from International Cultural Heritage Law

Lucas Lixinski*

1. Introduction

In 2012, the International Law Commission decided to start consideration of the topic of protection of the environment in relation to armed conflict.[1] Harm to the environment during armed conflict has been a concern for several thousand years.[2] It is thus a wonder that the topic has not warranted its own legal regime before. Granted, there are certain rules of international humanitarian law (IHL), both customary and treaty-based, which grant some sort of protection to the environment. However, in the modern international legal era, during which environmentalism has been a central topic since at least the 1972 Stockholm United Nations Conference on the Human Environment,[3] and much conflict-caused environmental harm has occurred, no dedicated legal regime for protection of the environment during armed conflict has been developed. Assuming there should be such a regime the question arises as to what that regime would look like.

An oft-used strategy when devising a new legal regime is to look for analogous regimes. In this respect, the regime for the protection of cultural heritage

---

* PhD in Law, European University Institute (Florence, Italy). Lecturer, Faculty of Law, The University of New South Wales, Sydney, Australia. I am very thankful to Professor Rosemary Rayfuse for her extensive comments to an earlier version. All errors remain my own.

1 United Nations, *Official Records of the General Assembly, Sixty-sixth Session, Supplement No. 10* (A/66/10), paras. 365–367.

2 For that history, *see* J. Wyatt, 'Law-making at the intersection of international environmental, humanitarian and criminal law: the issue of damage to the environment in international armed conflict', 92:879) *International Review of the Red Cross* (2010) pp. 593–646, at pp. 596–599. *See also* C. Thomas, 'Advancing the Legal Protection of the Environment in relation to Armed Conflict: Protocol I's Threshold of Impermissible Environmental Damage and Alternatives', in this volume.

3 Declaration of the United Nations Conference on the Human Environment (Stockholm, June 1972).

Rosemary Rayfuse (ed.), War and the Environment: New Approaches to Protecting the Environment in Relation to Armed Conflict
 ISBN 978-90-04-27064-0 pp. 157-234

in time of armed conflict may be a suitable candidate. This regime is currently comprised of the Convention for the Protection of Cultural Property in the Event of Armed Conflict and its two Protocols of 1954 and 1999[4] and has spawned a (mostly) successful regime for safeguarding cultural heritage during times of armed conflict. While the Convention and Protocols refer to cultural 'property' rather than 'heritage', the term 'heritage' is used here as being the more contemporary term.[5] The use of this comparator can be justified on the basis of the highly specialised nature of the two legal regimes. Moreover, like parts of the environment, much of heritage falls under the notions of 'global commons', or 'common heritage of mankind', thus making the two legal goods (heritage and the environment) somewhat comparable.

This study investigates what lessons, if any, can be drawn from the regime for the protection of cultural heritage in the event of armed conflict for the design of a new regime relating to protection of the environment with respect to armed conflict. Before doing so, however, it is necessary to provide an account as to why the environment has so far been mostly neglected in IHL. In this respect ecofeminism provides a useful theoretical framework. By feminising the environment, ecofeminism provides a narrative of the environment's relative neglect in certain fields (including the regulatory field). This explanation is necessary if we are to understand how we have arrived at this point, and whether a broader change of attitude towards the environment is necessary not only to ensure a regime is ever put into place, but that it is also embraced by States and becomes effective.

This study proceeds as follows: Section 2 introduces the ecofeminist perspective and how it bears on the relationship between environment, war and culture. Section 3 focuses more specifically on certain key features of the regime for the protection of heritage protection in wartime, stressing the extent to which these features could (or could not) be incorporated into an eventual regime for the protection of the environment in wartime. Section 4 concludes the study.

---

4 Convention for the Protection of Cultural Property in the Event of Armed Conflict, adopted at The Hague on 14 May 1954 (number of parties as of September 2013: 126); Protocol to the Convention for the Protection of Cultural Property in the Event of Armed Conflict, adopted at The Hague on 14 May 1954 (number of parties as of September 2013: 102); and Second Protocol to the Hague Convention of 1954 for the Protection of Cultural Property in the Event of Armed Conflict 1999, adopted at The Hague on 26 March 1999 (number of parties as of September 2013: 64).

5 On this terminological evolution in the specific context of armed conflicts, *see* M. Frigo, 'Cultural property v. cultural heritage: A "battle of concepts" in international law?', 86:854 *International Review of the Red Cross* (2004) pp. 367–378. On this evolution in general, *see* F. Francioni, 'A Dynamic Evolution of Concept and Scope: From Cultural Property to Cultural Heritage', in A. A. Yusuf (ed.), *Standard-Setting in UNESCO Vol 1: Normative Action in Education, Science and Culture* (Martinus Nijhoff and UNESCO Publishing, 2007) pp. 221–236; L.V. Prott and P. J. O'Keefe, '"Cultural Heritage" or "Cultural Property"?', 1 *International Journal of Cultural Property* (1992) pp. 307–320.

2. War, Environment and Cultural Heritage: Ecofeminist Perspectives

The insights of feminist theory into international law have been widely documented in many areas.[6] These insights do not appear, however, to have seeped into international environmental law, despite the existence of ecofeminism as a strand of discourse around the environment. Nevertheless, feminist international law (and feminist theory more generally) represents an important starting point for the present discussion; not as a means to suggest that environmental issues affect women in particular, or are a women's cause but, rather, as "a mode of analysis, a method of approaching life and politics, a way of asking questions and searching for answers, rather than a set of political conclusions about the oppression of women".[7]

One of the principal insights of the application of feminist theory to international law concerns the normative structure of international law, or, more specifically, the fact that "modern international law rests on and reproduces various dichotomies between the public and private spheres, and the 'public' sphere is regarded as the province of international law".[8] In this sense, the 'private' is restricted to the reserved domain of sovereignty, and excluded from international law-making. The public/private distinction arises from an insight of feminist theory through which the public is the domain of men, and the private that of women. The private is beyond the purview of the law-maker (in our example, the international community), and therefore escapes regulation.

The manner in which these insights are applicable to environmental matters is articulated in a strand of feminist thought known as ecofeminism. According to ecofeminism, "women and nature have been mutually associated and devalued in Western culture and … both can be elevated and liberated through direct political action".[9] By transposing the 'male / female' dichotomy to environmental matters, ecofeminism aims to understand the articulation between humankind

6 For more general approaches, *see* H. Charlesworth, C. Chinkin and S. Wright, 'Feminist Approaches to International Law', 85:4 *American Journal of International Law* (1991) pp. 613–645; and H. Charlesworth and C. Chinkin, *The boundaries of international law: A feminist analysis* (Manchester University Press 2000) (looking at issues of law-making, treaties, statehood, international organisations, human rights, use of force and peaceful settlement of disputes).

7 N. Hartsock, 'Feminist Theory and the Development of Revolutionary Strategy', in Z. R. Eisenstein (ed.), *Capitalist Patriarchy and the Case for Socialist Feminism* (1979), p. 58 cited by Charlesworth, Chinkin and Wright, *ibid.*, p. 614.

8 Charlesworth, Chinkin and Wright, *supra* note 6, p. 625.

9 C. Merchant, 'Ecofeminism and Feminist Theory', in I. Diamon and G. F. Orenstein (eds.), *Reweaving the Web: The Emergence of Ecofeminism* (Sierra Club Books, San Francisco, 1990) p. 100, at p. 101.

and the environment. Ecofeminism treats 'culture' as 'male', and 'environment' as 'female'.

According to Leach, ecofeminists argue that "women and nature have been subjected to a shared history of oppression by patriarchal institutions and dominant western culture."[10] Nevertheless, ecofeminists, despite having a few shared notions, are far from a uniform group. Rather, since the 1970s,[11] ecofeminism has developed a number of subgroups. Liberal ecofeminists, for example, generally argue that women, having been excluded from regulatory processes, lack a voice in environmental matters and should therefore be brought into the fold. Radical ecofeminists tend to focus on the revival of ancient rituals, and on the connection between women and nature being grounded in biology. Socialist ecofeminists generally ground their analysis "in capitalist patriarchy and would totally restructure, through a socialist revolution, the domination of women and nature inherent in the market economy's use of both as resources".[12]

Early ecofeminist discourse essentialised both women and nature by necessarily connecting all women to nature and treating both as fairly straightforward notions, without specifying the nature of the association between women and nature.[13] The essentialisation of women and nature led to a series of attacks on ecofeminism. However, essentialism was also vital in mobilising the ecofeminists around central themes (nature and female nature, in this case). Essentialism had the strength of demonstrating that this way of thinking was feasible and that it could work as a means to reverse a male-centric order.

Today, most ecofeminism thinking is no longer framed in essentialised terms.[14] Instead, "ecofeminism is highly critical of most current social and political institutions and thereby serves a deconstructive or dissembling function that supports political resistance".[15] Socialist ecofeminism is the branch of ecofeminism that has probably been most successful in moving beyond essentialist notions of women and nature. More specifically, "feminist green socialism would not assume that human society is so exclusively determined by its mode of production that all other social / biological / ecological structures will 'fall into line' if that mode of production is changed. It would accept that while there is no pre-

10 M. Leach, 'Earth Mother Myths and Other Ecofeminist Fables: How a Strategic Notion Rose and Fell', 38:1 *Development and Change* (2007) pp. 67–85, at p. 70.

11 C. Spretnak, 'Ecofeminism: Our Roots and Flowering', 3:2 *Ecospirit*, (1987) pp. 2–9, at p. 5.

12 Merchant, *supra* note 9, pp. 100–101.

13 C. Jackson, 'Women/nature or gender/history? A critique of ecofeminist "defelopment"', 20:3 *The Journal of Peasant Studies* (1993), pp. 389–418, at p. 413.

14 S. Buckingham, 'Ecofeminism in the twenty-first century', 170:2 *The Geographical Journal* (2004) pp. 146–154, at p. 147.

15 S. Lahar, 'Ecofeminist Theory and Grassroots Politics', 6:1 *Hypatia* (1991) pp. 28–45, at p. 35.

determined destiny in biology or ecology, we need to come to terms politically with their reality."[16]

What ecofeminism does is to explain ways in which the environment is often forgotten as a participant in and stage for the conduct of warfare. Coupled with feminist international law, it helps explain why the environment has thus far been neglected in the (very male) context of warfare. Because the environment is considered to be female, it belongs to the 'private', or the reserved domain of sovereignty of States.[17] States have a duty of 'care' towards the environment during wartime. However, under existing rules, only damage that reaches a very high degree of intensity becomes part of the public sphere and thus regulated by international law. The explanation of this neglect suggests that, in order for any future regime on the environment in times of armed conflict to be successful, a broader change in attitude is needed. More specifically, the environment should be seen not only as a defenceless casualty of conflict (a "damsel in distress"),[18] but primarily as an important resource that needs to outlive the conflict if parties to the conflict (and humanity as a whole) are to rebound. The environment needs to be protected not because it cannot defend itself, but because damage to the environment is damage to the common heritage of mankind.

However, if, as suggested by ecofeminist discourses, nature is in opposition to culture, how can a regime for cultural property in times of war help in the regulation of the environment during warfare? According to socialist ecofeminism, both culture and nature are the product of social and political forces of their time, and therefore historically and politically contingent. Rather than an opposition, there is a dialectical relationship between ecology and society, [19] with nature being a product of culture, even if they were both created through denying full participation to women.[20] In this way, ecofeminism can both explain why cultural heritage has received its own regime (after all, culture precedes nature in order of importance), and sufficiently connect the two (both being historically contingent products). The manner in which the heritage in wartime regime might work as a model for the design of a possible regime for the environment is addressed in the next section.

---

16 M. Mellor, 'Eco-feminism and eco-socialism: Dilemmas of essentialism and materialism', 3:2 *Capitalism Nature Socialism* (1992) pp. 43–62, at p. 60.

17 *Ibid.*, p. 61.

18 M. Kheel, 'From Heroic to Holistic Ethics: The Ecofeminist Challenge', in G. Gaard (ed.), *Ecofeminism: Women, Animals, Nature* (Temple University Press, 1993) pp. 243–271, at p. 243.

19 Mellor, *supra* note 16, p. 48.

20 Jackson, *supra* note 13, p. 395 (referring to Claude Levi Strauss).

3. Features of Heritage Protection in Times of War and Lessons for a Regime for the Environment

In considering the development of more detailed rules on the protection of the environment in relation to armed conflict it is necessary to consider whether what is needed is simply a set of legal obligations, or whether some sort of institutional arrangement is also needed. Given the paucity of existing rules a case can be made simply for the development of further norms, or for a clarification of those norms, without the setting up of any institutional mechanism. This approach is undoubtedly attractive to those concerned about the fragmentation of international law. Under this approach, implementation and/or enforcement of any such norms would be ascribed to pre-existing institutions,[21] thereby avoiding contributing to institutional fragmentation.[22] However, it is argued here that development of a dedicated institutional arrangement would provide a number of advantages over this approach. First, it would enable the more constant supervision of compliance with the norms adopted. Second, a dedicated institutional mechanism could assist in encouraging States to become parties to the treaty, thereby contributing to regime success. Third, the establishment of an institutional mechanism would lend more credibility to the regime. Finally, a dedicated mechanism or treaty body would be perfectly placed to promote the necessary change of attitude towards the environment in times of armed conflict that was identified above. The protection of cultural heritage in the event of armed conflict has benefitted from having its own institutional apparatus, some of the characteristics of which may provide a useful precedent for any new environmental regime.

The regime for the protection of cultural heritage in the time of armed conflict is based on the 1954 Convention on the Protection of Cultural Property in the Event of Armed Conflict and its two Protocols of 1954 and 1999. The 1954

21 Expressing this concern in the specific context of environmental protection during wartime, *see* Wyatt, *supra* note 2, pp. 594–596.

22 *See generally* International Law Commission, *Fragmentation of International Law: Difficulties Arising from the Diversification and Expansion of International Law*, Report of the Study Group, finalised by Martti Koskenniemi. UN Doc. A/CN.4/L.682, 13 April 2006. The report makes a distinction between institutional and substantive fragmentation, particularly at para. 489 (highlighting the focus of the report on substantive issues regarding fragmentation, including the emergence of treaty regimes and "functional clusters of rules and specialized branches of international law and on their relationship *inter se* and to general international law"). Pierre-Marie Dupuy calls these two types of fragmentation normative and organic/institutional fragmentation. P.-M. Dupuy, 'A Doctrinal Debate in the Globalisation Era: On the "Fragmentation" of International Law', 1 *European Journal of Legal Studies* (2007). For a critique of this report, *see* B. Conforti, 'Unité et Fragmentation du Droit International: "*Glissez, Mortels, N'Appuyez Pas!*"', 111 *Revue Générale de Droit International Public* (2007) p. 5.

Protocol deals with the export of cultural objects during conflict.[23] The Second Protocol (1999) is to a large extent an extensive overhaul of the original system in the 1954 Convention, even if it is framed as a complementary instrument.[24] The main purposes of these three instruments are to prevent the destruction and export of items of cultural heritage during conflict. In addition to imposing a blanket protection on items of cultural heritage (subject to military necessity), the main mechanisms created by the instruments are lists of cultural property that deserves a higher degree of protection, and the creation of an emblem that can be affixed to protected buildings so as to signal their importance. These features will be examined in more detail in the sections below, which will also present some of the critique against the 1954 Hague Convention and its Protocols. The following sections focus on specific aspects of the cultural heritage regime that may be instructive in contemplating the formulation of a new regime relating to protection of the environment in relation to armed conflict.

3.1. The Definition of Heritage for the Purposes of Protection

One of the first elements to consider is the definition of the thing to be protected by the regime. In this respect, the static definition of 'heritage' embodied in the Convention represents one of its main shortcomings. As defined in Article 1, the Convention, only applies very narrowly to cultural 'property', specified as including, among other things, monuments, sites, artefacts, archives, archaeological sites and book manuscripts. This definition reflects understandings of heritage at the time the Convention was enacted. During negotiation of the Second Protocol, proposals were made to change the definition of heritage in order to update and expand it. There was even consideration of the possibility of including natural heritage (therefore, the environment) under the purview of the Second Protocol. This change was rejected, however, because natural heritage was deemed to have too many peculiarities that would make it incompatible with the cultural heritage regime.[25] Even a general updating of the concept of heritage was rejected because of the need that the Second Protocol be seen as closely aligned with rather

23 1954 Protocol, Article 1.

24 V. Mainetti, 'De nouvelles perspectives pour la protection des biens culturels en cas de conflit armé: l'entrée en vaguer du Deuxième Protocole relative à la Convention de La Haye de 1954', 86:854 *International Review of the Red Cross* (2004) pp. 337–366, at pp. 338–339.

25 J. Toman, *Cultural Property in War: Improvement in Protection – Commentary on the 1999 Second Protocol to the Hague Convention of 1954 for the Protection of Cultural Property in the Event of Armed Conflict* (UNESCO Publishing 2009) pp. 50–51.

than replacing the Convention.[26] As a result, the Second Protocol merely refers to the Convention definition.[27]

The missed opportunity of updating the concept of cultural heritage in the Second Protocol may be persuasively justified in light of the limitations of a Protocol which needs to be aligned with the general instrument, as opposed to the freedom of negotiating an entirely new instrument. However, in contemplating a new instrument on protection of the environment in armed conflict, the possibility that its definition of 'environmental areas subject to protection', if too narrow, will only represent aspirations of the time must be considered. Thus, a more open definition that allows for future interpretation to adequately account for contemporaneous developments is to be preferred.[28]

3.2. *Temporalities of War*

A second aspect to consider relates to the temporal scope of application of the regime. The issue here is the manner in which the regime applies before, during and after a conflict. In this respect it is important to note that the current regime for cultural heritage applies both before and after the conflict. Before a conflict, parties are required to create inventories of the items they would wish to protect in the event of a conflict and to otherwise prepare in time of peace for the safeguarding of cultural property situated within their own territory against the foreseeable effects of an armed conflict, by taking such measures as they consider appropriate. These include the insertion of specific rules on the protection of heritage in military manuals, the employment of personnel specialised in cultural heritage protection as part of the armed forces, the preparation of inventories, planning of emergency measures, evacuation plans for cultural property and the designation of competent authorities domestically.[29] During a conflict parties are

26 *Ibid.*

27 Second Protocol, Article 1 "For the purposes of this Protocol… b. 'cultural property' means cultural property as defined in Article 1 of the Convention".

28 On this issue, *see particularly* the work of the International Law Commission on the interpretation of treaties over time. United Nations General Assembly, International Law Commission, First Report on Subsequent Agreements and Subsequent Practice in Relation to Treaty Interpretation. Special Rapporteur Georg Nolte. UN Doc. A/CN.4/660, of 19 March 2013.

29 1954 Hague Convention, Articles 3 and 7. Second Protocol, Article 5. For a commentary on these activities, *see* J.-M. Henckaerts, 'New rules for the protection of cultural property in armed conflict: the significance of the Second Protocol to the 1954 Hague Convention for the Protection of Cultural Property in the Event of Armed Conflict', in M. T. Dutli (ed.), *Protection of Cultural Property in the Event of Armed Conflict* (International Committee of the Red Cross, 2002) pp. 27–55, at pp. 30–32.

obliged not to destroy heritage that has been listed or otherwise identified with the requisite emblem.[30]

Nevertheless, despite these obligations, the regime fails to capture post-conflict effects and it downplays the roles of heritage in the other phases of the conflict. In this respect a significant shortcoming is the regime's failure to comprehend the mutability of heritage and its possible uses. As has been well documented, the living nature of cultural heritage[31] makes it more susceptible to being reinterpreted in accordance with the social and political ideas of the day. Indeed, cultural heritage has been used in many places as a means to construct national political identity, and sometimes at the expense of differing interpretations of the same heritage by different groups, sometimes by simply suppressing other bodies of heritage within the same State. In Burma/Myanmar, for example, the Buddhist heritage of the cultural elite has been promoted at the expense of more indigenous forms of intangible heritage in order to create a national unity. Whether intentional or not, this policy privileges the heritage of the dominating group and at the same time serves as a means to justify their political and social dominance.[32]

A similar situation can occur in conflict situations. Prior to conflict, as tensions grow between opposing social groups, the tendency is to reinterpret heritage so as to diminish the opposing group's importance, and even to re-evaluate the other group's heritage as being inferior.[33] Even worse, one group may appropriate the other group's heritage and ascribe to it meanings that serve their own interests.[34] By way of illustration, let us consider the following scenario. Groups A and B have lived in the same territory for several centuries. While originally very culturally distinct, gradually their cultures have started to share many characteristics in areas such as food, holidays, dress, traditional music and dance. The one cultural element that has remained clearly distinct between the two groups is religion. The two groups live peacefully and regularly interact with one another, even inter-marrying. The cultural belonging of these newly formed family units is determined by the male's cultural origin.

Traditionally, group B has been economically more affluent, and controls the vast majority of the economy, whereas group A is usually employed by group B and does not own the means of production. Business owners belonging primarily to group B start pursuing legislative reforms aimed at further enhanc-

30 1954 Hague Convention, Article 4.

31 On this notion, *see generally* L. Smith, *Uses of Heritage* (Routledge, 2006) p. 56.

32 *See for instance* J. Philp, 'The Political Appropriation of Burma's Cultural Heritage and its Implications for Human Rights', in M. Langfield, W. Logan, and M. N. Craith (eds.), *Cultural Diversity, Heritage and Human Rights: Intersections in Theory and Practice* (Routledge, 2010) pp. 83–100.

33 For several historical examples, *see generally* D. Lowenthal, *The Heritage Crusade and the Spoils of History* (Cambridge University Press, 1998).

34 *Ibid.*

ing their economic dominance, to the disadvantage of non-business owners, who are primarily from group A. While the reasons behind the political turmoil are economic, their effects can largely be traced along cultural lines. Because of this, it becomes politically convenient to contest these legislative reforms in terms of cultural divisions and discrimination, instead of looking at the issue in purely economic terms. Cultural tensions arise and grow. Religion becomes the initial yardstick of the cultural debate, but this soon escalates into other areas. Traditional dances that have been shared between the two groups now become a contested cultural space. Group A appropriates some, group B others. Out of some of those that become group B's dances, group A starts denigrating them for being silly and unsophisticated. Group B by its turn appropriates some of what had become group A's dances into their own repertoire by changing the costumes and changing some of the instruments used to play the background music, while maintaining the choreography. Costumes and instrumental arrangements are changed to incorporate foreign and contemporary notions of sophisticated, high culture. All of this happens before military conflict actually breaks out. However, it is an important phase of the contestation and reassessment of intangible heritage that assists in creating the necessary cultural divide to justify creating a distinct 'other' that can be later disliked and dehumanised. The same type of contestation can happen during and after conflict, as a means to redraw cultural lines and create new identities.

This hypothetical suggests a conflict along ethnic lines, which, because of their grounding on cultural identity is a catalyst for conflict. It demonstrates that the current regime for the protection of cultural property in the event of armed conflict fails to capture cultural heritage in a holistic way. When applied to nature and the environment it is important to remember that nature, too, can be an important part of identity. Just as the Mostar Bridge was a target in the war between Croatians and Bosniaks in the 1990s Yugoslavian conflict[35] because of its importance to the identity of the warring factions, certain animals, plants and even natural sites which are particularly important to a party's identity can easily spark a conflict, or become the target of a conflict, Natural resources – or rather the availability of, access to and control over natural resources – can also be a cause of war.[36] Thus any regime for protection of the environment in relation to armed conflict will have to address the environment as both target and as spark, or catalyst, for conflict.

Post-conflict reconstruction may also be relevant although the current cultural heritage regime is silent on the matter. The assumption seems to be that, as

---

35 For an in-depth discussion of the destruction of the Mostar Bridge, *see* S. Krishnamurthy, 'Memory and Form: An Exploration of the Stari Most, Mostar (BIH)', 11:4 *Journal of Ethnopolitics and Minority Issues in Europe* (2012) pp. 81–102.

36 *See* D. Dam-de Jong, 'From Engines for Conflict into Engines for Sustainable Development: The Potential of International Law to Address Predatory Exploitation of Natural Resources in Situations of Internal Armed Conflict', in this volume.

soon as the conflict is over, the array of peacetime instruments will be sufficient to re-establish order. However, this notion fails to consider that cultural heritage is fundamentally transformed by conflict. One interesting example of post-conflict heritage management is that of South Africa where much of the country's culture was re-written after 1994 to give it a post-colonial, post-apartheid meaning. While some of the physical symbols of apartheid and conflict were kept, the heritage behind them was re-defined. No longer are those places and cultural spaces symbols of oppression; rather, they are reminders of the past and hopeful catalysts for the future.[37]

Responsibility for destruction of cultural property is also a relevant consideration. Here, too, the current regime is silent. Responsibility for destruction of cultural heritage during conflict is not covered by the Convention or its Protocols. Rather the issue is primarily a matter for the secondary regime of State responsibility (see below), the applicability of which is circumscribed by the failure of norms on reparations in general international law to take into account the irreplaceable nature of much of cultural heritage.[38] Environmental resources may also be fundamentally transformed by conflict, in particular as a result of irreversible damage. Here, too, the secondary rules on State responsibility have not yet shown themselves to be sufficient to address the matter of reparations. Thus, in contemplating a new environment specific regime, norms that set out clear obligations for post-conflict reparations, or at least that provide minimum parameters for the relevant peace settlements, would be desirable.

3.3. *Obligations to Whom?*

The next question to be considered is the material scope of application of the regime. As provided in Articles 18 and 19 of the Convention, the current regime for the protection of cultural heritage in armed conflict applies to both international and non-international conflicts[39] while the Second Protocol is more decid-

---

37 *See for instance* L. Witz, C. Rassool and G. Minkley, 'Repackaging the Past for South African Tourism', in G. Corsane (ed.), *Heritage, Museums and Galleries: An Introductory Reader* (Routledge, 2005) pp. 308–319.

38 On this matter, *see generally* A. F. Vrdoljak, 'Reparations for Cultural Loss', in F. Lenzerini (ed.), *Reparations for Indigenous Peoples: International and Comparative Law Perspectives* (Oxford University Press, 2008) pp. 197–228.

39 1954 Hague Convention: Article 18 provides that the Convention applies "in the event of declared war or of any other armed conflict which may arise between two or more of the High Contracting Parties, even if the state of war is not recognized by, one or more of them" and "to all cases of partial or total occupation of the territory of a High Contracting Party, even if the said occupation meets with no armed resistance". With respect to non-international armed conflicts, Article 19 requires "each party to the conflict to apply, as a minimum, the provisions of the present Convention which relate to respect for cultural property" and to "endeavour to bring into

edly applicable to non-international conflicts.[40] The expanded applicability of the Second Protocol reflects the changing nature of warfare which has increasingly moved from the international to the non-international. Similar considerations will be central to the development of any new regime with respect to the environment. Even if it is not possible to apply the entirety of the instrument to non-international conflicts, a strong set of core norms should nevertheless apply.

Also relevant to the scope of application is the question of what happens when only one of the parties to a conflict is a party to the relevant instrument. The obligations of the cultural heritage regime also apply to parties to a conflict who are not parties to the relevant instruments, as long as at least one of the other parties to the conflict is a party to the instrument, and the parties all agree to apply the terms of the instrument and effectively apply them.[41] In this sense, the cultural heritage regime only applies on the basis of reciprocity.

This provision is drawn from Article 2 common to the 1949 Geneva Conventions, and follows its spirit, in the sense that acceptance of the terms of the instrument may be implied from *de facto* application of the rules.[42] The problem here is reciprocity, or the idea that international obligations to respect and protect cultural heritage only apply if the other party is willing (expressly or impliedly) to abide to the same obligations. However, if the safeguarding of cultural heritage, like the environment, is thought of as the duty of all of humankind, and all of humankind stands to lose from its destruction (as proclaimed in the Hague Convention's preamble), it is incongruous to require that these obligations only apply on the basis of reciprocity. The challenge for any regime for the protection of the environment will be to extend the obligations of parties to the instrument irrespective of whether the other party(ies) to the conflict is(are) also bound by the instrument.

3.4. *Multiple Levels of Protection*

Another issue to consider relates to the level of protection to be afforded to elements of the environment. In this respect the cultural heritage regime creates two means of protection during armed conflict. The first is a general regime which imposes a general prohibition on the targeting of cultural heritage (except in cases of military necessity).[43] The second is a regime for certain specific types of heritage which, as discussed further below, are subject to either special or enhanced protection and a heightened threshold of military necessity. The rationale

force, by means of special agreements, all or part of the other provisions of the present Convention".

40 Mainetti, *supra* note 24, pp. 340–341.

41 1954 Hague Convention, Article 18(3); Second Protocol, Article 3(2).

42 Toman, *supra* note 25, pp. 65–67

43 1954 Hague Convention, Article 4.

for this differentiation has to do with the perception that some items of heritage are considered more important than others.[44]

Given the imperatives of armed conflict, this bifurcated approach to protection may make sense from a pragmatic point of view. Nevertheless, commentators are highly critical of tiered systems of protection with respect to heritage, precisely because they open the opportunity for selectivity of heritage, essentially constituting an endorsed statement that certain manifestations of culture and of identity are more worthwhile than others. The problem, of course, is with who gets to make that decision, and what their (undisclosed) biases are in making that selection.[45]

At the same time, however, two-tiered systems are seen as necessary to making sense of what would otherwise be a paralyzing cacophony of manifestations of cultural heritage. Particularly in the fast-paced context of an armed conflict, such pragmatism, however imperfect, may well be needed. Moreover, the ability of states to 'showcase' some of their heritage for stronger protection works both as good publicity for and as further legitimation of the Convention thereby enhancing both its pull to membership and its pull to compliance. Similar considerations might be relevant with respect to the environment where certain protected areas might be set aside for special protection as areas in which any activities relating to armed conflict are prohibited.

3.5. *Listing*

This then begs the question as to the mechanisms by which areas or aspects of the environment might be identified for protection. Two levels of protection have been devised in respect of cultural heritage: the regime of special protection created by the 1954 Convention[46] and that of enhanced protection created by the 1999

---

44 C. Forrest, *International Law and the Protection of Cultural Heritage* (Routledge, 2010) p. 97.

45 On this matter, with particular regard to the intangible cultural heritage regime, *see* L. Lixinski, 'Selecting Heritage: The Interplay of Art, Politics and Identity', 22:1 *European Journal of International Law* (2011) pp. 81–100.

46 1954 Hague Convention, Chapter II (Special Protection): Article 8 provides that "[t]here may be placed under special protection a limited number of refuges intended to shelter movable cultural property in the event of armed conflict, of centers containing monuments and other immovable cultural property of very great importance, provided that they: (a) are situated at an adequate distance from any large industrial center or from any important military objective constituting a vulnerable point, such as, for example, an aerodrome, broadcasting station, establishment engaged upon work of national defense, a port or railway station of relative importance or a main line of communication; (b) are not used for military purposes." Military use is defined in the same Article as "use for the movement of military personnel or material, even in transit".

Second Protocol.[47] The mechanism by which these properties are identified is that of listing. Pursuant to the 1954 Convention a List of Cultural Property under Special Protection was created for cultural heritage refuges identified as being "of very great importance". A second criterion was that these properties had to be sufficiently far from important military objectives or large industrial centres, and not used for military purposes.[48] That the list was only open to this rarefied type of heritage "of very great importance" reinforced the idea of listing as a means to create hierarchies and privilege some heritage over other. However, the system proved to be excessively complex.[49] In addition to the detailed requirements of Article 8, a complex series of implementing regulations[50] also needed to be followed if property was to be inscribed on the list. Moreover, given that the rule of military necessity continued to apply as an exception to special protection,[51] there was little difference in the level of protection afforded to listed versus non-listed properties.[52] As a result, only five refuges were ever inscribed (Vatican City, three refuges in the Netherlands and one in Germany).[53]

One objection against the Convention listing system is the difficulty of complying with the condition of adequate distance from an industrial centre or military objective. Another more pertinent objection to the very concept of listing, as such, is that, in the specific context of armed conflict, a list would provide a potential adversary essentially with a 'hit list' of important sites, particularly valu-

---

47 Second Protocol, Chapter 3 (Enhanced Protection): Article 10 determines that "[c] ultural property may be placed under enhanced protection provided that it meets the following three conditions: a. it is cultural heritage of the greatest importance for humanity; b. it is protected by adequate domestic legal and administrative measures recognising its exceptional cultural and historic value and ensuring the highest level of protection; c. it is not used for military purposes or to shield military sites and a declaration has been made by the Party which has control over the cultural property, confirming that it will not be so used." Enhanced protection is granted, according to Article 11, if a list is submitted by the state party to the Committee, or by the International Committee of the Blue Shield or other accredited organisations. All parties to the Second Protocol may submit observations as to whether the heritage proposed should be inscribed on the list or not. A decision is made ultimately by the Committee. Enhanced protection can be granted on an emergency basis, too, upon the outbreak of hostilities.

48 1954 Hague Convention, Article 8(1).

49 Forrest, *supra* note 44, pp. 99–100.

50 Regulations to the 1954 Hague Convention, Articles 11–16.

51 1954 Hague Convention, Article 9. This Article determines that all property under special protection is immune from attacks, unless it is being used for military purposes.

52 Forrest, *supra* note 44, pp. 99–100.

53 *Ibid.*, p.102.

able if the other party to the conflict is not bound by the relevant instruments.[54] Despite these objections, however, Article 10 of the Second Protocol also creates a list, although it extends enhanced protection to cultural heritage "of the greatest importance for humanity", which is protected by domestic legislation "recognizing its exceptional ... value", and is "not used for military purposes or to shield military sites". An accompanying declaration by the State confirming that the property will not be used in these ways is also required.[55] The notion of "greatest importance for humanity" again reinforces the idea of hierarchies in listing while the other two requirements are fairly straightforward: the obligation of a mirror list of heritage worth protecting, and that the State protecting it will not employ the heritage for military purposes.

As Toman notes, "the objective of Article 10 and the following articles of the Second Protocol is to remove the obstacles created by the restrictive definition and unrealistic conditions preventing larger registration of property under special protection".[56] To that end, the Protocol creates a new List of Cultural Property under Enhanced Protection. The system is modelled, for the most part, on the 1972 World Heritage Convention.[57] Although the notion of simply incorporating cultural heritage on the World Heritage List into the Enhanced Protection List was rejected (partly because of the difference in the definition of 'heritage' between the two instruments, which affects their scope of application), the presence of cultural heritage on the World Heritage List serves as a powerful guide to the "greatest importance for humanity" threshold.[58] In fact, according to the guidelines implementing the Second Protocol, there is a presumption that heritage on the World Heritage List meets the criteria for enhanced protection.[59]

The system created by the Second Protocol appears to function better, and is decidedly less burdensome than the Convention system. The process for inscription is more streamlined and in line with listing processes for other instru-

---

54 J. Hladík, 'UNESCO's activities for the implementation and promotion of the 1954 Hague Convention for the Protection of Cultural Property in the Event of Armed Conflict and its two Protocols', in M. T. Dutli (ed.), *Protection of Cultural Property in the Event of Armed Conflict* (International Committee of the Red Cross, 2002) pp. 57–77, at p. 66.

55 Second Protocol, Article 10.

56 Toman, *supra* note 25, p. 187.

57 Convention concerning the Protection of the World Cultural and Natural Heritage, adopted in Paris on 16 November 1972 (parties as of September 2013: 190). Henckaerts, *supra* note 29, p. 43. UNESCO in 1993 even invited states to submit items of the World Heritage List for consideration for inscription in the Special Protection List. No nominations resulted from this effort. *See* Hladík, *supra* note 54, p. 66.

58 Toman, *supra* note 25, p. 188.

59 Guidelines for the Implementation of the 1999 Second Protocol to the Hague Convention of 1954 for the Protection of Cultural Property in the Event of an Armed Conflict (March 2012), Guideline 36.

ments in the field of heritage. However, it is still tied to the original Convention. Even if the Second Protocol is fairly clear in that the enhanced protection regime replaces the special protection regime for parties to the Second Protocol,[60] the drafting history of the Second Protocol makes it clear that the necessity of staying within the parameters of the Convention was still very much in the mind of the drafters.[61] Clearly, in devising any new system for the protection of the environment in relation to armed conflict pre-existing substantive protections embodied in IHL would need to be considered although, in the absence of any existing institutional mechanism innovative solutions might be more freely pursued. For example, while the notion of borrowing from other lists has been rejected in the case of the cultural heritage regime, the approach might be revisited in the context of developing a new regime for the protection of the environment. This could result in the alleviation of significant bureaucratic and financial burdens on States and promote the continuing and contemporaneous development of any new instrument consistent with the changing environmental obligations of the parties. A number of international environmental instruments already create lists of either protected areas or species,[62] and the notion of listing was already mentioned in the drafting of Additional Protocol I to the 1949 Geneva Conventions.[63] Presumably these lists could form the starting point for any new listing of environmental areas or species to be protected under any new environmentally targeted agreement.

---

60 Second Protocol, Article 4 on the Relationship between Chapter 3 (on enhanced protection) and other provisions of the Convention and this Protocol provides:

> The application of the provisions of Chapter 3 of this Protocol is without prejudice to:
>
> a. the application of the provisions of Chapter I of the Convention and of Chapter 2 of this Protocol [both on general provisions regarding protection];
>
> b. the application of the provisions of Chapter II of the Convention [special protection regime] save that, as between Parties to this Protocol or as between a Party and a State which accepts and applies this Protocol in accordance with Article 3 paragraph 2, where cultural property has been granted both special protection and enhanced protection, only the provisions of enhanced protection shall apply.

61 Toman, *supra* note 25, pp. 190–194.

62 For instance the Ramsar Convention, which establishes a List of Wetlands of International Importance, discussed by M. Bothe, C. Bruch, J. Diamond and D. Jensen, 'International law protecting the environment during armed conflict: gaps and opportunities', 92:879 *International Review of the Red Cross* (2010) pp. 569–592, at p. 582.

63 *See* C. Droege and M.-L. Tougas, 'The Protection of the Natural Environment in Armed Conflict – Existing Rules and Need for Further Legal Protection', in this volume.

3.6. *Marking: The Emblem*

Of course, listing is only one step in the protective process. As provided by Article 6 of the Hague Convention, a consequence of listing is that cultural heritage on one of the lists can be marked with a distinctive emblem. While no such specific provision is found in the Second Protocol, its guidelines for implementation indicate that parties to the Second Protocol are "entitled to mark such cultural property in accordance with Article 6 of the Convention".[64] Once marked the properties are more easily identified as protected for the purposes of the Hague Convention and its Second Protocol. The emblem thus serves an important function, akin to that of the Red Cross/Red Crescent/Red Diamond emblems under the 1949 Geneva Conventions and its protocols.

The question that deserves asking is whether an emblem could similarly be used in the environmental context. Clearly, the marking of individual animals or members of stocks or species would not be possible. Similarly, application of emblems to large natural reserves would be significantly more difficult to achieve. Nevertheless, one might imagine, for example, that an emblem could be easily affixed to trees in much the same way that international hiking marks are affixed to trees, or displayed at the entrances to natural 'refuges' such as greenhouses, zoos or parks. While the practical difficulties associated with such an approach are acknowledged, the possibilities could at least be considered.

3.7. *Funds*

Another important feature of the cultural heritage regime, and an innovation of the Second Protocol, is the existence of a specific Fund for the Protection of Cultural Property in the Event of Armed Conflict.[65] The Fund is meant to support preparatory measures during peacetime, including the preparation of inventories for inclusion in the enhanced protection list, as well as fund emergency assistance and post-conflict recovery. Although the idea of a fund was already mentioned as desirable during the drafting of the 1954 Convention,[66] it was only established by the Second Protocol. The Fund's resources come from voluntary contributions, precisely as a means to avoid the imposition of additional burdens on the parties. As mentioned by the delegate of Argentina during the negotiation of the Second Protocol,[67] the Fund was designed in this way to avoid the difficulties experi-

64 Guidelines for the Implementation of the 1999 Second Protocol to the Hague Convention of 1954 for the Protection of Cultural Property in the Event of an Armed Conflict (March 2012), Guideline 95.

65 Second Protocol, Article 29.

66 Toman, *supra* note 25, p. 597.

67 *Ibid.*, p. 600.

enced with implementation of the World Heritage Fund.[68] Given the potential gravity of conflict related environmental damage such as contamination from oil and chemical spills and the costs and difficulties of remediation, perhaps a useful purpose a dedicated environmental regime might serve would be to establish a funding mechanism, along the lines of that included in the Second Protocol, to help defray the costs of preparation of inventories, emergency environmental protection measures and post-conflict environmental remediation

3.8. *Individual and State Responsibility*

The regime for the protection of cultural heritage in armed conflict imposes clear obligations upon States and individuals with respect to responsibility for, and criminalisation of, acts against cultural heritage during conflict. While the 1954 Convention is silent on matters of State responsibility, Article 38 of the Second Protocol makes clear that State responsibility and the obligation to make reparation subsists, even in the face of the ascription of individual criminal responsibility.[69] The issue of responsibility was of paramount importance during the negotiation of the Second Protocol,[70] with the parties cognizant of the work of the International Law Commission on the Responsibility of States for Internationally Wrongful Acts.[71] The wording of Article 38 of the Second Protocol, which draws on several general IHL instruments, most notably Article 91 of the 1977 Additional Protocol 1,[72] thus envisages the application of the general rules on State responsibility.

With respect to individual criminal responsibility for acts against cultural property, Article 28 of the 1954 Hague Convention only provides that States should adopt domestic legal measures to prosecute and impose sanctions upon persons who breach the Convention.[73] The Second Protocol dedicates an entire chapter to the matter which goes much further than the 1954 Hague Convention in specifying what crimes should be covered by national criminal law and States' obligations in this area.[74] When the 1954 Hague Convention was drafted the concept of individual criminal responsibility under international law was still in its

68 On the fund, *see generally* F. Lenzerini, 'Articles 15–16: World Heritage Fund', in F. Francioni (ed.), *The 1972 World Heritage Convention: A Commentary* (Oxford University Press, 2008) pp. 269–288.

69 Second Protocol, Article 38.

70 Toman, *supra* note 25, p. 665.

71 International Law Commission, 'Draft Articles on the Responsibility of States for Internationally Wrongful Acts', (2001) *Yearbook of the International Law Commission*, vol. II.

72 Toman, *supra* note 25, p. 666.

73 1954 Hague Convention, Article 28.

74 Second Protocol, Articles 15–21.

infancy.[75] By 1962, however, during the First Meeting of the High Contracting Parties, the unsuitability of Article 28 came to the fore. Much of the criticism came from countries that even during the drafting of the 1954 Convention wanted the instrument to have stronger language on sanctions, including particularly countries of the Socialist bloc.[76] With the subsequent evolution of individual criminal responsibility, through developments including the 1977 Additional Protocols to the 1949 Geneva Conventions,[77] the work of the International Law Commission on the Code of Crimes against the Peace and Security of Mankind[78] and the Statute of the International Criminal Court,[79] as well as the ad hoc tribunals for ex-Yugoslavia[80] and Rwanda,[81] momentum was built for a more extensive regime with respect to individual criminal responsibility.[82]

The Second Protocol contains specific rules on matters such as crimes against cultural heritage,[83] jurisdiction,[84] the obligation *aut dedere aut judicare*,[85] extradition,[86] and mutual assistance.[87] This extensive and fairly detailed regime draws on the significant evolution of international criminal law and serves as a valuable model for developing individual criminal responsibility for damage to the environment in relation to armed conflict beyond that already provided for in the Geneva Conventions and Protocol I, particularly in light of the growing criminalisation of environmental harm in domestic and international law.[88]

---

75 Toman, *supra* note 25, p. 254.

76 *Ibid.*, p. 256.

77 Protocol Additional to the Geneva Conventions of 12 August 1949, and relating to the Protection of Victims of International Armed Conflicts (Protocol I), 8 June 1977 (parties as of September 2013: 172). Protocol Additional to the Geneva Conventions of 12 August 1949, and relating to the Protection of Victims of Non-International Armed Conflicts (Protocol II), 8 June 1977 (parties as of September 2013: 166).

78 International Law Commission, 'Draft Code of Crimes against the Peace and Security of Mankind', *Yearbook of the International Law Commission*, vol. II (1954).

79 Rome Statute of the International Criminal Court, 17 July 1998 (parties as of September 2013: 122).

80 Statute of the International Criminal Tribunal for Former Yugoslavia, UN Security Council Resolution 827, 25 May 1993.

81 Statute of the International Criminal Tribunal for Rwanda, UN Security Council Resolution 955, 6 November 1994.

82 Toman, *supra* note 25, at pp. 259–272.

83 Second Protocol, Article 15.

84 Second Protocol, Article 16.

85 Second Protocol, Article 17.

86 Second Protocol, Article 18.

87 Second Protocol, Article 19.

88 Documented by, among others, Wyatt, *supra* note 2, pp. 614–632 and pp. 642–645.

3.9. International Bureaucracies

The discussion above highlights several aspects of the cultural heritage regime that might serve as precedents in the development of a new regime for the protection of the environment during armed conflict. What the discussion above has by and large neglected, however, is the issue of institutionalisation and the question of what the bureaucracy for a new regime might look like. Bearing in mind the risks associated with the further fragmentation of international law through the development of yet another self-contained regime, it is suggested here that any such bureaucracy could perhaps best be established under the auspices of the United Nations Environmental Programme (UNEP) and modelled on the cultural heritage regime which is under the auspices of United Nations Educational, Scientific and Cultural Organization. Within this framework, the Second Protocol creates a specific Committee for the Protection of Cultural Property in the Event of Armed Conflict.[89] This Committee, like many other features of the Second Protocol, is based on the model of the World Heritage Convention's Intergovernmental Committee for the Protection of the Cultural and Natural Heritage of Outstanding Universal Value (World Heritage Committee).[90] The functions of the Committee are to develop guidelines for implementation of the Protocol, make determinations about enhanced protection (including maintenance of the List), monitor implementation of the Protocol, consider requests for international assistance, and manage the Fund. The Committee is expected to cooperate with international and national governmental and non-governmental organisations performing activities in the area of protection of heritage during armed conflict, and can invite these organisations to attend its meetings in advisory capacity.[91] The Committee relies on the UNESCO Secretariat for assistance with preparatory work.[92]

One shortcoming of the cultural heritage regime is that it relies excessively on governmental agents and experts, and does not include members of the affected populations.[93] More inclusive and participatory solutions might be preferable in the case of protection of the environment. In addition, it must be admitted that the experience with a separate committee under UNESCO's umbrella is not entirely positive. Despite the fact that the bodies implementing different heritage instruments under UNESCO are all located in the same physical space and deal with the same subject-matter (cultural heritage), effective communication and the exploitation of possible functional synergies are lacking, although beyond its own confines, UNESCO actively cooperates with the International Committee

89 Second Protocol, Article 24.

90 Toman, *supra* note 25, p. 526.

91 Second Protocol, Article 27.

92 Second Protocol, Article 28.

93 Second Protocol, Article 24(4).

of the Red Cross (ICRC) in the implementation of the 1954 Hague Convention and its Protocols.[94] This kind of institutional and inter-regime cooperation would also be necessary in the environmental context.

4. Concluding Remarks

Ecofeminism, coupled with feminist international law, helps explain why the protection of the environment in relation to armed conflict has been neglected as a topic of international regulation. It also demonstrates that a deeper change in attitude towards the environment is needed if the move towards a new regime on the protection of the environment during armed conflict is to succeed. Assuming that attitudinal change is forthcoming, the regime for the protection of cultural heritage during armed conflict can serve as a useful guide for the design of any new regime with respect to the environment. If one considers that many of the significant innovations brought about by the 1999 Second Protocol to the 1954 Hague Convention were inspired by the World Heritage Convention, an instrument which protects both natural and cultural sites of significance, the connection is even stronger. The cultural heritage regime can teach important lessons with respect to regime design relating to, *inter alia*, listing, individual and State responsibility, and the design and functioning of a bureaucracy. Ultimately, however, it is up to States to decide whether a further regime is needed to protect the environment from the scourges of armed conflict for generations to come.

---

94 Hladík, *supra* note 54, pp. 60–61.

8 The Role of Multilateral Environmental Agreements in Armed Conflict: 'Green-keeping' in Virunga Park. Applying the UNESCO World Heritage Convention in the Armed Conflict of the Democratic Republic of the Congo

Britta Sjöstedt*

1. Introduction

The Virunga National Park (the Park) is situated in the east of the Democratic Republic of the Congo (the DRC). Because of the outstanding value of its nature in 1979 the Park was included on the World Heritage List and protected under the 1972 United Nations Educational, Scientific and Cultural Organization (UNESCO) World Heritage Convention (the WHC).[1] However, since 1996 the unique environment of the Park has been imperilled due to armed conflicts taking place in and around the Park.[2]

Damage occurring during armed conflict, including environmental damage, is primarily regulated and assessed under the law of armed conflict. However, there is a common understanding among scholars that the law of armed conflict has thus far proven inadequate to deal with environmental wartime damage.[3]

---

* PhD Candidate, Faculty of Law, Lund University, Sweden

1 The DRC ratified the WHC on 23 September 1974; *see* <www.whc.unesco.org/en/statesparties>, visited 30 September 2012. The DRC has five natural world heritage sites protected under the WHC including the Salonga National Park, Okapi Wildlife Reserve, Kahuzi-Biega National Park and Garamba National Park. For the full text of the 1972 UNESCO World Heritage Convention, *see* the UNESCO World Heritage Centre website <www.whc.unesco.org/en/ conventiontext>.

2 Already in 1994 the Park was adversely affected by persons displaced because of the Rwandan genocide. Approximately 720,000 displaced persons settled inside and around the Park. Although many of them have left the Park, it has been adversely affected due to the exploitation of the Park's resources. *See* A. Crawford and J. Bernstein, *MEAs, Conservation and Conflict – A Case Study of Virunga National Park, DRC* (International Institute for Sustainable Development, Winnipeg, 2008) pp. 15–16.

3 For further reading, *see* M. Bothe *et al.*, 'International Law Protecting the Environment During Armed Conflict: Gaps and Opportunities', 92:879 *International Review of the Red Cross* (2010) pp. 569–592; Y. Dinstein, 'Protection of the Environment

Rosemary Rayfuse (ed.), War and the Environment: New Approaches to Protecting the Environment in Relation to Armed Conflict
 ISBN 978-90-04-27064-0 pp. 179-234

Attention has therefore turned to the analysis of the potential role of multilateral environmental agreements (MEAs) to address environmental damage in times of armed conflict. The continued applicability of MEAs during armed conflict may overlap or even conflict with the law of armed conflict and other regimes that regulate the same subject matter.[4] In a situation where several overlapping and perhaps conflicting international legal obligations may apply the question must be asked: what rules are the States obliged to follow?

The purpose of this study is to analyse the role of the WHC in addressing environmental damage during armed conflict and to examine how the rules of the WHC relate to other relevant legal regimes. In particular, the study focuses on the capacity of the WHC, with its typically general and vague provisions, to deal with the environmental damage resulting from the armed conflicts in and around the Park, during the time between 2000 and 2011.

The following section describes the consequences of the warfare for the Park's environment. Section 3 then provides a brief overview of the law applicable to the situation in the Park. Section 4 discusses the potential role of the WHC in addressing the environmental damage caused to the Park by the conflicts by scrutinising the legal nature and powers of the WHC, while section 5 examines the decisions and recommendations concerning the Park that have been adopted by the World Heritage Committee (the Committee), the executive organ of the WHC. The study concludes with a discussion of the consequences of applying the WHC during the armed conflict and whether other relevant legal regimes may be affected by such application.

2. The Impacts of the Armed Conflicts on Virunga Park

Virunga Park covers an area of approximately 800,000 hectares encompassing active volcanoes, wetlands, rainforest, savannah, snow-capped mountains

---

in International Armed Conflict', 5 *Max Plank Yearbook of United Nations Law* (2001) pp. 523–546; R. Falk, 'Evaluating the Adequacy of Existing International Law Standards', in J. Austin and C. Bruch (eds.), *The Environmental Consequences of War* (Cambridge University Press, Cambridge, 2000) pp. 137–155; W. Verwey, 'Protection of the Environment in Times of Armed Conflict: In Search of a New Legal Perspective', 8 *Leiden Journal of International Law* (1995) pp. 7–40; S. Simonds, 'Conventional Warfare and Environmental Protection', 29 *Stanford Journal of International Law* (1992–1993) pp. 165–221; S. Vöneky, 'Peacetime Environmental Law as a Basis of State Responsibility for Environmental Damage Caused by War', in J. Austin and C. Bruch (eds.), *The Environmental Consequences of War* (Cambridge University Press, Cambridge, 2000) pp. 190–193.

4 For further reading on specialised regimes regulating the same subject matter, *see* N. Matz-Lück, 'Norm Interpretation across International Regimes: Competences and Legitimacy', in M. Young (ed.), *Regime Interaction in International Law Facing Fragmentation*(Cambridge University Press, Cambridge, 2012) pp. 201–234.

and woodlands.[5] The Park was inscribed on the World Heritage List in 1979 as a natural site due to its exceptional biological diversity and astonishing beauty in accordance with Articles 2 and 11(3) of the WHC.[6] The Park hosts a wealth of wildlife, including lions, buffalos, hippopotamus and elephants. The Park is particularly known for its mountain gorillas, a critically endangered species listed on the Appendix I of the 1973 Convention on the Illegal Trade on Endangered Species (CITES).[7] Humans, too, live in the Park. In 2001 it was reported that over 20,000 families were living in the central and northern parts of the Park where they engaged in fishing and livestock herding activities.[8]

Since 1996, a number of armed conflicts, both international and non-international in nature, have taken place in the DRC. The ongoing warfare has had severe impacts on the Park. Because the Park offers shelter, foodstuff, water and charcoal for cooking and heating, persons displaced by the fighting, as well as armed groups engaged in the fighting, have taken refuge inside the Park.[9] The cutting of firewood and wildlife poaching by the displaced population in camps installed inside and around the Park has adversely effected the environment.[10] Moreover, armed groups have used the inaccessible nature of the Park for strategic purposes both as a hiding place and as a place to set up base camps for planning and launching attacks.[11] Economic motives have also been influential in attracting armed groups to the Park with members of armed groups having been involved in illegal[12] exploitation of the Park's natural resources through mining

5 UNESCO World Heritage Centre Publication, *World Heritage in the Congo Basin* (2010) p. 20.

6 UNESCO World Heritage Centre website <www.whc.unesco.org/en/list/63>, visited on 30 September 2012.

7 The mountain gorilla has been included since 1975 on Appendix I of the 1973 Convention on the Illegal Trade on Endangered Species (CITES). Appendix I lists species that are the most endangered among CITES-listed animals and plants (*see* Article 2(1) of the Convention). *See* CITES website <www.cites.org/eng/app/appendices.php>, visited 30 September 2012.

8 UNESCO World Heritage Committee, Doc. WHC-01/CONF.208/24, 8 February 2002, p. 17.

9 *See* Crawford and Bernstein, *supra* note 2, pp. 15–16. *See also* UNESCO World Heritage, *State of conservation of the properties inscribed on the List of World Heritage in Danger*, Doc. WHC-08/32.COM/7A, 22 May 2008, p. 10.

10 Crawford and Bernstein, *supra* note 2, p. 15.

11 UNESCO World Heritage Committee, Doc. WHC-01/CONF.208/24, 8 February 2002, p. 17. For example, between 2008 and 2009, armed rebel groups occupied the gorilla sector. *See also* UNESCO World Heritage Committee, *State of conservation of the properties inscribed on the List of World Heritage in Danger*, Doc. WHC-09/33.COM/7A, 11 May 2009, p. 12.

12 The term 'illegal' in this study is used in the same sense as in the 'Report of the Panel of Experts on the Illegal Exploitation of Natural Resources and Other Forms of Wealth in the Democratic Republic of the Congo' meaning all activities includ-

activities and charcoal production used both to sustain their military operations and for personal gain.[13] Additionally, armed groups using automatic weapons have been involved in large-scale poaching of the Park's protected animal species for food purposes and for war-sustaining trade in ivory and bush meat.[14] This has led to serious consequences for the protected wildlife of the Park where, for example, the hippopotamus population[15] has now been taken to the brink of extinction.[16]

The presence of the rebel groups in the Park has also resulted in the corresponding conduct of military operations by the DRC army inside the Park aimed at defeating the rebel groups.[17] These operations have been conducted in a way that has jeopardised the integrity of the Park by, for example, cutting down trees to deny the rebels cover, and placing army posts and training camps inside the Park.[18] In addition, poor discipline, irregular pay and lack of food have resulted in the growing participation of military personnel in illegal activities, including

---

ing extraction, production, commercialization and exports occurring in the DRC without being approved by the DRC government; not in accordance with existing national regulations; not according to accepted practices in trade and business as conducted in the DRC; and/or in violation with international law. For further explanations, *see* UN Security Council, UN Doc. S/2001/357, 21 April 2001, para. 15.

13 *See* UNESCO World Heritage Committee, *State of conservation of the properties inscribed on the List of World Heritage in Danger*, Doc. WHC-06/30.COM/7A, 26 May 2007, p. 27; *State of conservation of the properties inscribed on the List of World Heritage in Danger*, Doc. WHC-07/31. COM/7A, 10 May 2007, p. 9; *State of conservation of the properties inscribed on the List of World Heritage in Danger*, Doc. WHC-08/32. COM/7A, 22 May 2008, p. 8. *See also* Crawford and Bernstein, *supra* note 2, pp. 17–18.

14 *See* UNESCO World Heritage Committee, *State of conservation of the properties inscribed on the List of World Heritage in Danger*, Doc. WHC-07/31.COM/7A, 10 May 2007, p. 9; *State of conservation of the properties inscribed on the List of World Heritage in Danger*, Doc. WHC-08/32. COM/7A, 22 May 2008, p. 8.

15 Hippopotamus have been listed in Appendix II of the CITES since 1995. *See* CITES website <www.cites.org/eng/app/appendices.php>, visited 30 September 2012.

16 Crawford and Bernstein, *supra* note 2, p. 20.

17 UNESCO World Heritage Committee, *State of conservation of the properties inscribed on the List of World Heritage in Danger*, Doc. WHC-07/31.COM/7A, 10 May 2007, p. 9.

18 In 2006 it was reported that four brigades totalling 12,000 soldiers were deployed inside or close to the Park, some of them with their families. *See* UNESCO World Heritage Committee, *State of conservation of the properties inscribed on the List of World Heritage in Danger*, Doc. WHC-06/30.COM/7A, 26 May 2006, p. 27; *State of conservation of the properties inscribed on the List of World Heritage in Danger*, Doc. WHC-08/32.COM/7A, 22 May 2008, p. 10. *See also* J. Kalpers, 'Overview of the Armed Conflict and Biodiversity in Sub-Saharan Africa: Impact, Mechanisms and Responses', 2001 Biodiversity Support Program, Washington DC, 2001, p. 13.

artisanal mining, charcoal production and wildlife poaching.[19] Several members of the DRC army have also collaborated with rebels in the illegal charcoal trade in the Park.[20] Even though the DRC army has agreed to cooperate with the Park rangers to protect the Park, the army's involvement in illegal activities has made such cooperation difficult, with violent confrontations having occurred between the DRC army and the Park staff.[21] In one particularly noteworthy incident in November 2006, the head of one of the Park ranger stations was tortured by the commander of the army camp in Rutshuru, which lies inside the Park, probably to deter the efforts of the Park rangers to control the charcoal activities involving members of the army.[22]

The Park's richness in natural resources has made control over the Park an important feature in the armed conflicts for both strategic and economic reasons. The Park areas function as hiding places and bases to launch attacks and as an income generator for funding the conflict.[23] As a consequence of the military activities, the job of the Park rangers has become extremely dangerous and has even resulted in the rangers being themselves targeted.[24] Between the start of the armed conflicts in 1996 and 2008 more than 190 Park rangers were reportedly killed while performing their duties.[25] By the same token, members of the Park staff have also been accused of corruption and involvement in illegal activities.

---

19 *See* UNESCO World Heritage Committee, *State of conservation of the properties inscribed on the List of World Heritage in Danger*, Doc. WHC-04/28.COM/15A Rev, 21 June 2004, p. 8; *State of conservation of the properties inscribed on the List of World Heritage in Danger*, Doc. WHC-10/34. COM/7A, 1 June 2010, p. 11.

20 *Final Report of Groups of Experts on the DRC*, UN Security Council, UN Doc. S/2008/773, 12 December 2008, para. 113.

21 *See* UNESCO World Heritage Committee, *State of conservation of the properties inscribed on the List of World Heritage in Danger*, Doc. WHC-04/28.COM/15A Rev, 21 June 2004, p. 8; *State of conservation of the properties inscribed on the List of World Heritage in Danger*, Doc. WHC-06/30. COM/7A, 26 May 2006, p. 27; *State of conservation of the properties inscribed on the List of World Heritage in Danger*, Doc. WHC-10/34.COM/7A, 1 June 2010, p. 11; *State of conservation of the properties inscribed on the List of World Heritage in Danger*, Doc. WHC-10/34.COM/7A.Add, 22 June 2010, pp. 82-83.

22 Following an international protest, the Minister of Defence in the DRC ordered an investigation of this event. *See* UNESCO World Heritage Committee, *State of conservation of the properties inscribed on the List of World Heritage in Danger*, Doc. WHC-07/31.COM/7A, 10 May 2007, p. 9.

23 Crawford and Bernstein, *supra* note 2, pp. 17–18.

24 UNESCO World Heritage Committee, *State of conservation of the properties inscribed on the List of World Heritage in Danger*, Doc. WHC-98/CONF.203/7, 30 September 1998, p. 4.

25 UNEP, *The Last Stand of the Gorilla, Environmental Crime and Conflict in the Congo Basin*(2010), p. 21. <www.unep.org/pdf/GorillaStand_screen.pdf>, visited 30 September 2012.

In one notable incident, in the summer of 2007, the chief warden of the Park, Honoré Mashagiro, was arrested for being involved in the charcoal trade and in an incident concerning the killing of ten gorillas.[26]

3. Applicable International Law Relating to Environmental Damage in Armed Conflict

When addressing the environmental damage occurring in the Park from an international law perspective, a first reflection is that several legal regimes may be applicable. These legal regimes include, among others, international environmental law and the law of armed conflict. Several provisions in the law of armed conflict are aimed, directly or indirectly, at protection of the environment. In terms of direct protection, Articles 35(3) and 55(1) of the 1977 Additional Protocol I to the 1949 Geneva Conventions (Protocol I) and the 1976 Convention on the Prohibition of Military or Any Other Hostile Use of Environmental Modification Techniques (ENMOD Convention) specifically refer to the environment. Both Protocol I and the ENMOD Convention only apply in international armed conflict. The ENMOD Convention regulates intentional environmental modification techniques and has a more narrow scope of protection than Articles 35(3) and 55(1) in Protocol I. The ENMOD Convention is not relevant in the case of the Park given that the warfare does not involve any attempt to intentionally modify the environment. For their part, Articles 35(3) and 55(1) set an extremely high threshold by including the cumulative requirement of "widespread, long-term and severe damage to the natural environment". The definition of these terms remains unclear; however, it is evident that, in any case, the damage has to be of an exceptional nature. In addition, as required by Article 35(3), the environmental damage must also be a result of the application of means and methods of warfare. Thus, although extensive damage to the environment has occurred in the Park, it is highly unlikely that such damage would reach the threshold set out in Articles 35(3) and/or 55(1).[27]

While Protocol I and the ENMOD Convention are applicable in international armed conflicts, the armed conflicts in the DRC have changed character over time, vacillating between non-international and international and back to

---

26 Crawford and Bernstein, *supra* note 2, p. 22.

27 For further reading on the definitions of the requirements set out in Articles 35(3) and 55 in Protocol I, *see* K. Hulme, *War Torn Environment: Interpreting the Legal Threshold* (Hotei Publishing, Leiden, 2004) pp. 88–100; Y. Dinstein, *The Conduct of Hostilities under the Law of International Armed Conflict* (Cambridge University Press, Cambridge, 2004) pp. 181–186; M. Schmitt, 'Green War: An Assessment of Environmental Law of International Armed Conflict', 22 *Yale Journal of International Law* (1997) pp. 68–81.

non-international.[28] This further complicates the application of the law of armed conflict, rendering much of that body of law inapplicable in the case of the Park. The rules relevant to non-international armed conflicts are scarce, consisting primarily of common Article 3 in the Geneva Conventions of 1949 and the provisions of the 1977 Additional Protocol II to the Geneva Conventions of 1949 (Protocol II). However, emerging customary international norms have extended the application of many provisions regulating international armed conflicts to non-international armed conflicts. According to the study on the current status of international customary law completed by the International Committee of the Red Cross (the ICRC), Articles 35(3) and 55(1) constitute customary international law and can thus arguably be applied in non-international armed conflicts as well.[29]

The law of armed conflict also provides the environment with indirect protection as a civilian object. Article 52(1) of Protocol I prohibits attacks against civilian objects, that is all objects that are not 'military objectives'. Article 52 of Protocol I represents customary law and the prohibition of attacks on civilian objects thus applies in non-international armed conflict as well.[30] Nevertheless, the environment can represent a military objective if it "by nature, location, purpose or use makes an effective contribution to military action and [if its] total or partial destruction, capture or neutralization, in the circumstances ruling at the time, offers a definite military advantage".[31] Thus, protection of the environment as a civilian object is relatively weak because environmental elements can turn

28 The First Congo War lasted between 1996–1998 and involved Rwanda, Uganda and Angola. The second Congo War lasted between 1998–2000 and involved DRC, Rwanda, Uganda, Zimbabwe, Burundi, Angola, Namibia, Chad, Eritrea and Sudan to varying degrees. A peace agreement was signed between warring parties in April 2002. The fighting has however continued with such intensity and organisation among the concerned armed groups, including the DRC army, that it should be classified as a conflict of non-international character (although it still may have some international elements). The lines are however blurring. *Cf.* with OCHA, *Democratic Republic of the Congo Mapping Exercise* (2010) pp. 8–10, documenting the most serious violations of human rights and international humanitarian law 1993–2003, <www.ohchr.org/Documents/Countries/ZR/DRC_MAPPING_REPORT_FINAL_EN.pdf>, visited September 2012. *See also* Crawford and Bernstein, *supra* note 2, pp. 6–8, and *Prosecutor* v. *Tadić*, Opinion and Judgment, Case IT-94-1-T (May 7, 1997) for classification of armed conflict.

29 *See* Rules 43-45 in J.-M. Henckaerts and L. Doswald-Beck (eds.), *Customary International Humanitarian Law Study* (Cambridge University Press, Cambridge, 2005) vol. I, pp. 143–158.

30 *Ibid.*, pp. 25–35. Rules 7–10 in the Customary Law Study by ICRC expand the application to also include non-international armed conflict.

31 Article 52(2) of the Additional Protocol I (1977). Incorporated as Rule 8 in the Customary Law Study and applies to non-international armed conflicts. *See* Henckaerts and Doswald-Beck, *supra* note 29, pp. 29–32.

into military objectives depending on their use.[32] This is illustrated in the case of the Park where, for example, armed groups use the Park as a hiding place or base of operations thereby turning at least parts of the Park into military objectives.

In sum, the law of armed conflict does not contain a clear assertion of the degree of environmental damage that can be tolerated.[33] Thus a substantial amount of damage can be done to the environment so long as it is proportionate in relation to the military advantage anticipated of an attack in accordance with the proportionality principle[34] or does not reach the threshold in Articles 35(3) or 55(1).

The inadequacy of the law of armed conflict to protect the environment has been well studied.[35] This has led to the recognition that international environmental law may provide alternative approaches to address environmental damage in times of armed conflict. Indeed, the applicability of MEAs during armed conflict is increasingly recognised in international law. As long ago as 1993, UN General Assembly resolution 47/37 urged States to comply with international law protecting the environment during armed conflict.[36] In the course of its work on the 'Effects of Armed Conflict on Treaties', the UN International Law Commission (ILC) concluded, in its Draft Article 3, that "the existence of an armed conflict does not *ipso facto* terminate or suspend the operation of treaties".[37] Annexed to Draft Article 7, the ILC incorporated an indicative list of treaties whose subject matter implies continued application during armed conflict. This list includes environmental treaties.[38] This shows that there is a general presumption by the ILC that MEAs continue to apply during armed conflict.[39]

The DRC is a State party to several MEAs that could be of interest for addressing the environmental damage in the Park. In addition to the WHC and CITES

---

32 Bothe *et al.*, *supra* note 3, p. 576.

33 M. Schmitt, 'War and the Environment: Fault Lines in the Prescriptive Landscape', in J. Austin and C. Bruch (eds.), *The Environmental Consequences of War* (Cambridge University Press, Cambridge, 2000) p. 113.

34 The principle of proportionality in attack is codified in Article 51(5)(b) in Protocol I. It is also included in the ICRC Customary Law Study in Rule 14 and applies in both international and non-international armed conflict. *See* Henckaerts and Doswald-Beck, *supra* note 29, pp. 46–50. For further reading on the proportionality principle and environmental damage in armed conflict, see Bothe *et al.*, *supra* note 3, pp 577–578.

35 *See* various sources, *supra* note 3.

36 UN General Assembly, *Protection of the Environment in Times of Armed Conflict*, UN Doc. A/47/37, 25 November 1993.

37 Draft Articles on the Effects of Armed Conflicts on Treaties, with Commentaries, adopted at the 63rd session of the ILC (2011), Draft Article 3, <untreaty.un.org/ilc/texts/instruments/english/commentaries/1_10_2011.pdf>.

38 *See ibid.*, Draft Article 7 and annexed indicative list of treaties.

39 *See ibid.*, Commentaries attached to the indicative list of treaties.

these include: the 1992 Biological Diversity Convention; the 1979 Convention on the Conservation of Migratory Species of Wild Animals; the 1971 Convention on Wetlands of International Importance; and the 2003 African Convention on the Conservation of Nature and Natural Resources. The chosen focus of this study is the WHC because the natural world heritage sites in the DRC, including the Park, have been put on the Danger List due to the threat posed by the armed conflicts taking place in and around the sites. In addition, in 2000 a project[40] was launched by the WHC in the DRC with the expressed goal of protecting the world heritage sites in times of armed conflict. This makes the WHC of particular interest and relevance when assessing the role of MEAs during armed conflict.

4. The World Heritage Convention

The WHC protects world heritage sites of outstanding universal value. Pursuant to Article 4 of the WHC the States parties to the Convention are under the obligation to ensure the identification, protection, preservation, presentation and transmission, for future generations, of the cultural and natural heritage situated in their territory. Article 6(3) of the WHC requires States parties to refrain from deliberately causing damage to the world heritage sites situated in the territory of other States parties, whether directly or indirectly. To enhance the protection, pursuant to Article 11(2), States parties can nominate sites in their territory to be inscribed on the World Heritage List. For designation to that List, a site has to fulfill the requirements set out in Articles 1 and 2 of the WHC.[41] The World Heritage List is supported by a separate 'List of World Heritage in Danger' (the 'Danger List') provided for in Article 11(4). Sites on the Danger List are prioritised for international assistance under the WHC according to Article 21(2). The 'outbreak of an armed conflict' is expressly identified as such a danger in Article 11(4).[42] The explicit reference to 'outbreak of an armed conflict' in Article 11(4) strengthens the notion that the WHC should continue to apply in times of armed conflict

40 For more information regarding the project, *see* section 5 below.

41 In accordance with Articles 1 and 2, these sites must all have elements that are of outstanding universal value.

42 Other serious and specific dangers listed in Article 11(4) of the WHC include: 'threat of disappearance caused by accelerated deterioration, large-scale public or private projects or rapid urban or tourist development projects; destruction caused by changes in the use or ownership of the land; major alterations due to unknown causes; abandonment for any reason whatsoever; calamities and cataclysms; serious fires, earthquakes, landslides; volcanic eruptions; changes in water level, floods and tidal waves'.

and, indeed, several scholars share this view.[43] Importantly, the Virunga Park has been on the Danger List since 1994.[44]

4.1. The Legal Mandate of the World Heritage Convention

Regardless of whether MEAs continue to operate during armed conflict, it must be asked whether this body of law can play a meaningful role in such situations. International environmental law is often criticised for being nothing more than a 'negotiation system' with poor implementation even in peacetime.[45] Given the particular nature of environmental problems, MEAs often consist merely of frameworks general principles and vague obligations.[46] This is also the case in respect of the WHC. For example, Article 4 of the WHC requires States parties to do all they can to protect world heritage sites "to the utmost of [their] own resources". Similarly, Article 5 proposes measures that each State party is merely to 'endeavour' to undertake to safeguard the world heritage within its territory. The wording used in both of these articles permits a degree of flexibility for States parties to choose measures adjustable to the particular problems within the national context. In other words, it is up to the State party to decide what the appropriate action will consist of. This flexibility renders the obligations vague since there are no expressed tangible requirements of what States parties must do to comply with the instrument.[47] As a result, State responsibility is difficult to enforce. Moreover, and particularly germane to this study, the WHC does not contain any specific provisions or mechanisms to protect world heritage sites during armed conflict.[48] In the absence of concrete enforceable obligations, the

---

43 *See* Bothe *et al.*, *supra* note 3, p. 582; Vöneky, *supra* note 3, pp. 224–225; J. Austin and C. Bruch, 'Legal Mechanisms for Addressing Wartime Damage to Tropical Forests', 16 *Journal of Sustainable Forestry* (2003) pp. 171–172.

44 UNESCO World Heritage Committee, Decision 18COM IX adopted at 18th session on 12–17 December 1994, Doc. WHC-94/CONF.003/16, 31 January 1995. The massive movement of displaced persons from the Rwandan civil war who sheltered in Virunga Park created adverse impacts on the Park resulting in stipulations for inscription on the List of Danger. *See also* UNESCO World Heritage Committee, *State of conservation of the properties inscribed on the List of World Heritage in Danger*, Doc. WHC-09/33.COM/7A, 11 May 2009, p. 11.

45 D. Bodansky, *The Art and Craft of International Environmental Law* (Harvard University Press, Cambridge, 2011) p. 226.

46 P. Birnie *et al.*, *International law & the environment* (Oxford University Press, Oxford, 2009) p. 17.

47 *See* G. Carducci, 'Articles 4–7, National and International Protection of Cultural and Natural Heritage', in F. Francioni (ed.), *The 1972 World Heritage Convention: A Commentary* (Oxford University Press, Oxford, 2008) p. 145.

48 *See* W. Burhenne, 'The Prohibition of Hostile Military Activities in Protected Areas', 27:4 *Environmental Policy and Law* (1997) p. 373; Verwey, *supra* note 3, p. 15; R. Tarasofsky, 'Protecting Specially Important Areas during International Armed Conflict:

Convention's ability to create meaningful environmental protection in times of armed conflict is thus questionable.

The lack of discrete substantive obligations in the WHC is neither unusual nor entirely unhelpful but rather just a manifestation of the constitutive and dynamic character of MEAs. As Bodansky explains it, "the treaty text itself represents just the tip of the normative iceberg".[49] The constitutive element in MEAs enables them to create systems of governance for specific issues by establishing institutions that develop the treaty provisions into substantive rules.[50] In the case of the WHC, it is the World Heritage Committee that defines and develops the provisions of the WHC by adopting decisions, recommendations and guidelines.[51] In particular, the Committee has adopted a set of Operational Guidelines[52] that provide directions for the application of the WHC. In contrast to other MEAs, the WHC has assigned all the decision-making competences to the Committee as opposed to the General Assembly of the State parties to the Convention.[53] The Committee is also empowered to adopt recommendations and executive decisions in regard to specific world heritage sites.[54] The Operational Guidelines together with the recommendations and decisions of the Committee are thus relevant to the assessment of the role of the WHC in relation to the armed conflicts occurring in and around the Park.

Like other MEAs, the WHC lacks an enforcement mechanism. Rather, it penalises non-compliance through 'international exposure and embarrassment'.[55] In exceptional cases, delisting of a site from the World Heritage List may also

---

A Critique of the IUCN Draft Convention on the Prohibition of Hostile Military Activities in Protected Areas', in J. Austin and C. Bruch (eds.), *The Environmental Consequences of War* (Cambridge University Press, Cambridge, 2000) p. 568.

49 Bodansky, *supra* note 45, p. 155.

50 *Ibid.*, p. 158.

51 The Committee is composed of 21 member States and meets at least once a year. *See The Operational Guidelines for Implementation of the WHC (hereinafter the Operational Guidelines)* (November 2011) available at <whc.unesco.org/archive/opguide11-en.pdf>, visited 30 September 2012.

52 *Ibid.*

53 The General Assembly corresponds to a conference of the parties, which is usually the supreme decision-making organ in MEAs. *See* D. Zacharias, 'The UNESCO Regime for the Protection of World Heritage as Prototype of an Autonomy-Gaining International Institution', 9 *German Law Journal* (2008) p. 1842.

54 *Ibid.*, p. 1838.

55 *See* Bodansky, *supra* note 45, pp. 226–227. For further reading on compliance under the WHC, *see* E. Goodwin, 'The World Heritage Convention, the Environment, and Compliance', 20:2 *Colorado Journal of International Environmental Law & Policy* (2009) p. 157.

occur.[56] However, more positively, the WHC uses measures or tools to facilitate compliance and works with States parties to overcome causes of non-compliance rather than engaging in robust enforcement measures.[57] International assistance (discussed below), the World Heritage Fund[58] and the Operational Guidelines are all tools designed to enhance compliance by States parties.

4.2. *International Assistance*

An important feature of the WHC, designed to augment compliance, is the system of international assistance. States parties may make requests for international assistance to the Committee for the purposes of securing the protection, conservation, presentation or rehabilitation of the world heritage sites.[59] International assistance may consist of studies, the provision of experts, skilled labour, training of staff and specialists, the supply of equipment, low-interest or interest-free loans or the granting of non-repayable subsidies.[60] The Committee decides whether action should be taken; the nature and extent of the assistance; it makes the necessary arrangements with the government of the concerned State party; and sets the priority for the assistance.[61] Interestingly, although the provisions of the WHC allow only States parties to request international assistance for world heritage sites situated in their territories,[62] for sites on the Danger List, paragraph 177(d) of the Operational Guidelines authorises any Committee member or the Secretariat – the administrative body of the WHC[63] – to make requests concerning international assistance. Indeed, in such cases, the Committee is empowered

56 The Committee suggested starting a process to delist the cultural site – the Cologne Cathedral – in Germany, unless Germany reconsidered its building projects. Germany halted the building plans and the Cologne Cathedral was kept on the World Heritage List. In 2007, the Committee decided to remove the 'Arabian Oryx Sanctuary', as hydrocarbon exploration activities inside the World Heritage Site reduced its outstanding value. *See* T. Scovazzi, 'Articles 8–11, World Heritage Committee and World Heritage List', in F. Francioni (ed.), *The 1972 World Heritage Convention: A Commentary* (Oxford University Press, Oxford, 2008) pp. 170–171.

57 *See* Bodansky, *supra* note 45, pp. 226–227, in regard to MEAs in general, and in particular on the WHC compliance mechanism, *see* Goodwin, *supra* note 55, p. 157.

58 The World Heritage Fund is a trust fund for the protection of the World Heritage Sites consisting of compulsory and voluntary contributions by State parties. The Fund is established in accordance with Article 15 of the WHC.

59 The Committee grants the requests in accordance with Article 13(1) of the WHC.

60 WHC, Article 22.

61 WHC, Articles 13(3) and (4).

62 Only State parties can make a request for a world heritage site within their territory according to Articles 13, 19 and 21 of the WHC.

63 The role of the Secretariat to the World Heritage Committee is to assist the Committee as provided by Article 14(2) of the WHC.

not only to make such a request, but also to decide on the action that should be taken in regard to the site in accordance with Article 13(3) in the WHC. Hence, theoretically, a State may be the subject of international assistance for a site on the Danger List located in its territory without requesting or consenting to it.

The possibility for a Committee member or the Secretariat, as opposed to the territorial State, to request international assistance is a significant development resulting from the Committee's practice under the Convention. It is often conduct of the territorial State that contributes to the endangered status of a site leading to its inscription on the Danger List.[64] In situations preceding such inscription, it is understandably difficult to obtain the consent of the territorial State concerned. This tension between respect for State sovereignty and the international interest in protecting world heritage sites is embodied in Article 6(1) of the WHC, which establishes a duty on the international community to cooperate to protect world heritage while 'fully respecting' State sovereignty. The protection of a collective or an international interest of the States parties and the non-reciprocal character of Articles 6(1) and 7 suggest that the obligations are so-called *erga omnes partes* obligations. According to the International Court of Justice (the ICJ), *erga omnes* obligations are owed towards the international community as a whole, and can be distinguished from other obligations of a reciprocal character owed to another State. *Erga omnes* obligations constitute a concern of all States and all States therefore have a legal interest in protecting such concern.[65] Similarly, the protection of the world heritage sites represents a universal interest that all States parties to the WHC have a legal obligation to uphold. Article 7 establishes a system for international cooperation under the WHC enabling international assistance to protect this common interest. Thus, international assistance embodies the protection of a collective interest of the States parties by the international community.[66] Therefore, Articles 6(1) and 7 in the WHC constitute *erga omnes partes* obligations.[67] This may imply that the protection of a universal

---

64 G. P. Buzzini and L. Condorelli, 'Article 11, List of World Heritage in Danger and Deletion ofa Property from the World Heritage List', in F. Francioni (ed.), *The 1972 World Heritage Convention, A Commentary* (Oxford University Press, Oxford, 2008) p. 185.

65 *Case concerning the Barcelona Traction, Light and Power Company Limited (Belgium v. Spain)*, 5 February 1970, ICJ, Judgment, para. 33. <www.icj-cij.org/docket/files/50/5387.pdf>, visited on 30 September, 2012.

66 Carducci, *supra* note 47, pp. 119–120 and pp. 131–132. *See also* UNESCO World Heritage Committee, *Legal considerations concerning the inscription of properties on the List of World Heritage in Danger and the deletion of properties from the World Heritage List*, Doc. WHC-02/CONF.202/8, 21 May 2002, para. 34–35. For further reading in particular on the WHC and obligations *erga omnes/erga omnes parks, see* Carducci, *ibid.*, pp. 132–145.

67 *Erga omnes partes* obligations must be distinguished from *erga omnes* obligations. *Erga omnes partes* obligations are established to protect a common interest of a group of State parties to a specific regime. These 'collective obligations' are bind-

value of a world heritage site may, in some situations, supersede State sovereignty and justify the granting of international assistance even in the absence of State consent. States parties have, after all, agreed to constrain their sovereignty in relation to the world heritage sites in accordance with the binding obligations in the WHC.[68] The possibility for a non-territorial State to make a request for international assistance, as provided in the Operational Guidelines, corresponds with the *erga omnes partes* nature of the obligations of the WHC in protecting a global concern.[69]

Nevertheless, Article 4 of the WHC acknowledges that the duty to protect world heritage belongs first and foremost to the territorial State. Even if the Committee is able to request international assistance without State consent, the reality is that without State cooperation such international assistance will be impractible to carry out.[70] Accordingly, once the Committee approves an international assistance request, the Secretariat concludes an agreement with the concerned State defining the conditions for how the international assistance is to be performed pursuant to Article 26 in the WHC. As per Article 4, however, the State receiving the assistance retains the primary obligation to continue to safeguard the site.[71] In this respect, international assistance is only a supplement to national resources and is only given to enable a State party to meet its obliga-

---

ing for the group of States and are often concerned with extra-State interests of a non-reciprocal character. *Erga omnes* obligations are owed to the international community as a whole. The distinction between the two categories is blurred in practice, because *erga omnes partes* obligations may also have *erga omnes* effect in some cases if they have been recognised as customary law. Therefore obligations with the same content may concurrently belong to both categories. *See* ILC Commentary on Draft Article 48 in Draft Articles on Responsibility of States for Internationally Wrongful Acts, with commentaries, p. 126, paras. 6–9, available at <untreaty.un.org/ilc/texts/instruments/english/commentaries/9_6_2001.pdf>; *see also* L. A. Sicilianos, 'The Classification of Obligations and the Multilateral Dimension of the Relations ofInternational Responsibility', 13 *The European Journal of International Law* (2002) p. 1136; E. de Wet, 'The International Constitutional Order', 55:1 *International and Comparative Law Quarterly* (2006) p. 55.

68 Buzzini and Condorelli, *supra* note 64, p. 178. *See also* UNESCO World Heritage Committee, *Legal considerations concerning the inscription of properties on the List of World Heritage in Danger and the deletion of properties from the World Heritage List*, Doc. WHC-02/CONF.202/8, 24 May 2002, para. 33.

69 *Ibid.*, p. 183.

70 A. F. Vrdoljak, 'Article 14, the Secretariat and Support of the World Heritage Committee', in F. Francioni (ed.), *The 1972 World Heritage Convention: A Commentary* (Oxford University Press, Oxford, 2008), pp. 226–227.

71 A. Lemaistre and F. Lenzerini, 'Articles 19-26, International Assistance', in F. Francioni (ed.), *The 1972 World Heritage Convention: A Commentary* (Oxford University Press, Oxford, 2008) p. 323.

tions under the WHC.[72] The fact remains, however, that where a State party is unwilling to receive international assistance, the Committee cannot intervene. This was graphically illustrated in March 2001, when the Taliban government of Afghanistan destroyed the sculptures of the Buddhas of Bamiyan, despite the efforts made by the Director General of UNESCO and the Committee to prevent the act.[73] Furthermore, a State party that does not approve the measures adopted by the Committee has the option to denounce the WHC in accordance with Article 35.

5. The Application of the World Heritage Convention in Virunga Park

Despite the limitations noted above, the WHC has played a pivotal role in attempting to protect the environment of the Virunga Park from the adverse consequences of the ongoing armed conflicts in the DRC. In 2000 the WHC launched its pilot project on 'Biodiversity Conservation in Regions of Armed Conflict: Conserving World Heritage sites in the Democratic Republic of the Congo'.[74] The activities that have taken place under the auspices of the project illustrate how MEAs can play a role in protecting the environment during armed conflict. The project consists of a partnership including the World Heritage Secretariat and the Congolese Wildlife Authority, a Congolese State organ entrusted with the management of the national parks, including the Virunga Park. Other UN agencies and UN programmes, States, international and national governmental and non-governmental organisations active in the DRC are also involved in the project.[75]

---

72 Operational Guidelines, para. 233, *supra* note 51.

73 For further reading, *see* F. Francioni and F. Lenzerini, 'The Destruction of the Buddhas of Bamiyan and International Law', 14:4 *European Journal of International Law* (2003) pp. 619–651.

74 UNESCO World Heritage Committee, Decision 23.COM.X.A4 adopted at 23rd session on 29 November–4 December 1999, Doc. WHC-99/CONF.209/22, 2 March 2000, p. 22.

75 The partnership consists of the UNESCO's World Heritage Centre and Division of Ecological Sciences in cooperation with Institut Congolais pour la Conservation de la Nature (ICCN), the International Union for Conservation of Nature (IUCN), German Technical Cooperation (GTZ), and a task force of conservation NGOs including International Rhino Foundation, International Gorilla Conservation Programme, Wildlife Conservation Society, the World Wide Fund for Nature, and the Gilman International Conservation. In addition, the European Union and States (*i.e.* Belgium, Italy and Germany) as well as UN agencies or programmes (*i.e.* UN Development Programme, UN Environmental Programme) and the UN Mission to DRC (MONUC) collaborate with the Committee and the World Heritage Centre to address issues relating to the safeguarding of World Heritage properties in the DRC. *See* L. Patchett, 'Articles 17–18, Activities to support the World Heritage Fund', in F. Francioni (ed.), *The 1972 World Heritage Convention: A Commentary* (Oxford

The expressed ambition of this ongoing project is to ensure that basic protection of the universal values of world heritage is maintained by international law, even in times of armed conflict, and to prepare the international community to respond in such situations.[76]

5.1. Calling for Removal of Armed Groups and to Halt Military Activities inside the Park

As discussed above, the presence of rebel groups and the DRC army has had negative environmental impacts on the Park. Therefore, the Committee has urged the DRC to remove all armed groups and to halt all military activities inside the world heritage sites.[77] The DRC has also been urged to reduce the number of military positions inside the Park and to place army posts at a satisfactory distance from the world heritage sites.[78]

A call to remove all military activity from the Park may be justified on the basis of Article 5 of the WHC when seen from a strictly environmental and conservation perspective. However, this recommendation clearly has the capacity to interfere with the ability of the DRC to conduct its military operations against armed groups hiding in or operating from the Park. For example, the settlement of camps by the DRC army in the Park and the decisions to cut down trees to locate the rebels may be acts taken against military objectives in accordance with the law of armed conflict, and therefore permissible. This runs, however, contrary to the obligation in Articles 4 and 5 of the WHC not to directly or indirectly harm the world heritage sites. In addition, the immediate removal of the DRC army, as requested by the Committee, could obstruct efforts to protect civilians and the displaced population inside the Park. The position adopted by the Committee does not inevitably mean that there is a clash between the obligations in the WHC and the law of armed conflict, since the DRC could avoid taking action that would harm the Park without breaching any obligation in the law of armed

---

University Press, Oxford, 2008) p. 298; and World Heritage website <whc.unesco.org/en/congobiodiversity>, visited on 30 September 2012.

76 UNESCO World Heritage Committee, Report of the Rapporteur on the 23rd session of the Bureau of the World Heritage Committee, Doc. WHC-99/CONF.209/4, 11 October 1999, p. 5. For the latest report on the project *see* UNESCO World Heritage Committee, *State of conservation of the properties inscribed on the List of World Heritage in Danger*, Doc. WHC-12/36.COM/7A.Add, 1 June 2012 p. 6.

77 *See* UNESCO World Heritage Committee, Decision 27 COM 7A.2 adopted at 27th session on 30 June–5 July 2003, Doc. WHC-03/27.COM/24, 10 December 2003, p. 10; Decision 28 COM 15A.3 adopted at 28th session on 28 June–7 July 2004, Doc. WHC-04/28/COM/26, 29 October 2004, p. 52.

78 *See* UNESCO World Heritage Committee, Decision 28 COM 15A.3 adopted at 28th session on 28 June–7 July 2004, Doc. WHC-04/28/COM/26, 29 October 2004, p. 52; Decision 31 COM 7A.7 adopted at 31st session on 23 June–2 July 2007, Doc. WHC-07/31.COM/24, 31 July 2007, p. 11.

conflict. However, it raises the question of whether the actions suggested by the Committee imply that the outstanding values of the world heritage of mankind should take precedence over military necessity in an armed conflict context.

For its part, the Committee has acknowledged the role of the military to ensure security in the Park, which is important for Park rangers to be able to perform their conservation work. Given the ongoing hostilities within the Park the Committee has construed cooperation with the army as an alternative measure to protect the Park. Through military operations, the DRC army has succeeded, as required by the Committee, to drive rebel groups out from several of their positions in and around the Park. As a result, Park rangers have been able to regain control over their Park stations and the Park areas.[79] The DRC army and the Park rangers have also conducted joint operations to prevent poaching and illegal exploitation of the natural resources by the rebels.[80] In the Garamba Park, another world heritage site in the DRC, the army has even installed an army brigade with the specific mandate to protect the world heritage site.[81]

However, the cooperation between the army and the Park rangers is complicated. As noted above, the involvement of the army in illegal resource exploitation within the Park has resulted in the deaths of several Park rangers. The Committee has therefore urged the DRC to follow up the illegal activities of the army soldiers.[82] While the law of armed conflict does not directly address the issue of exploitation of the natural resources, under certain circumstances such exploitation for pure personal profit could amount to the war crime of pillage.[83] The prohibition of pillage prohibits destruction and seizure of civilian State-owned or private property. Whether natural resources could constitute civilian property was dealt with in the judgment of the ICJ in regards to the *Armed Activities on the Territory of the Congo (Democratic Republic of the Congo* v. *Uganda)* case where the government of Uganda was held internationally responsible under the law of

79 UNESCO World Heritage Committee, *State of conservation of the properties inscribed on the List of World Heritage in Danger*, Doc. WHC-10/34.COM/7A, 1 June 2010, p. 10.

80 UNESCO World Heritage Committee, *State of conservation of the properties inscribed on the List of World Heritage in Danger*, Doc. WHC-06/30.COM/7A, 26 May 2006, p. 27.

81 UNESCO World Heritage Committee, *State of conservation of the properties inscribed on the List of World Heritage in Danger*, Doc. WHC-11/35.COM/7A.Add, 27 May 2011, p. 13.

82 *See* UNESCO World Heritage Committee, Decision 34 COM 7A.4 adopted at 34th session on 25 July–3 August 2010, Doc. WHC-10/34.COM/20, 3 September 2010, p. 20; *see also State of conservation of the properties inscribed on the List of World Heritage in Danger*, Doc. WHC-10/34. COM/7A, 1 June 2010, pp. 11–12.

83 The prohibition of pillage is laid down in Articles 28 and 47 of the 1907 Hague Regulations, Article 33(2) of the 1949 Geneva Convention IV and also in Article 4(2)(g) of 1977 Additional Protocol II of the 1949 Geneva Conventions. Hence, such crime is forbidden both in international and non-international armed conflicts.

armed conflict for looting, plundering and exploiting the DRC's natural resources by failing to prevent members of its army from the commission of these acts during the armed conflicts when Uganda was occupying areas of the DRC.[84] The ICJ stated that exploitation of natural resources constitutes plunder or pillage as set out in the law of armed conflict.[85] In this context, the recommendation from the Committee to punish the illegal exploitation activities is both consistent with and strengthens the law of armed conflict.

Overall, the Committee is divided over the question as to how the army should behave in regard to the world heritage sites. On the one hand, the Committee wants the army to refrain from entering the sites at all, but on the other hand, it requests the army to demobilise and disarm rebel groups in the Park and cooperate with the Park rangers. The Committee seems to be unclear as to how to balance security and conservation needs, in particular since these needs appear to be interrelated. Should the DRC army only function as a force assisting the rangers to remove rebels inside the Park? Does not the army have both a right and an obligation to fight rebels inside the Park? If the army does not have such a right, would this mean that conservation of the Park, at least in part, contradicts and supersedes the law of armed conflict? The request from the Committee does not express any consideration of the need for the DRC army to defend its territory through military operations that sometimes need to take place inside the Park. The restriction on military operations as imposed by WHC could impede the law of armed conflict by denying the application of the doctrine of military necessity. At the very least, in the specific case, the practical outcome is one where the WHC's protection of the environment informs the interpretation and application of the law of armed conflict to a certain degree. This suggests that although there is no existing obligation in the law of armed conflict not to turn natural world heritage sites into military objectives, such obligation could arise when interpreting the law of armed conflict in light of the obligations set out in the WHC. In particular, as the rules of law of armed conflict are often considered inadequate to protect the environment, to interpret them using the obligations set out in international environmental law could fill gaps and clarify ambiguities.

---

84 *Armed activities on the territory of the Congo (Democratic Republic of the Congo v. Uganda)*, 19 December 2005, ICJ, Judgment, paras. 242–246. <www.icj-cij.org/docket/files/116/10455.pdf>, visited 30 September 2012.

85 *Ibid.*, paras. 219 and 242–246. The ICJ based its decision on customary international law corresponding to Article 47 in the Hague Regulations and 33 of the 1949 Geneva Convention IV. The Hague Regulations have become part of customary law and are binding on both parties of the conflict, in this case Uganda and the DRC.

5.2. Strengthen the Role of the Park Rangers

Prior to the start of the WHC project, Park rangers regularly left their posts due to a number of reasons, including non-payment of salaries, lack of equipment and the insecure situation in general. In response, the WHC project has provided funding for salaries, equipment and training activities for the Park rangers.[86] Facilities at the Park stations and patrol posts have been rehabilitated and reconstructed.[87] The Park rangers have been able to continue their work to protect the Park because of the international assistance provided under the WHC project. Management by the Park rangers has been strengthened by the acquisition of key equipment including trucks, speedboats, an airplane, communication systems and computer systems.[88] In 2011, it was reported that all Park stations in the Park have mobile phone coverage, which enables coordination of the Park activities.[89] The supply of such equipment is granted according to Article 22(4) of the WHC.[90] In addition, the Committee has called for improved staff training among the Park rangers.[91] Training constitutes an essential element in the international assistance, as provided in Article 22(3) under the WHC. In 2011 a major training effort was reported to be underway, consisting of high-level paramilitary training by specialists of the Belgian Special Forces.[92] There is no explanation in the report

86 During the first phase of the pilot project (2001 to 2005) approximately USD 900,000 was spent on salaries, equipment, *etc. See* UNESCO World Heritage Committee, *State of conservation of the properties inscribed on the List of World Heritage in Danger*, Doc. WHC-06/30.COM/7A, 26 May 2006, p. 26.

87 UNESCO World Heritage Committee, *State of conservation of the properties inscribed on the List of World Heritage in Danger*, Doc. WHC-11/35.COM/7A.Add, 27 May 2011, p. 4.

88 This equipment was financed under a separate project launched by the European Union, one of the partners within the WHC project. *See* UNESCO World Heritage Committee, *State of conservation of the properties inscribed on the List of World Heritage in Danger*, Doc. WHC-11/35. COM/7A.Add, 27 May 2011, p. 4.

89 *See* UNESCO World Heritage Committee, *State of conservation of the properties inscribed on the List of World Heritage in Danger*, Doc. WHC-10/34.COM/7A, 1 June 2010, p. 12.

90 According to Article 22(4) of the WHC, assistance in the form of equipment supply should be of such nature that the State party does not possess or is not in a position to acquire it – which seems to be the case here.

91 *See* UNESCO World Heritage Committee, Decisions 30 COM 7A.7 adopted at 30th session on 8–16 July 2006, Doc. WHC-06/30.COM/19, 23 August 2006, p. 17. *See also State of conservation of the properties inscribed on the List of World Heritage in Danger*, Doc. WHC-10/34.COM/7A, 1 June 2010, p. 12.

92 No further report has been made on whether the military training actually took place or whether the military training was requested by the Committee. It appears that the training has been provided either as a part of the activities undertaken within the umbrella of the WHC project, or as part of a separate project closely

of the context in which Park rangers are expected to make use of the military training, however, it can be inferred that the paramilitary training may be useful when the rangers take part in disarming operations, dealing with poachers or illegal exploitation of the natural resources in the Park. An advance Park ranger force was fully operational in 2007 and has been effective in securing parts of the Park that were occupied by the rebels.[93]

According to the principle of restrictive interpretation, a treaty should be interpreted in a manner that favours the sovereign freedom of States. Although this principle has limited use in international law, it implies that where a choice of two possible options to interpret a treaty provision exists, one should prefer the one that affects the State sovereignty the least.[94] There are several passages in the WHC provisions whose ordinary meaning is not unclear, but which lack substantive content and are therefore dependent on elaboration by the Committee in order to become meaningful obligations. Furthermore, the States parties have agreed to conclude a constitutive agreement using flexible wording and providing the Committee with both expressed and implied powers to elucidate the substantive content of the WHC, as long as the Committee acts in compliance with its mandate and does not engage in revision of the WHC. Looking at the military training, as described above, provided by the Belgian Special Forces, it seems that the Committee has favoured a more extensive interpretation when clarifying the content of the WHC and that it may have gone beyond the intention of negotiators of the Convention, by relying on the vague language of the Convention. Examining how the Committee uses the vague language is an important issue that needs further exploration.

5.3. Collaboration with the UN Peacekeeping Forces – 'Green-keeping' Operation

In the case of the Park, the WHC is not only enforced through the State organs of the DRC, but also through other actors. The Committee has invited the UN peacekeeping forces deployed in the DRC, the UN Organization Mission in the DRC (MONUC), which since 2010 has acted under the title the UN Organization

related to the WHC project. *See* UNESCO World Heritage Committee, *State of conservation of the properties inscribed on the List of World Heritage in Danger*, Doc. WHC-11/35.COM/7A.Add, 27 May 2011, p. 4.

93 UNESCO World Heritage Committee, *State of conservation of the properties inscribed on the List of World Heritage in Danger*, Doc. WHC-07/31.COM/7A, 10 May 2007, p. 10.

94 The rule of restrictive interpretation has been used sparsely in international law. *See* U. Linderfalk, *On the Interpretation of Treaties* (Springer, Dordrecht, 2010) pp. 280–281.

Stabilization Mission in the DRC (MONUSCO),[95] to provide assistance to disarm and evacuate armed rebel groups from the world heritage sites.[96] The MONUC/MONUSCO is deployed in accordance with Chapter VII of the UN Charter because the situation in the DRC constitutes a threat to international peace and security.[97] The Security Council has authorised the MONUC/MONUSCO to use all necessary – including military – means to support the DRC in protecting civilians and humanitarian workers, disarming belligerents or armed groups, collecting arms, preventing entry of military materiel and enhancing the security situation in the region of the Park.[98]

Pursuant to Article 13(7) of the WHC, the Committee is empowered to cooperate with other organisations, bodies and individuals to implement projects and programmes funded with international assistance. On this basis, since October 2003, MONUC/MONUSCO has collaborated with the Committee and has performed military operations putting an end to many of the hostilities in and around the world heritage sites in the DRC.[99] This cooperation demonstrates the potential of the overlapping application of the WHC and the UN Charter and Security Council decisions in regard to disarming rebels and restoring security in the Park region. MONUC/MONUSCO has helped the rangers to monitor the Park through helicopter reconnaissance flights over the Park area.[100] The peacekeepers have also agreed to conduct disarmament operations of rebel groups in cooperation with the Park rangers.[101] Although such cooperation has not been formalised between MONUC/MONUSCO and the Committee, mixed patrols

---

95 Since the end of June 2010, it operates under the name MONUSCO with a decreased number of personnel. *See* UN Security Council Resolution, UN Doc. S/Res/1925, 28 May 2010, para. 1.

96 *See* UNESCO World Heritage Committee, Decision 27 COM 7.A.2 adopted at 27th session on 30 June–5 July 2003, Doc. WHC-03/27.COM/24, 10 December 2003, p. 10; *see also* Decision 30 COM 7A.7 adopted at 30th session on 8–16 July 2006, Doc. WHC-06/30.COM/19, 23 August 2006, p. 18.

97 UN Security Council Resolution, UN Doc. S/RES/1493, 28 July 2003, in preamble para. 12.

98 *See* UN Security Council Resolutions UN Doc. S/RES/1493 (2003), paras. 17–20 and 25–26; UN Doc. S/RES/1565 (2004), paras. 4–6; UN Doc. S/RES/1592 (2005), para. 7; UN Doc. S/RES/1756 (2007), paras. 2–4; UN Doc. S/RES/1856 (2008), paras. 3–5; UN Doc. S/RES/1906 (2009), paras. 5–6; UN Doc. S/RES/1925 (2010), paras. 11–12; UN Doc. S/RES/1991 (2011), para. 1.

99 UNESCO World Heritage Committee, Decision 28 COM 15A.3 adopted at 28th session on 28 June–7 July 2004, Doc. WHC-04/28/COM/26, 20 October 2004, p. 53.

100 UNESCO World Heritage Committee, *State of conservation of the properties inscribed on the List of World Heritage in Danger*, Doc. WHC-10/34.COM/7A, 1 June 2010, p. 13.

101 UNESCO World Heritage Committee, *State of conservation of the properties inscribed on the List of World Heritage in Danger*, Doc. WHC-04/28.COM/15A Rev, 21 June 2004, p. 7.

with the peacekeeping forces and the rangers have been regularly organised in the Park. This has allowed the Park rangers to access areas previously unreachable due to security concerns.[102]

Pursuant to Security Council Resolution 1493 all States, including the DRC, are legally bound to prevent the direct and indirect supply of weapons and related materiel, and also to prevent the provision of any advice or training related to the military activities to all armed groups operating in the territory in the region of the Park.[103] This weapons embargo does not apply to supplies for MONUC/MONUSCO, the integrated DRC army and police forces or supplies of non-lethal equipment for humanitarian purposes only.[104] Thus, the military training that the Park rangers have received from the Belgian Special Forces complicates the maintenance of the weapons embargo. Should the Park rangers be viewed as an integrated part of the DRC army there would be no breach of the weapons embargo. However, the Park rangers may then be considered as belligerents in accordance with the law of armed conflict if they take a direct part in the hostilities as members of the armed forces on a continuing basis.[105] On this analysis, the Park rangers are legitimate military objectives pursuant to the law of armed conflict and may be the subject of an attack. If, however, the Park rangers are not an integrated part of the DRC army or the peacekeeping forces, but act as an independent group, then the military training provided to the Park rangers would appear to constitute a violation of the weapons embargo. According to Article 103 of the UN Charter, obligations under the UN Charter prevail in relation to obligations

---

102 UNESCO World Heritage Committee, *State of conservation of the properties inscribed on the List of World Heritage in Danger*, Doc. WHC-09/33.COM/7A, 11 May 2009, p. 14. In 2011, it was reported that the Committee remained in contact with the UN peacekeeping troops, but that little direct support was provided to the Park. *See* UNESCO World Heritage Committee, *State of conservation of the properties inscribed on the List of World Heritage in Danger*, Doc. WHC-11/35. COM/7A.Add, 27 May 2011, p. 5.

103 UN Security Council Resolution, UN Doc. S/RES/1493 (2003), paras. 20–21. The weapons embargo has been reaffirmed in UN Security Council Resolutions UN Doc. S/RES/1533 (2004), para. 1; UN Doc. S/RES/1807 (2008), para. 5; UN Doc. S/RES/1896 (2009), para.1; UN Doc. S/RES/1952 (2010), para. 1; UN Doc. S/RES/2021 (2011), para. 1.

104 UN Security Council Resolution, UN Doc. S/RES/1493, 28 July 2003, paras. 20–21.

105 Membership in a national guard, customs or police force can qualify as armed forces if they assume the function of armed forces in a non-international armed conflict. Also, just as in an international armed conflict, membership in irregular State armed forces includes members of militia, volunteer or paramilitary groups if having a continuous combat function. *See* N. Melzer, 'Interpretive Guidance on the Notion of Direct Participation in Hostilities under International Humanitarian Law, Adopted by the Assembly of the International Committee of the Red Cross on 26 February 2009', 90:872 *International Review of the Red Cross* (2008) p. 1005.

stemming from other instruments. Thus, the Security Council decision adopting a weapons embargo supersedes obligations arising under the WHC.

This informal collaboration between the Park rangers and the UN peacekeeping forces is surprising, particularly given that it is not within the ordinary tasks of UN peacekeeping forces to participate in conservation operations in a world heritage site. However, the Security Council has acknowledged that there is a link between illegal exploitation of natural resources and the outbreak, escalation or continuation of armed conflict.[106] In the case of the DRC, the Security Council has noted that exploitation of natural resources is one of the main elements fuelling the armed conflict.[107] Thus, there is an impetus for the Security Council to engage in security issues related to exploitation of the environment.[108] In 2000, the Security Council established a Panel of Experts to examine the illegal exploitation of natural resources and its connection to the continuation of the armed conflict in the DRC and to inform the mandate of peacekeeping forces.[109] The Panel recommended increased institutional capacity of the DRC authority to control and govern the natural resources.[110] This recommendation was considered in the revised mandate and, consequently, from 2008 the Security Council has empowered MONUC/MONUSCO to fight the illegal exploitation of and trade in natural resources using military means. It should be noted that the mandate of MONUC/MONUSCO is limited to dealing with the armed rebels only and excludes unlawful exploitation or trade activities carried out by the DRC army.[111] The mandate also does not include protection of the world heritage

---

106 UN Security Council Resolution, UN Doc. S/RES/1625, 14 September 2005, para. 6.

107 UN Security Council Resolution, UN Doc. S/RES/1457, 24 January 2003, paras. 3 and 8, which has been reaffirmed in several of the following resolutions adopted by the Security Council.

108 UNEP recommended that the UN peacekeeping force should be more involved in the monitoring of exploitation of natural resources to support peace and stabilisation. *See* UNEP, 'Greening the Blue Helmets, Environment, Natural Resources and UN Peacekeeping Operations' (2012) pp. 81–82, <postconflict.unep.ch/publications/UNEP_greening_blue_helmets.pdf>, visited 30 September 2012.

109 *See Report of the UN Panel of Experts on the Illegal Exploitation of Natural Resources and Other Forms of Wealth of the Democratic Republic of the Congo*, UN Doc. S/2001/357, 12 April 2001.

110 *Final Report of the Groups of Experts on the DRC, pursuant to Security Council Resolution 1698 (2006)*, UN Doc. S/2007/423, 18 July 2007, p. 11, para. 40. *See also* UNEP, 'Greening the Blue Helmets, Environment, Natural Resources and UN Peacekeeping Operations' (2012) p. 53.

111 *See* UN Security Council Resolution, UN Doc. S/RES/1856, 22 December 2008, paras. 3(j) and 5; UN Doc. S/RES/1906, 23 December 2009, para. 21(d); UN Doc. S/RES/1925, 28 May 2010, para. 12(r); UN Doc. S/RES/1991, 28 June 2011, para. 1.

sites *per se*, but only where such sites are directly linked to the armed conflict, as in the case of the Virunga Park.[112]

This informal institutional arrangement of the Committee and the MONUC/MONUSCO can be referred to as a 'green-keeping' operation,[113] which enables the Committee to acquire assistance from an external actor to secure and protect the environment in world heritage sites. In this way the Committee and MONUC/MONUSCO can buttress the competence of each other to address common goals and balance security and conservation needs. The peacekeeping forces can secure the safety in the Park to enable the rangers to monitor the Park, while the peacekeeping forces can be assisted by the Park rangers to control the exploitation of resources. Undoubtedly the Committee would have preferred that military activities did not occur in the Park at all. However, given the reality of the situation and the cooperation with MONUC/MONUSCO represents an interesting, albeit not entirely unproblematic, approach to dealing with the situation.

Regime interaction in the form of a 'green-keeping' operation may thus serve as an arrangement to overcome fragmentation issues[114] and facilitate coherence among the various legal systems within international law.[115] The mechanism of 'green-keeping' could, for example, be used to harmonise the otherwise apparently incompatible decisions of the Committee with those of the Security Council. Admittedly, such collaboration may be controversial, but it is not contrary to international law, provided of course both the Security Council and the Committee act within in their mandates. Such collaboration between international institutions established under different international regimes may also provide some normative influence on their operational activities and consequently further expand the possibilities of action under either or both regimes.[116] In this case, of course, it will remain an open question as to whether States have,

---

112 UNESCO World Heritage Committee, *Reflection on the trends of the state of conservation*,Doc. WHC-12/36.COM/7C, 15 June 2012, para. 26.

113 R. J. Parsons uses 'green-keeping' to describe the role of the US army to enforce the law pertaining to environmental protection during armed conflict. *See* R. J. Parsons, 'The Fight to Save the Planet: US Armed Forces, "Greenkeeping," and Enforcement of the Law Pertaining to Environmental Protection During Armed Conflict', 10 *The Georgetown International Environmental Law Review* (1997–1998) pp. 441–500.

114 For further reading on institutional arrangements, *see* M. Young, 'Regime Interaction in Creating, Implementing and Enforcing International Law', in M. Young (ed.), *Regime Interaction in International Law Facing Fragmentation* (Cambridge University Press, Cambridge, 2012) pp. 97–99.

115 Matz-Lück, *supra* note 4, p. 209.

116 *See* J. L. Dunhoff, 'A New Approach to Regime Interaction', in M. Young (ed.), *Regime Interaction in International Law Facing Fragmentation* (Cambridge University Press, Cambridge, 2012) pp. 166–167.

directly or indirectly, consented to such actions and whether the actions then are in conformity with the law.[117]

6. Conclusions

International environmental treaties are frequently criticised as lacking the capacity to create concrete and substantive obligations. This may undermine their ability to address wartime environmental damage. However, MEAs establish systems of governance, in which the convention bodies may be empowered to develop the framework rules of the relevant MEA by adopting operational guidelines, decisions and recommendations for the States parties. Hence, the fact that the treaties themselves are infused with general and flexible language does not mean that they lack significance and that they cannot be effectively applied during armed conflicts.

In the case of the WHC and its application to the Virunga Park, the flexible provisions of the Convention have been utilised to craft novel approaches to accomplishing the object and purpose of the Convention. Through its executive role, the Committee has developed the provisions of the WHC to operate and respond to environmental problems in an armed conflict context. As a result of the efforts of the Committee, the Park rangers have been able to continue their work in protecting the Park. The international assistance granted under the WHC has provided the Park rangers salaries, equipment and training. Through its requests, the Committee has ensured support for the Park rangers from the DRC army and UN Peacekeeping forces deployed in the DRC. Even though the integrity of the Park is still under threat due to the continuing armed conflicts, the WHC – taking its operational activities and their effects into account – should not be considered as a meaningless convention incapable of addressing the environmental damage being caused by the ongoing armed conflict.

Particularly with respect to sites on the Danger List, the Committee has an extensive mandate to decide on the appropriate action needed. While this may result in disagreement between a State party and the Committee in regard to the action required under the WHC, it should be remembered that a State party has, by ratifying the WHC, agreed to restrict its sovereignty with respect to sites inscribed on the World Heritage List. Thus, the Committee is permitted to act in the interest of the international community to protect that world heritage in accordance with the WHC. In the case of the Virunga Park, the Committee has acted to ensure its protection and, although the DRC has not implemented all the decisions and recommendations of the Committee fully, neither has the DRC expressly opposed them.

Arguably, the decisions and recommendations that have been adopted by the Committee constrain the ability of the DRC to engage in legitimate military operations as permitted under the law of armed conflict. However, it is suggested

117 *See* Young, *supra* note 114, pp. 97–99.

here that the law of armed conflict should be interpreted in a manner that construes consistency with the legal obligations in the WHC. Interpreting the law of armed conflict in the light of the obligations set out in the WHC (and other MEAs) will help to achieve the harmonisation and application of compatible obligations among the relevant regimes applicable to the Park, and also overcome the inadequacy of international law relating to the protection of the environment in armed conflict.

The outstanding value of world heritage constitutes a universal interest of the international community. It is acknowledged that this interest must be balanced with other concerns such as the need for the DRC to conduct military operations to defend and protect its territory and population or with the UN peacekeepers' task of restoring international peace and security in the DRC and elsewhere. As demonstrated above, on both the institutional level and the operational level, the Committee has made noteworthy efforts to collaborate with other relevant actors to overcome these conflicting interests. The 'green-keeping' operation in Virunga Park represents an attempt to reconcile the interests and mandates of the Committee and the UN Security Council and can be viewed as a bridge between the two different international legal regimes of the UN and the WHC. This regime interaction on an institutional level is an interesting, albeit controversial, attempt to overcome the problems of fragmentation in international law in order to create solutions for addressing the specific problem of protection of the environment in relation to armed conflict.

9 From Engines for Conflict into Engines for Sustainable Development: The Potential of International Law to Address Predatory Exploitation of Natural Resources in Situations of Internal Armed Conflict

Daniëlla Dam-de Jong*

1. Introduction

The exploitation of natural resources in order to finance an armed conflict is today one of the most prevalent causes of environmental damage during armed conflict.[1] Extensive logging by all parties to the armed conflict in Cambodia, for example, significantly diminished the country's forest cover.[2] Likewise, highly organised and systematic exploitation activities within and around United Nations Educational, Scientific and Cultural Organization (UNESCO) World Heritage Sites in the Democratic Republic of the Congo (DR Congo), including ivory poaching, logging and mining, have posed a significant threat to the integrity of these biodiversity reserves.[3] Similarly, substantial diamond mining during the conflict in Sierra Leone caused extensive land degradation. Exhausted mining sites were not rehabilitated, resulting in severe environmental degradation.[4]

---

* LL.M., M.A. Doctoral Candidate and Lecturer, Grotius Centre for International Legal Studies Leiden University, Leiden, The Netherlands.
The author expresses gratitude to Prof. Nico Schrijver, Dr. Erik Koppe and the anonymous reviewer for providing useful comments on a draft of this paper.

1 *Cf.* K. Hulme, 'Environmental Security: Implications for International Law', 19 *Yearbook of International Environmental Law* (Oxford University Press, Oxford, 2008) p. 15.

2 For more details on the links between logging and the armed conflict in Cambodia, *see* P. Le Billon and S. Springer, 'Between War and Peace: Violence and Accommodation in the Cambodian Logging Sector', in W. de Jong, D. Donovan and K. Abe (eds.), *Extreme Conflict and Tropical Forests* (Springer, New York, 2007) pp. 17–36.

3 *Interim report of the Panel of Experts on the Illegal Exploitation of Natural Resources and Other Forms of Wealth of the Democratic Republic of the Congo*, UN Doc. S/2002/565, paras. 50 and 52.

4 *See* UNEP, *Sierra Leone: Environment, Conflict and Peacebuilding Assessment*, February 2010, p. 45.

Rosemary Rayfuse (ed.), War and the Environment: New Approaches to Protecting the Environment in Relation to Armed Conflict

ISBN 978-90-04-27064-0 pp. 205-234

Although unsustainable patterns of resource exploitation are not specific to the situation of armed conflict only, the examples above show that resource exploitation during an armed conflict poses a special threat to the environment. The prospects for parties to an armed conflict to gain 'easy' profits from resource exploitation, either in order to finance their armed struggle or for their personal benefit, encourage these parties to resort to destructive exploitation methods that are highly detrimental to environmental conservation.

This study explores the issue of predatory behaviour by parties to an armed conflict[5] which causes severe damage to the very natural resources that are the basis for development. The principal question addressed concerns the role that international law should play in addressing this problem. This study argues that international law should first and foremost provide an adequate legal framework to govern the exploitation of natural resources during armed conflict. This is currently not the case. Rather, the existing international legal framework is both fragmented and imprecise. It is posited that this is problematic because it provides parties to an armed conflict with possibilities to bypass the few rules that are in place.

A second role that international law should play is to provide structural solutions to break the link between natural resources and armed conflict. It is argued that this is an essential part of the process of conflict resolution and peace-building. This study focuses on the role of the Security Council in addressing these issues. Sanctions have been the prevalent tool used by the Security Council to address predatory resource exploitation in recent armed conflicts.[6] These sanctions regimes have increasingly moved away from direct crisis management to more systematic approaches aimed at breaking the link between natural resources and armed conflict. This study embraces this development and argues in favour of an enhanced role for the Security Council in this regard.

The following section discusses the role of natural resources in fuelling armed conflict. Sections 3 and 4 examine the regulatory framework for the exploitation of natural resources during armed conflict. In section 5 this study examines the structural approach adopted by the Security Council in some of its recent sanctions regimes aimed at breaking the link between natural resources and armed conflict. Since most of the armed conflicts in which predatory resource exploitation take place are internal in nature, this study focuses exclusively on these conflicts.

---

5 Ballentine and Nitzschke refer in this regard to 'resource predation'. *See* K. Ballentine and H. Nitzschke (eds.), *Profiting from Peace: Managing the Resource Dimensions of Civil War* (Lynne Rienner Publishers, Boulder 2005) p. 2.

6 Direct commodity sanctions have been imposed *inter alia* in the conflicts in Angola, Sierra Leone, Liberia and Côte d'Ivoire, while ancillary sanctions (asset freezes and travel bans against persons implicated in predatory resource exploitation) have been imposed in the conflict within the DR Congo.

2. The Role of Natural Resources in Fuelling Armed Conflicts

Natural resources are at the heart of many present-day armed conflicts. Examples include the conflicts in Cambodia, Angola, Sierra Leone and Liberia in the 1990s and the ongoing conflicts in the DR Congo and Côte d'Ivoire. Even if these conflicts are not strictly motivated by the drive to obtain access to lucrative natural resources, natural resources have played a major role in sustaining these armed conflicts.[7] In this way, they have helped shape the dynamics of these conflicts.

In some cases, natural resources have proven to be an adequate replacement for Cold War funding by the major superpowers. This may be illustrated by the armed conflict in Cambodia between 1979 and 1991. For a long time, this conflict was funded through the support of other States. The Soviet Union sponsored the government side, while China and the United States funded the ousted Khmer Rouge regime. It was only after these revenues had started to dry up that natural resources came into the picture. Both the government and the Khmer Rouge started logging timber to fund their armed struggle.[8] The conflict in Angola between 1975 and 2002 is also illustrative. During the Cold War, the Angolan government received funding from the Soviet Union and Cuba, while the opposing National Union for the Total Independence of Angola (UNITA) received funding from the United States, France and South Africa. From the early 1990s on, the government switched to oil, while UNITA discovered diamonds as a new source of revenue.[9]

In other cases, the role of natural resources during the conflict evolved from a mere source of funding into a motivation to continue fighting. Gaining control over the Sierra Leonean diamond fields, for example, became one of the principal aims of the opposing Armed Forces Revolutionary Council (AFRC) and the Revolutionary United Front (RUF) in the conflict that raged through Sierra Leone in the 1990s, especially in the final phase of the conflict.[10] After the conflict, the leaders of both armed groups were charged before the Special Court for Sierra Leone for sharing a "common plan, purpose or design (joint criminal enterprise) which was to take any actions necessary to gain and exercise political power and control over the territory of Sierra Leone, in particular the diamond

---

7 *See e.g.* K. Ballentine and J. Sherman (eds.), *The Political Economy of Armed Conflict: Beyond Greed and Grievance* (Lynne Rienner Publishers, Boulder 2003); Ballentine and Nitzschke (eds.), *supra* note 5.

8 *See* Le Billon and Springer, *supra* note 2, pp. 17–36.

9 *See* Ballentine and Sherman, *supra* note 7, pp. 23–24.

10 Report of the Sierra Leone Truth and Reconciliation Commission, *Witness to Truth*, Volume 3b: Chapter 1: Mineral Resources, their Use and their Impact on the Conflict and the Country, available through <www.sierra-leone.org/TRCDocuments.html>, visited on 31 July 2012.

mining areas".[11] Likewise, obtaining access to lucrative minerals in the DR Congo continues to be a motivation for armed groups fighting in the eastern provinces of the DR Congo today.[12]

Natural resource revenues constitute an important source of income for rebel groups and the government alike. In the conflict in the DR Congo, for example, minerals provide both the rebel groups and the government with an important source of income to fund their military campaign.[13] Likewise, in the conflict in Côte d'Ivoire, diamonds provided the rebel groups with income, while the government funded its military campaign through cocoa and coffee.[14] Other examples include Angola (oil and diamonds), Cambodia (timber and gemstones) and Sierra Leone (diamonds). Although it is often difficult to establish the extent to which resource exploitation by States is used directly to fund an armed conflict, reports by relevant UN Panels of Experts have demonstrated the existence of a link between resource revenues and military expenditure. In the case of Côte d'Ivoire, for example, the UN Group of Experts established a clear link between natural resources, in particular cocoa, and extra-budgetary military spending by the Ivorian government.[15]

Resource exploitation by parties to an armed conflict is not carried out solely to obtain revenues to fund the armed conflict. There are also cases in which natural resource exploitation is undertaken for the personal benefit of individuals. A report of the Group of Experts on the DR Congo, for example, reveals that

---

11 *See* the indictment in the case of *The Prosecutor* v. *Sesay, Kallon and Gbao (RUF Case)*, Case No. SCSL-2004-15-PT, para. 36; and the indictment in the case of *The Prosecutor* v. *Brima, Kamara and Kanu (AFRC Case)*, Case No. SCSL-2004-65-PT, para. 33, both before the Special Court for Sierra Leone.

12 *See* the *Final Report of the Group of Experts on the Democratic Republic of the Congo prepared pursuant to paragraph 6 of Security Council resolution 1896 (2009)*, UN Doc. S/2010/596 of 29 November 2010, p. 76, where the Group of Experts comes to the conclusion that "economic motivations are increasingly driving a significant portion of armed actors".

13 *See* the *Report of the Panel of Experts on the Illegal Exploitation of Natural Resources and Other Forms of Wealth of the Democratic Republic of the Congo*, UN Doc. S/2001/357 of 12 April 2001 and the *Addendum to the Report*, UN Doc. S/2001/1072 of 13 November 2001.

14 *Midterm report of the Group of Experts submitted in accordance with paragraph 11 of Security Council resolution 1842 (2008)*, UN Doc. S/2009/188 of 8 April 2009; *Final report of the Group of Experts on Côte d'Ivoire, prepared in accordance with paragraph 14 of Security Council Resolution 1980 (2011)*, UN Doc. S/2012/196 of 14 April 2012.

15 *See e.g.* the *Report of the Group of Experts submitted in accordance with paragraph 7 of resolution 1584 (2005)*, UN Doc. S/2005/699, paras. 22–42. *See also* the *Final Report of the Group of Experts on Côte d'Ivoire, prepared in accordance with paragraph 14 of Security Council resolution 1980 (2011)*, *supra* note 14, paras. 92–95 for a link between natural resources and violations of the arms embargo by the Ivorian government.

exploitation activities are carried out both by armed groups and by factions within the Congolese army for their personal enrichment.[16] Thus, it is often difficult or even impossible to make neat distinctions between resource exploitation for the purpose of funding an armed conflict and for the personal benefit of members of armed groups. The two purposes are often inextricably linked.

While all of these activities keep the armed conflict ongoing, both the actors involved and their motivations have implications for the rules that apply to specific instances of predatory resource exploitation. With this in mind, the following sections examine the existing legal framework for the exploitation of natural resources during armed conflict.

3. General Remarks on the Applicability of Various Sets of Rules

In order to properly understand the legal framework governing the exploitation of natural resources during armed conflict, this section discusses the interplay between the different fields of international law that shape the legal framework. These fields include international humanitarian, environmental, human rights and general international law.

First of all, international humanitarian law, the law which is designed specifically to regulate the situation of armed conflict, provides two basic rules. Protection of the environment and natural resources under this field of international law is provided primarily through provisions on the protection of civilian objects and of property. The most relevant provisions relate to the protection of objects indispensable to the survival of the civilian population (Article 14 of Additional Protocol II); and the prohibition of pillage (Article 4(2)(g) of Additional Protocol II to the Geneva Conventions). Moreover, additional protection is provided through the prohibition on the destruction or seizure of the property of the adversary, derived from Article 23(g) of the 1907 Hague Regulations. This prohibition is not expressly codified for internal armed conflicts, but its application to these conflicts may be derived from international criminal law (Article 8(2)(e)(xii) of the 2002 International Criminal Court (ICC) Statute).[17]

In addition, international environmental, human rights and general international law, although not designed specifically to deal with situations of armed conflict, also provide relevant rules.[18] These fields of international law apply at all times, including during armed conflict. Yet, in those cases where international

---

16 *See* the *Final Report of the Group of Experts on the Democratic Republic of the Congo prepared pursuant to paragraph 6 of Security Council resolution 1896 (2009)*, *supra* note 12, pp. 47–76.

17 A more detailed discussion of these provisions follows.

18 The recently adopted ILC articles on the effects of armed conflict on treaties formulate a presumption of continued applicability of international environmental and human rights treaties. *See Draft articles on the effects of armed conflicts on treaties, with commentaries*, adopted at the 63rd session of the ILC (2011).

humanitarian law provides relevant rules, international environmental, human rights and general international law are set aside. This is due to the status of international humanitarian law as the prevailing *lex specialis* during an armed conflict.[19]

However, this is not to say that these fields of international law lose their relevance entirely. Where international humanitarian law does contain relevant rules, international environmental, human rights and general international law continue to play a role in the background as other rules of international law which must be taken into account in the interpretation of international humanitarian law provisions on the basis of Article 31(1) and (3)(c) of the Vienna Convention on the Law of Treaties.[20] On the basis of Article 31(1) of the Vienna Convention, international environmental, human rights and general international law can be taken into account in order to clarify the ordinary meaning of the terms of international humanitarian law provisions. In addition, Article 31(3)(c) of the Vienna Convention prescribes that treaty provisions are to be interpreted in the light of other rules of international law applicable between the parties to the treaty.

Relevant rules from international environmental, human rights and general international law include the principle of sustainable development and related principles, such as sustainable use, equity and good governance.[21] Another important principle, derived from State sovereignty and the right of peoples to self-determination, is the principle of permanent sovereignty over natural resources

---

19 On the interplay between international humanitarian law and other fields of law during armed conflicts, *see* the following documents related to the ILC study on the effects of armed conflict on treaties: *Second report on the effects of armed conflicts on treaties by Ian Brownlie, Special Rapporteur*, UN Doc. A/CN.4/570, 16 June 2006, para. 41 and the *Third report on the effects of armed conflicts on treaties by Ian Brownlie, Special Rapporteur*, UN Doc. A/CN.4/578, paras. 29–31 and 49–55; *Effects of Armed Conflict on Treaties, Comments and information received from Governments*, UN Doc. A/CN.4/622, 15 March 2010; the *Memorandum of the UN Secretariat on the Effect of Armed Conflict on Treaties: an Examination of Practice and Doctrine*, UN Doc. A/CN.4/550 of 1 February 2005.

20 Article 31(1) of the Vienna Convention provides that "[a] treaty shall be interpreted in good faith in accordance with the ordinary meaning to be given to the terms of the treaty in their context and in the light of its object and purpose". Article 31(3)(c) determines that, "[t]here shall be taken into account, together with the context: … any relevant rules of international law applicable in the relations between the parties".

21 *See* in this regard the *ILA New Delhi Declaration of Principles of International Law Relating to Sustainable Development*, UN Doc. A/57/329 of 31 August 2002, which distinguishes seven principles relating to sustainable development. For a recent analysis of international case-law relevant to the principles of sustainable development, *see* the *2010 Hague Conference Report of the ILA Committee on International Law on Sustainable Development*, available through <www .ila-hq.org>, visited on 26 March 2012.

and the corresponding obligation to use natural resources for national development and the well-being of the people. This principle has found expression in the landmark Declaration on Permanent Sovereignty over Natural Resources and has also been laid down in identical Articles 1(2) of the 1966 International Covenant on Civil and Political Rights (ICCPR) and International Covenant on Economic, Social and Cultural Rights (ICESCR).[22] This provision formulates a right for peoples to freely dispose of their natural resources as well as a prohibition to deprive peoples of their means of subsistence. This prohibition applies in all circumstances.

4. Legal Framework for Resource Exploitation during Armed Conflict

The current section examines the legal framework for the exploitation of natural resources during internal armed conflicts. The objectives of this section are to determine the extent to which the current legal framework addresses the issue of predatory resource exploitation and to establish the weaknesses of the current framework.

For this purpose, this section focuses first of all on the basic rules of international humanitarian law relating to the exploitation of natural resources that apply to all parties to an internal armed conflict, whether rebel groups or the national army. In addition, the current section examines the extent to which peacetime law closes the gaps left open by the international humanitarian law rules.

4.1. International Humanitarian Law

International humanitarian law does not contain specialised rules governing the exploitation of natural resources. Nonetheless, it does contain some rules that are relevant to the issue of natural resource exploitation. These are the prohibition on the taking or destruction of objects indispensable to the survival of the civilian population (Article 14(2) of Additional Protocol II); the prohibition of pillage (Article 4(2)(g) of Additional Protocol II) and the prohibition on the seizure or destruction of the property of the adversary (derived from Article 23(g) of the 1907 Hague Regulations). It is posited in this regard that natural resources may constitute property, since they are capable of ownership.

It is to be noted that the prohibition on taking or destroying objects indispensable to the survival of the civilian population and the prohibition of pillage

22 For the *Declaration on Permanent Sovereignty over Natural Resources*, *see* UN General Assembly Resolution 1803 (XVII), adopted on 14 December 1962. For a detailed analysis of the genesis of this principle as well as its contents, *see* N.J. Schrijver, *Sovereignty over Natural Resources: Balancing Rights and Duties* (Cambridge University Press, Cambridge, 1997).

are laid down in Additional Protocol II,[23] which is applicable to internal armed conflicts between government troops on the one side and one or more organised armed groups on the other. Internal armed conflicts which do not involve government armed forces or otherwise do not reach the threshold set by Additional Protocol II are governed by the rules formulated in common Article 3 of the Geneva Conventions[24] and by customary international law.

In this regard, it should be noted that Article 3 contains an obligation of humane treatment. This obligation may be interpreted as a prohibition on depriving the population of their basic needs for survival. It thus resembles the prohibition contained in Article 14 of Additional Protocol II. In addition, the prohibition of pillage has attained the status of customary international law.[25] As such, it also applies to armed conflicts that do not satisfy the criteria set by Additional Protocol II. Thus, in practice, the regulatory regime for conflicts reaching the threshold of Additional Protocol II and those that do not, is quite similar.

4.1.1. Prohibition to Take or Destroy Objects Indispensable to the Survival of the Civilian Population

Article 14 of Additional Protocol II prohibits parties to an armed conflict to "attack, destroy, remove or render useless" objects that may be considered indispensable to the survival of the population. This prohibition is subject to the overarching prohibition on starving the civilian population. This implies that the prohibition on taking or destroying objects that are indispensable to the civilian

---

23 In this regard, Article 4(2)(g) of Additional Protocol II to the Geneva Conventions, adopted on 8 June 1977 (1125 UNTS 609), determines that pillage against persons who do not take a direct part or who have ceased to take part in hostilities remains prohibited at any time and in any place whatsoever. Article 14(2) of Additional Protocol II stipulates that "[s]tarvation of civilians as a method of combat is prohibited. It is therefore prohibited to attack, destroy, remove or render useless, for that purpose, objects indispensable to the survival of the civilian population, such as foodstuffs, agricultural areas for the production of foodstuffs, crops, livestock, drinking water installations and supplies and irrigation works." Both provisions are discussed in more detail in the following sections.

24 Article 3, which is common to all four Geneva Conventions, adopted on 12 August 1949 (75 *UNTS* 287), contains a set of minimum rules applicable in internal armed conflicts aimed at protecting the human dignity of persons not taking part in hostilities.

25 Both the Appeals Chamber of the ICTY and the Special Court for Sierra Leone have expressly held the prohibition of pillage to be part of customary law applicable to non-international armed conflict. *Hadzihasanovic, Alagic and Kubura* (IT-01-47), ICTY, 11 March 2005, Decision on Joint Defence Interlocutory Appeal of Trial Chamber Decision on Rule 98bis Motions for Acquittal, para. 37; *The Prosecutor* v. *Moinina Fofana and Allieu Kondewa*, Special Court for Sierra Leone, 28 May 2008, Appeals Chamber Judgment, para. 390.

population requires some form of intent on behalf of the perpetrator to do harm to the civilian population. Arguably, this intent may take the form of direct intent or of reckless disregard by a party to an armed conflict for the consequences of its actions.

Article 14 of Additional Protocol II provides a safety net for the population of a State mixed up in an internal armed conflict, which secures their right to retain access to the basic needs for survival. The provision is generally understood to provide protection to parts of the environment that supply the population with foodstuffs and other primary goods necessary for their survival.[26] Thus, in the first instance it prohibits practices like the targeting of water supply systems and the destruction of crops, as, for example, reportedly done by the rebel group RUF during the conflict in Sierra Leone.[27]

A question of interest in this regard is whether and to what extent the prohibition covers valuable natural resources. Can valuable natural resources be considered 'indispensable to the survival of the population'? Although this seems far-fetched at first blush, it must be remembered that many civilians in conflict regions are highly dependent on particular natural resources to generate a basic income. In fact, it seems that the dependency of the local population on artisanal mining in the DR Congo constituted one of the principal reasons for the Security Council to abstain from imposing commodity sanctions to curb the trade in natural resources originating from the DR Congo.[28]

It is posited here that the phrase 'objects indispensable to the survival of the civilian population' in Article 14 of Additional Protocol II should be interpreted extensively to cover natural resources that provide a basic income for the local population. This can be achieved through an interpretation of Article 14 of Additional Protocol II in the light of identical Article 1(2) of the ICESCR and the ICCPR. This provision determines that a people may not be deprived of its own means of subsistence. An interpretation of Article 14 of Additional Protocol II in light of Article 1(2) of the ICESCR and the ICCPR would therefore extend the protection provided by the provision to all objects which provide the population with the means of subsistence, including particular natural resources that generate a basic income for the local population. Following this interpretation, parties to an armed conflict may, under certain circumstances, be prohibited from

26 Article 14 of Additional Protocol II contains a non-exhaustive list of objects which are considered indispensable to the survival of the population, including "foodstuffs, agricultural areas for the production of food-stuffs, crops, livestock, drinking water installations and supplies and irrigation works".

27 UNEP, *Sierra Leone, Environment, Conflict and Peacebuilding Assessment, Technical Report*, February 2010, p. 45.

28 A report prepared by the Secretary-General had warned against the negative impacts of such sanctions on the local population. *See* the *Report of the Secretary-General pursuant to paragraph 8 of resolution 1698 (2006) concerning the Democratic Republic of the Congo*, UN Doc.S/2007/68 of 8 February 2007, paras. 62–63.

cutting-off the civilian population from the mining sites or forests under their control.

4.1.2. Prohibition of Pillage

Article 4(2)(g) of Additional Protocol II formulates a prohibition of pillage. This prohibition traditionally applies to acts of theft, either by individual soldiers or through forms of organised plundering.[29] The provision is sufficiently broad to capture all types of natural resources, whether state-owned or privately-held; extracted natural resources or forests and mines; as well as rights relating to the exploitation of natural resources, such as concessions.[30]

Nonetheless, the prohibition contains some important restrictions. These restrictions are not explicit in the provision, but may be derived from international criminal law. The Elements of Crime that define the crimes listed in the ICC Statute restrict pillage to appropriation for private or personal use.[31] In section 2 above it was argued that the exploitation of natural resources by parties to an armed conflict may serve two purposes. Natural resources are either exploited to fund an armed conflict or for the personal benefit of individuals. In the latter case, the requirement of appropriation for private or personal use is easily satisfied. Thus, the prohibition of pillage may be said to apply to acts of predatory resource exploitation by members of rebel groups or the national army for their personal gain.

It is also within this context that the prohibition of pillage was applied by the International Court of Justice (ICJ) in the case of the DR Congo against Uganda. In this case, the DR Congo contended that members of the Ugandan army had systematically exploited the DRC's natural resources for their personal benefit.[32]

---

29 *See* the *Commentary to the Additional Protocols*, p. 1376; and G. Carducci, 'Pillage', in R. Bernhardt, *Encyclopedia of Public International Law*, Max Planck Institute for Comparative Public Law and International Law (Heidelberg and Oxford University Press, 2012).

30 The prohibition of pillage applies to property. According to the *Commentary to the Additional Protocols*, p. 1376, this includes both State-owned and private property as well as immovable and movable property. In addition, the Nuremberg Tribunals have extended its scope to physical and intangible property. *See* the *I.G. Farben* case, *Trials of War Criminals before the Nuremberg Military Tribunals under Control Council Law No. 10*, vol. VIII (1952), p. 1134.

31 Elements of Crimes, *Official Journal of the International Criminal Court*, available at <www .icc-cpi.int/library/about/officialjournal/Element_of_Crimes_English.pdf>, visited on 1 August 2012. *See further* K. Dörmann, *Elements of War Crimes under the Rome Statute of the International Criminal Court: Sources and Commentary* (International Committee of the Red Cross, Cambridge University Press, Cambridge, 2002).

32 *Armed Activities on the Territory of the Congo (Democratic Republic of the Congo* v. *Uganda)*, I.C.J., 19 December 2005, Judgment, *I.C.J. Reports* 2005, paras. 222–229.

The International Court of Justice concluded that "whenever members of the UPDF were involved in the looting, plundering and exploitation of natural resources in the territory of the DRC", they acted in violation of the prohibition of pillage.[33]

However, fitting resource exploitation for the purpose of funding an armed conflict into the definition of pillage is far more problematic. An interpretation that confines pillage to the appropriation of natural resources for private or personal use seems to exclude from the definition of pillage the exploitation of natural resources for the purpose of funding an armed conflict.

This is at least true for the government that uses resource revenues to fund its military campaign. After all, military expenditure constitutes by definition a public purpose. For rebel groups this may be different. The application of pillage to resource exploitation by rebel groups for the purpose of funding an armed conflict may depend on the qualification of the armed struggle itself. Is the struggle ideologically motivated or is it primarily motivated by self-interest? This makes it a very difficult issue to deal with *in abstracto*.

Unfortunately, specific case law from modern international criminal tribunals applying the war crime of pillage to the exploitation of natural resources is lacking. Until now, none of these tribunals have applied the provision to instances of natural resource exploitation. Notwithstanding the potential of the war crime to capture these instances, counts of pillage before modern international criminal tribunals have been confined to the appropriation of personal belongings of civilians, mostly in relation to the raiding of villages.[34] Even in the cases against Charles Taylor and the leaders of the RUF and the AFRC before the Special Court for Sierra Leone, where there was a close nexus between the exploitation of natural resources and the committing of other crimes, pillage of natural resources was not among the charges.[35]

In the absence of case law which may provide more specific guidance to the interpretation of pillage in relation to natural resources, it may be concluded in general that the prohibition of pillage applies first and foremost to the exploitation of natural resources for purposes of self-enrichment. It seems less appropriate to apply the prohibition to exploitation for the purposes of funding an armed conflict. These instances may however be covered by the prohibition to destroy or seize the property of the adversary, which is discussed in the following section.

---

33 *Ibid.*, para. 245.

34 For examples of relevant practice by international criminal tribunals, *see* the *ICRC Customary International Humanitarian Law Database*, Rule 52, available through <www.icrc.org/customary-ihl/eng/docs/home>, visited on 27 January 2012.

35 For a detailed discussion of the crime of pillage and its applicability to the exploitation ofnatural resources, *see* L. J. van den Herik and D. A. Dam-de Jong, 'Revitalizing the Antique WarCrime of Pillage: The Potential and Pitfalls of Using International Criminal Law to Address Illegal Resource Exploitation During Armed Conflict', 22:3 *Criminal Law Forum* (2011)pp. 237–273.

4.1.3. Prohibition to Destroy or Seize the Property of the Adversary

Whereas the prohibition of pillage relates to the appropriation of property for personal use, the prohibition on 'seizing' the property of the adversary relates to the appropriation of property for public purposes. This may be exemplified by the Commentary to the prohibition of pillage, which states that the latter prohibition "leaves intact the right of requisition or seizure".[36] In addition, the Special Court for Sierra Leone has explicitly confirmed that 'seizure' relates to the appropriation of property for public purposes.[37]

In addition, the prohibition covers the destruction of property, bringing some forms of environmental damage within its ambit. Both the Special Court for Sierra Leone and the International Criminal Court have addressed instances of the burning of property as falling within the definition of destruction.[38] This implies, for example, that the burning of parts of a forest to clear mining sites or for large-scale timber extraction may fall within the ambit of the prohibition.

The prohibition is based on Article 23(g) of the 1907 Hague Regulations, which formulates a prohibition on the destruction or seizure of enemy property unless imperatively demanded by the necessities of war. Unfortunately, an express provision for internal armed conflicts is lacking. Its applicability to internal armed conflicts may nonetheless be derived from Article 8(2)(e)(xii) of the ICC Statute, which criminalises the destruction and seizure of the property of an adversary.

However, the provision contains considerable impediments. A first relates to the condition that the property must belong to the adversary. This condition in fact limits the material scope of the war crime considerably. The question of ownership of natural resources is determined through national law. Many national constitutions vest the ownership of natural resources in the State. Therefore, the prohibition would primarily apply to rebel groups exploiting natural resources belonging to the State or to persons affiliated to the State.

Another impediment relates to the exception of military necessity. The prohibition on the destruction or seizure of the property of an adversary does not apply in cases of military necessity. In relation to natural resources, this prohibition may be understood as authorising acts of exploitation if strictly necessary to

---

36 J. Pictet and O. M. Uhler, *The Geneva Conventions of 12 August 1949: commentary, Part 4 on the Geneva Convention relative to the protection of civilian persons in time of war*, Geneva: International Committee of the Red Cross (1958), p. 227.

37 *See The Prosecutor* v. *Moinina Fofana and Allieu Kondewa*, Special Court for Sierra Leone, *supra* note 22, para. 392, note 770.

38 *The Prosecutor* v. *Moinina Fofana and Allieu Kondewa*, *supra* note 22, para. 389. *See further* the Warrants of Arrest issued on 27 April 2007 by the ICC in the cases against Harun and Kushayb in relation to the conflict in Sudan.

overcome the adversary.[39] Although the exception of military necessity may thus only be invoked in extreme circumstances, it may not be ruled out entirely that the exception covers exploitation for the purposes of financing an armed conflict. This seems at least the case when resource revenues are used to satisfy the primary needs of members of armed groups, such as food, clothing and shelter.

Unfortunately, there is no relevant case law elaborating on these questions. Most of the existing case law with respect to the prohibition on the destruction or seizure of the property of an adversary relates to the destruction of property, in particular of houses and other property belonging to civilians.[40]

In conclusion, the prohibition on the destruction or seizure of the property of the adversary may be regarded as the counterpart of the prohibition of pillage. The latter formulates a prohibition for parties to an armed conflict to appropriate property for personal interests while the former relates to appropriation for public purposes. The prohibition on the destruction or seizure of the property of the adversary applies first and foremost to exploitation of natural resources by rebel groups. It prohibits exploitation unless there is a military necessity to do so. The scope of the prohibition thus depends in particular on the contents of the exception of military necessity in relation to the exploitation of natural resources.

4.2. *Peacetime Law*

The previous section demonstrated that international humanitarian law contains a few elementary rules relating to the exploitation of natural resources. These rules apply first and foremost to rebel groups exploiting natural resources. The rules seem less apt to cover the exploitation of natural resources by the domestic State in times of armed conflict, except when members of the national army exploit natural resources for their personal benefit.

However, this does not imply that a State is entitled to exploit the domestic natural resources as it sees fit. According to the general framework set out in section 3, peacetime law continues to apply, unless these rules are set aside by more specific rules of international humanitarian law. In section 4.1 it was demonstrated that international humanitarian law does not contain specific rules to

---

39 Consider in this regard the *Hostage case*, where the Nuremberg Military Tribunal held in relation to the destruction of property that the Hague Regulations require the military necessity to be "urgent" and that there must be a "reasonable connection between the destruction of property and the overcoming of the enemy forces". The Tribunal also recognised that destruction as an end in itself is a violation of international law. *Hostage case*, Trials of War Criminals before the Nuernberg Military Tribunals Under Control Council Law No. 10, Nuremberg, October 1946–April 1949, Vol. XI, Washington: Government Printing Office (1959), pp. 1253–1254.

40 For examples of cases before criminal tribunals, *see* the ICRC Customary International Humanitarian Law Database under Rule 50, available through <www.icrc.org/customary-ihl/eng/docs/home>, visited on 6 August 2012.

deal with natural resource exploitation by States participating in internal armed conflicts. Therefore, arguably, the peacetime framework for the exploitation of natural resources continues to apply in these circumstances.

The key rules that apply to the exploitation of natural resources by States ensue from the principle of permanent sovereignty over natural resources which is recognised by the International Court of Justice as a principle of customary law.[41] Pursuant to this principle, natural resource ownership is vested within each State and people.[42] A government, as the legal representative of a State and its people,[43] is thus entitled to exploit domestic natural resources.

Nonetheless, this right entails duties as well.[44] First of all, States must exploit natural resources in a sustainable way. This condition ensues from the principle of sustainable use, which has been embodied in numerous international environmental treaties that qualify the rights of a State to dispose of their natural resources for the purposes of environmental protection. Suspension of the operation of these treaties – if possible at all – is not likely to affect the obligations contained therein, at least in as far as these treaties aim to protect the common interests of the international community. This is, for example, the case for the Convention on Biological Diversity, which qualifies the conservation of biological diversity as a "common concern of humankind".[45] Thus, large scale logging

---

41 *See Armed Activities on the Territory of the Congo (Democratic Republic of the Congo* v. *Uganda), supra* note 29, para. 244.

42 For a more thorough discussion of the principle of permanent sovereignty and the holders of the rights related to it, *see* Schrijver, *supra* note 21. For an analysis of the principle of permanent sovereignty over natural resources within the specific context of resource related armed conflicts, *see* P. N. Okowa, 'Natural Resources in Situations of Armed Conflict: Is there a Coherent Framework for Protection?', 9 *International Community Law Review* (2007) pp. 237–262; and D. A. Dam-de Jong, 'International Law and Resource Plunder: The Protection of Natural Resources during Armed Conflict', in O. K. Fauchald, D. Hunter and W. Xi (eds.), 19 *Yearbook of International Environmental Law* (Oxford University Press, Oxford, 2008) pp. 27–57.

43 A government is generally presumed to be the legal representative of a State, unless it is no longer recognised as such. In this regard it is interesting to mention the example of Libya. Not long after the beginning of the insurrection in February 2011, the international community started to recognise the insurrectional movement as the legitimate representative of the Libyan people and thus as the new government entitled to decide on the oil reserves of the country. This example shows that a government may lose its status as the legal representative of a State due to its course of actions during an armed conflict.

44 *See* Schrijver, *supra* note 21.

45 *See* the preamble of the Convention on Biological Diversity, adopted on 5 June 1992 (1760 *UNTS* 79) which "affirm[s] that the conservation of biological diversity is a common concern of humankind". Of course, there may be other impediments to observation of the obligations contained within such treaties. The Biodiversity Con-

"with little regard to sustainable forest practices", such as happened in Liberia under Charles Taylor, is not permitted.[46]

Second, States must exploit the domestic natural resources for the benefit of the population. This condition ensues first of all from the Declaration on Permanent Sovereignty over Natural Resources.[47] It has since been reaffirmed in several legal instruments, including resolutions of the Security Council dealing with the inter-linkage between natural resources and armed conflict.[48] Of course, using the proceeds of resource exploitation to fight rebel forces may perfectly well fit into this description. However, a State that uses the proceeds of natural resource exploitation to commit gross human rights violations may be said to act contrary to the principle of permanent sovereignty over natural resources.

The armed conflict in Libya in 2011 provides a relevant example. During this conflict, the government of Libya, led by Colonel Qadhafi, carried out large-scale and systematic attacks against the civilian population. In response, the Security Council imposed an asset freeze against the Libyan authorities, which included the assets of the Libyan National Oil Corporation as a "potential source of funding for [Qadhafi's] regime".[49]

Furthermore, States must respect resolutions adopted by the Security Council, pursuant to Article 25 of the UN Charter. Some of these resolutions contain additional measures to be implemented by governments, restricting their right to freely dispose of the State's natural resources.[50] Relevant measures include the establishment of a certificate of origin regime for natural resources, such as for rough diamonds originating from Sierra Leone and Liberia, or the implementation of a system aimed at promoting transparency and accountability in particular natural resources sectors, such as for the timber industry in Liberia.[51] These measures are discussed in section 5 below.

---

vention, for example, makes implementation of most of its obligations conditional on the conditions and capabilities of the implementing State.

46 *Report of the Panel of Experts on Liberia established pursuant to Security Council Resolution 1343 (2001), paragraph 19, concerning Liberia*, UN Doc. S/2001/1015 of 26 October 2001, para. 33.

47 *See* the *Declaration on Permanent Sovereignty over Natural Resources*, UN General Assembly Resolution 1803 (XVII), adopted on 14 December 1962.

48 *See e.g.* UN Security Council Resolution 1457 (2003), operative para. 4; and Resolution 1521 (2003), operative para. 13.

49 UN Security Council Resolution 1973 (2011), 17 March 2011, Annex II.

50 The measures are formulated as encouragements and not as hard legal obligations. However, due to the close connection between these measures and sanctions imposed against natural resources, they are to be regarded as imperative in nature. For examples, *see* section 4.2 of this study.

51 On diamonds, *see* UN SC Resolution 1306 (2000) for Sierra Leone and UN SC Resolution 1343 (2001) for Liberia. On timber, *see* UN Security Council Resolution 1521 (2003) on Liberia.

4.3. *Appraisal of the Current Legal Framework for Resource Exploitation in Situations of Internal Armed Conflict*

It may be concluded from the above that the current regulatory framework dealing with the exploitation of natural resources by parties to an armed conflict is very fragmented. The prohibitions contained in international humanitarian law apply first and foremost to rebel groups, while States derive their obligations mostly from peacetime law.

In addition, the existing regulatory framework provides major loopholes for parties to an armed conflict. Examples of such loopholes include the definition of military necessity in relation to the prohibition on the destruction or seizure of the property of an adversary as well as the determination of what constitutes 'for the benefit of the population' in relation to the exercise of permanent sovereignty over natural resources.

Related to these loopholes is the concern of legal uncertainty. The rules are not tailored to cover the specific situation of predatory resource exploitation. In the near absence of relevant case law, it is therefore extremely difficult to provide guidance in respect of the precise scope and contents of the rules in relation to the issue of predatory resource exploitation.

The judgment of the International Court of Justice in the DR Congo-Uganda case, which legally qualified the illicit exploitation of Congolese natural resources by Ugandan troops, may therefore be welcomed. This is especially so since the ICJ is the only international court which has explicitly addressed the issue of predatory resource exploitation in modern armed conflicts. However, this judgment touches upon only some of the issues. There is thus an urgent need to clarify the existing rules, both through case law and through codification and progressive development of these rules.

5. Security Council Sanctions Regimes

This section examines some of the sanctions regimes imposed by the Security Council in order to break the link between natural resources exploitation and the continuation of armed conflicts. The purpose of this section is twofold. First, it assesses the extent to which the sanctions regimes imposed by the Security Council provide a practical response to the imperfections of the regulatory framework discussed in the previous sections. Second, it assesses the role played by the Security Council in addressing the link between natural resources and armed conflict.

5.1. *General Remarks on Resource-Related Sanctions*

Sanctions are one of the most important tools of the UN Security Council to address threats to international peace and security. Pursuant to Article 41 of the UN Charter, the Security Council is entitled to take measures not involving the use of military force to maintain or restore international peace and security. The Council may do so in all phases of the conflict, once it has determined the existence of a threat to the peace, a breach of the peace or an act of aggression under Article 39 of the UN Charter.

Measures taken by the Security Council under Article 41 of the UN Charter prevail over the obligations of UN Member States under treaties to which they are party.[52] For present purposes, this implies that Security Council sanctions may, for example, further restrict the rights of parties to an armed conflict under international humanitarian law. Likewise – and of the utmost importance for the cases discussed below – Security Council sanctions may qualify the right of a State to exercise permanent sovereignty over its natural resources if necessary to maintain or restore international peace and security.

Sanctions addressing predatory resource exploitation have generally targeted the trade in natural resources from regions where these natural resources have fuelled armed conflicts. In most cases, the Security Council has established Panels of Experts to make a factual assessment of the situation before imposing sanctions. Panel reports have extensively documented the role that natural resources played in the conflicts discussed in this study. In addition, their findings concerning the breaking of sanctions in particular conflicts, such as those in Angola and Sierra Leone, have been instrumental in the Security Council's embracing of new approaches to tackle the trade in 'conflict resources', such as through the Kimberley Process for the Certification of Rough Diamonds.[53]

Some of the sanctions regimes imposed by the Security Council in order to break the link between natural resources and armed conflict have directly addressed the trade in particular natural resources, while other sanctions regimes have rather targeted persons or entities involved in resource exploitation. Relevant examples of commodity sanctions include the diamond sanctions discussed below. Relevant examples of targeted sanctions include the asset freeze and travel ban targeting individuals or entities supporting armed groups in the DR Congo through illicit trade in natural resources[54] and the asset freeze against the Libyan National Oil Company during the 2011 Libyan civil war.[55]

This section focuses on two examples of structural approaches adopted by the Security Council in order to break the link between natural resources and armed conflict: certificate of origin schemes for particular commodities, and reform plans for the natural resources sector. In both cases, the Security Council has conditioned the lifting of sanctions upon the effective implementation of these measures.

---

52 Article 103 of the UN Charter determines that in the event of a conflict between the obligations of Members of the United Nations under the UN Charter and their obligations under any other treaty, their obligations under the Charter prevail.

53 *See* Section 4.2 for more details.

54 UN Security Council Resolution 1857 (2008), operative paragraph 4(g).

55 UN Security Council Resolution 1973 (2011), *supra* note 46.

In practice, the Security Council has resorted to the imposition of resource related sanctions in the phase of conflict resolution and has maintained these in the early stages of post-conflict reconstruction. The two approaches discussed in the current section are representative of the steps taken by the Security Council in this regard. Certification schemes are usually introduced in the phase of conflict resolution, while reform plans are generally introduced in the phase of post-conflict reconstruction.

5.2. *Certificate of Origin Schemes*

Certificate of origin schemes seek to prevent the trade in natural resources from fuelling armed conflict by providing a certificate for natural resources from which their origin can be established. To date there have been four instances in which the Security Council has turned to a certificate of origin scheme to exempt particular natural resources from a sanctions regime it has adopted. All address the trade in rough diamonds.

The first time the Security Council referred to a certificate of origin regime was in relation to the conflict in Angola. The diamond trade constituted one of the primary sources of income for the rebel movement UNITA. In order to end the violence in Angola, the Security Council decided in Resolution 1173 (1998) that all States must take the necessary measures "to prohibit the direct or indirect import from Angola to their territory of all diamonds that are not controlled through the Certificate of Origin regime of the [Angolan government]".[56] In a subsequent resolution, the Security Council specified that the implementation of the measures contained in resolution 1173 requires "an effective Certificate of Origin regime".[57]

Also in relation to Sierra Leone, the Security Council installed a sanctions regime on all rough diamonds and requested the government of Sierra Leone "to ensure, as a matter of urgency, that an effective Certificate of Origin regime for trade in diamonds is in operation in Sierra Leone" which would exempt diamonds traded through this regime from the measures.[58] In subsequent resolutions, the Security Council renewed the diamond sanctions but exempted diamonds controlled by the Certificate of Origin Regime that the government had put in place, to wit, the Kimberley Process certification scheme.[59] The sanctions were finally

---

56 Security Council Resolution 1173 (1998), operative para. 12(b).

57 Security Council Resolution 1295 (2000), operative para. 16.

58 Security Council Resolution 1306 (2000), operative paras. 1, 2 and 5.

59 *See* Resolutions 1385 (2001) and 1446 (2002) for the extensions of the diamond sanctions. The Kimberley Process Certification Scheme is a voluntary mechanism to stop the trade in rough diamonds that are used by non-State armed groups to finance their armed struggle. It was set up in 2002 by States, the diamond industry and non-governmental organisations in response to calls by the UN General Assembly and the Security Council for an international certification scheme for rough diamonds.

lifted in 2003 in light of the government's "increased efforts to control and manage its diamond industry and ensure proper control over diamond mining areas, and the Government's full participation in the Kimberley Process".[60]

The third instance concerns the imposition of diamond sanctions against Liberia, principally to address the role of Liberia in the smuggling of Sierra Leonean diamonds.[61] The Security Council demanded that the government of Liberia "cease all direct or indirect import of Sierra Leone rough diamonds which are not controlled through the Certificate of Origin regime of the Government of Sierra Leone" and called upon the government "to establish an effective Certificate of Origin regime for trade in rough diamonds that is transparent and internationally verifiable".[62]

In subsequent resolutions, adopted in the phase of post-conflict reconstruction, the Security Council went a step further. In Resolution 1478 (2003), the Security Council called upon the Liberian government "to establish a Certificate of Origin regime for Liberian rough diamonds that is transparent, internationally verifiable and fully compatible with the Kimberley Process".[63] In a later resolution, the Security Council reiterated its call upon the government and encouraged it "to take steps to join the Kimberley Process as soon as possible".[64]

Finally, in the case of Côte d'Ivoire, the Security Council installed a sanctions regime targeting the whole diamond industry in Côte d'Ivoire.[65] These sanctions were imposed upon the request of the Ivorian government, which had already imposed a national ban on the export of diamonds in order to take away from the opposition forces their principal source of funding.[66] In the same resolution, the Security Council expressly referred to the Kimberley Process. It welcomed the measures agreed by participants in the Kimberley Process Certification Scheme to prevent the export of all rough diamonds from the territory of Côte d'Ivoire and called upon the States in the region which are not participants in the Kimberley Process "to intensify their efforts to join the Kimberley Process in

---

See e.g. UN General Assembly Resolution 55/56 of 29 January 2001. For more details on this Certification Scheme, *see* <www.kimberleyprocess. com/>, visited on 30 July 2012.

60 *See* UN Doc. SC/7778 of 5 June 2003 for a press statement by the president of the Security Council.

61 UN Security Council Resolution 1343 (2001), operative para. 6.

62 *Ibid.*, operative paras. 2(c) and 15.

63 UN Security Council Resolution 1478 (2003), para. 13.

64 UN Security Council Resolution 1521 (2003), operative paras. 7 and 9.

65 UN Security Council Resolution 1643 (2005), operative para. 6.

66 *Report of the Group of Experts submitted in accordance with paragraph 7 of resolution 1584 (2005)*, UN Doc. S/2005/699, para. 48.

order to increase the effectiveness of monitoring the import of diamonds from Côte d'Ivoire".[67]

In response to political changes that took place in Côte d'Ivoire in 2011, the Security Council offered the Ivorian government an opportunity for the modification or lifting of sanctions. The Security Council conditioned the modification or lifting of the sanctions on the creation and implementation of an action plan by the Ivorian authorities to enforce the Kimberley Process rules in Côte d'Ivoire.[68] A further condition stipulated that the authorities "closely work with the Kimberley Process Certification Scheme to conduct a review and assessment of Côte d'Ivoire's internal controls system for trade in rough diamonds and a comprehensive geologic study of Côte d'Ivoire's potential diamond resources and production capacity".[69]

These resolutions reveal a growing tendency of the Security Council to use sanctions as a tool to provide structural solutions to break the link between natural resources and armed conflict. First of all, the resolutions develop standards for a certificate of origin scheme. In its resolutions concerning Angola and Sierra Leone, the Security Council asked for an *effective* regime to be set up. In its resolutions against Liberia, the Security Council elaborated upon this requirement by demanding that the Certificate of Origin regime must be transparent and internationally verifiable.

In addition, the Security Council has increasingly relied upon one particular certificate of origin scheme, the Kimberley Process Certification Scheme. Whereas in earlier resolutions the Council refers to the Kimberley Process as a model for an effective certificate of origin scheme, in later resolutions it refers to the Kimberley Process as the only viable option.

5.3. *Reform Plans for Natural Resources Sectors*

The Security Council has also used its powers under Chapter VII to set out reforms for particular natural resource sectors. The Liberian timber industry may serve as a primary example. After the diamond sanctions had been installed against Liberia, the government led by Charles Taylor increasingly resorted to logging as a means of generating revenue in order to finance the armed conflict in the region. Therefore, the Security Council called upon the government of Liberia to "take urgent steps, including through the establishment of transparent and internationally verifiable audit regimes, to ensure that revenue derived by the Government of Liberia from the … Liberian timber industry is used for legitimate social, humanitarian and development purposes".[70] Having no effect,

67 UN Security Council Resolution 1643 (2005), operative para. 6.

68 UN Security Council Resolution 2045 (2012), operative para. 6.

69 *Ibid.*, operative para. 21.

70 UN Security Council Resolution 1408 (2002), operative para. 10.

the Security Council decided in a subsequent resolution to impose sanctions on Liberian timber.[71]

After Charles Taylor had been ousted from power, these sanctions remained in place as part of the post-conflict reconstruction phase. In Resolution 1521 (2003), the Security Council urged the government of Liberia "to establish its full authority and control over the timber producing areas, and to take all necessary steps to ensure that government revenues from the Liberian timber industry are not used to fuel conflict or otherwise in violation of the Council's resolutions but are used for legitimate purposes for the benefit of the Liberian people, including development".[72] It also encouraged the government "to establish oversight mechanisms for the timber industry that will promote responsible business practices, and to establish transparent accounting and auditing mechanisms to ensure that all government revenues … are not used to fuel conflict or otherwise in violation of the Council's resolutions but are used for legitimate purposes for the benefit of the Liberian people, including development".[73] Moreover, these objectives include "the promotion of responsible and environmentally sustainable business practices in the timber industry".[74]

In order to implement the measures set out in resolution 1521 (2003), the Liberian government developed two programmes with the aid of other States and international organisations. The first concerns the Liberia Forest Initiative, aimed at improving transparency and accountability for timber revenues as well as sustainable forest management.[75] The second programme, the Governance and Economic Management Assistance Program (GEMAP), has a more general scope and is aimed at improving transparency and accountability in government revenues and expenditure.[76]

In Resolution 1647 (2005), the Security Council embraced both programmes. With respect to the forest initiative, the Security Council considered that its implementation would "ensure transparency, accountability and sustainable forest management and contribute towards the lifting of the measures on timber in accordance with paragraphs 11 and 12 of resolution 1521 (2003)".[77] Likewise, the Security Council encouraged the government of Liberia to implement the

---

71 UN Security Council Resolution 1478 (2003), operative para. 16.

72 UN Security Council Resolution 1521 (2003), para. 11.

73 *Ibid.*, para. 13.

74 *Ibid.*, para. 15.

75 For more information on this initiative, *see* the website of the UN Food and Agriculture Organization, at <www.fao.org/forestry/lfi/en/>, visited on 30 January 2012.

76 The GEMAP document is available through the website of the World Bank, at <siteresources.worldbank.org/LIBERIAEXTN/Resources/GEMAP.pdf>, visited on 30 January 2012.

77 UN Security Council Resolution 1647 (2005), operative para. 3.

Governance and Economic Management Assistance Program which would "expedite the lifting of the measures imposed by resolution 1521 (2003)".[78]

These resolutions reveal a tendency of the Security Council to expand its tasks with regard to the maintenance of international peace and security. The resolutions in relation to Liberia go far beyond direct crisis management. The Security Council asks for great structural reforms and makes the lifting of sanctions conditional upon effective implementation of these reforms. In addition, it sets all kinds of requirements with respect to the contents and objectives of these reform programmes. The programmes must establish transparent and internationally verifiable audit regimes; they must promote responsible and environmentally sustainable business practices; and they must ensure that government revenues are used for legitimate social, humanitarian and development purposes for the benefit of the Liberian people. In this way, the Security Council has contributed in a more structural way to efforts of peace-building in Liberia, ensuring that Liberian natural resources are managed in a sustainable way for the purpose of development rather than conflict.

6. Adequacy of the Overall Legal Framework

This study has examined the role played by current international law in addressing the problem of predatory resource exploitation by parties to an armed conflict. It has discussed the regulatory framework applicable to the exploitation of natural resources in internal armed conflicts and has examined the practice of the Security Council in relation to armed conflicts fuelled through resource revenues. In particular, it has analysed two of the more systematic approaches of the Council's recent sanctions regimes to break the link between natural resources and armed conflict.

From the analysis above it is clear that the current regulatory framework for the exploitation of natural resources during internal armed conflicts is fragmented. International humanitarian law deals principally with obligations for rebel groups, while States derive most of their obligations from peacetime law. Especially relevant in this regard are international environmental, human rights and general international law. This fragmentation of obligations under international law creates uncertainties with regard to the applicable law.

In addition to being fragmented, the current regulatory framework is imprecise, leading to uncertainties regarding the interpretation of the obligations themselves. Notions such as 'military necessity', the distinction between exploitation for public and for private purposes and a determination of what constitutes exploitation 'for the benefit of the population' create uncertainties with regard to the substantive obligations of parties to an armed conflict.

Uncertainties within the regulatory framework, whether they result from questions concerning the applicable law or from the nature and scope of the sub-

78 UN Security Council Resolution 1647 (2005), operative para. 4.

stantive obligations, are problematic in situations of armed conflict. These situations call for clear and unequivocal rules for both sides to the conflict. This would increase the likelihood of the parties to an armed conflict respecting the rules. In order to address these inadequacies, the existing legal framework thus needs to be clarified and, preferably, expanded.

As discussed above, the Security Council has found ways to address the problem of predatory resource exploitation in a more structural way in the past decades through the use of sanctions and, in particular, by tying the modification or lifting of sanctions to the implementation of certificate of origin regimes and reform plans for particular natural resources sectors. One of the advantages of sanctions regimes is that these can be imposed against all parties to an armed conflict, without touching directly upon questions concerning the legality of resource exploitation. There may, for example, be good reasons for the Security Council to impose sanctions upon a party to an armed conflict, while the resource exploitation itself is perfectly legal. In addition, the prospect of the lifting of sanctions may pose an incentive to States to engage in structural reforms of their natural resource sectors. These structural reforms not only reduce the likelihood for that country to relapse into conflict but they may also help to turn natural resources into an engine for sustainable development.

In sum, it is only through a combination of different approaches that the link between the exploitation of natural resources and armed conflict can properly be addressed. The sanctions regimes imposed by the Security Council may provide solutions to particular instances where natural resources are used to fund an armed conflict. One of the most important advantages of sanctions regimes is that they can be tailored to address specific situations. Nonetheless, dealing with the issue of predatory resource exploitation in such an *ad hoc* manner is not sufficient. It is also of the utmost importance to provide parties to an armed conflict with clear rules to which they can adhere. This may not, in itself, put an end to the exploitation of natural resources for the purposes of funding an armed conflict. However, in the long run, it may significantly enhance the possibilities of turning natural resources from engines for conflict into engines for sustainable development.

Index

V

W

Y